The Background to Contemporary Critical Theory

The Background to Contemporary Critical Theory

From Kant to Lévi-Strauss

Edited by
Jon Simons

RAWAT PUBLICATIONS
Jaipur • New Delhi • Bangalore • Guwahati • Kolkata

ISBN 978-81-316-0904-0

Indian Reprint, 2017

First published in 2002 by
Edinburgh University Press Ltd.
22 George Square, Edinburgh EH8 9LF
www.eup.ed.ac.uk

Published by
Prem Rawat for **Rawat Publications**
Satyam Apts., Sector 3, Jawahar Nagar, Jaipur - 302 004 (India)
Phone: 0141 265 1748 / 7006 Fax: 0141 265 1748
E-mail : info@rawatbooks.com
Website: rawatbooks.com

New Delhi Office
4858/24, Ansari Road, Daryaganj, New Delhi 110 002
Phone: 011-23263290

Also at *Bangalore, Guwahati* and *Kolkata*

Printed and bound in India.

Contents

Acknowledgements

This volume, which I have edited, should be recognised as a collective effort. Without the expertise of the authors of the individual chapters, there would simply be no book. My debt of gratitude to the contributors is larger than that, however, as they have done more than write their own chapters. I thank them for reading and commenting on each other's chapters, including my own, thereby enhancing the quality of and coherence between the chapters. I am also grateful to the contributors for their valuable comments on both the introduction to the volume and on my brief introductions to each chapter. Indeed, I had so much help from other contributors with those introductions that they should be considered as co-authors of them, though I am responsible for any errors remaining in the introductions. On behalf of all the contributors I would like to thank David Owen for reading and commenting on all the chapters with his usual insight and acuity. Jackie Jones at Edinburgh University Press generously showed confidence in the original proposal and guided it through until its acceptance, while the production staff at the Press have made the publishing process as smooth as possible.

The inspiration for producing this book has come from the students at the University of Nottingham who have attended an annual lecture series on the 'Tradition of Critique' which began in 1995. Students on the M.A. in Critical Theory, the M.A. in Architecture and Critical Theory, and more recently research students from a variety of disciplines as well as a new M.A. in Cultural Studies and Critical Theory have been engaged and enquiring audiences for the lectures which are the basis for this book. All but two of the chapters in this volume have been developed from lectures which have benefited from the questions and comments of those students over the years. Those students' interest in and enthusiasm for the 'Tradition of Critique' has made this project worth while.

Jon Simons
January 2002

Notes on Contributors

Dr Matt F. Connell teaches social theory in the Department of English and Media Studies at Nottingham Trent University. He has published papers on Adorno and Freud in *Body and Society*, *Theory, Culture and Society* and *Radical Philosophy*. He is currently working on an introduction to Adorno for Pluto Press.

John Ellis teaches cultural studies, with special interests in design and visual culture, at the Open University and Nottingham Trent University. His current research is a comparative study of Weber's and Arendt's approaches to modernity, with a particular focus on the public sphere.

William Hutson is currently completing a Ph.D. on Husserl and the question of history. In addition to Husserl and the phenomenological tradition, he is particularly interested in Heidegger and pre-Socratic philosophy.

Professor Christopher Johnson is Professor of French at the University of Nottingham. He is author of *System and Writing in the Philosophy of Jacques Derrida* (Cambridge University Press, 1993), and *Derrida: The Scene of Writing* (Phoenix, 1997). He is currently preparing a book on Lévi-Strauss and French anthropology. He is a member of the editorial board of *Paragraph: A Journal of Modern Critical Theory*.

Professor Richard H. King is Professor of American intellectual history in the School of American and Canadian Studies at the University of Nottingham. He is the author of *A Southern Renaissance* (1980), which focused, among other things, on the Freudian themes of mourning and melancholy in classic writing from the US South, and also of *Civil Rights and the Idea of Freedom* (1992), which addresses Arendt's notions of politics.

Professor Stuart Sim is Professor of English Studies at the University of Sunderland. He has published widely on continental philosophy and cultural theory. His most recent books are *Contemporary Continental Philosophy: The New Scepticism* (Ashgate Press, 2000), *Post-Marxism: An Intellectual History* (Routledge, 2000), and *Lyotard and the Inhuman* (Icon Press, 2001).

Dr Jon Simons is Senior Lecturer in Critical Theory in the Postgraduate School of Critical Theory and Cultural Studies at the University of Nottingham. He is the author of *Foucault and the Political* (Routledge, 1995) as well as many journal articles and contributions to books on feminist, political and cultural theory. He is currently working on a book, *Critical Political Theory in the Media Age,* which will be published by Edinburgh University Press and New York University Press. He is on the editorial board of the journal *Culture, Theory and Critique.*

Dr Nicholas H. Smith is Senior Lecturer in Philosophy at Macquarie University, Sydney, Australia. He is the author of *Strong Hermeneutics: Contingency and Moral Identity* (Routledge, 1997), *Charles Taylor: Meaning, Morals and Modernity* (Polity, 2002), and is the editor of *Reading McDowell: On Mind and World* (Routledge, 2002).

Dr Simon Tormey is Senior Lecturer in Political Thought at the University of Nottingham. He is the author of *Making Sense of Tyranny: Interpretations of Totalitarianism* (Manchester University Press, 1995), *Politics at the Edge* (co-edited with C. Pierson, Macmillan, 1999), and *Agnes Heller: Socialism, Autonomy and the Postmodern* (Manchester University Press, 2001).

Dr David Woods is Senior Lecturer in the Department of English and Media Studies at Nottingham Trent University. He has written on Derrida and Homi Bhabha and is currently planning a book on continental philosophical approaches to notions of community.

1

Introduction

Jon Simons

This volume offers fourteen introductory essays on key thinkers in a modern European tradition of thought, which is both critical itself and also constitutes the intellectual background for many contemporary critical theorists. Critical theory in a broad sense includes the trends of Marxism and post-Marxism, semiotics and discourse analysis, structuralism and poststructuralism, ideology critique of all varieties, deconstruction, feminism, queer theory, psychoanalysis, postcolonialism, as well as the descendants of the Frankfurt School of Critical Theory. Those critical tendencies can be found across all the disciplines and interdisciplinary areas of the humanities, from architecture to theology, from American Studies to visual culture. The book is thus designed to be instructive for people with one or two areas of interest, which are the critical tradition itself and the contemporary theorists who are influenced significantly by their precursors whose thought is the intellectual background to contemporary theory. This book is intended to be a good enough introduction to the critical tradition that constitutes the background to contemporary critical theory for readers to get going with an understanding of at least some of that immense intellectual background. If this book succeeds in its aims, it will have whetted its readers' appetites to learn more about the critical tradition it introduces. The following section explains how best to use this book to satisfy either or both of the interests mentioned above. The subsequent sections of the introduction explain why the book has the scope it has and what is meant by a 'tradition of critique'.

How to use this Book

As stated above, this book is intended to be helpful for people with one or two areas of intellectual interest, which are the critical tradition itself and the contemporary theorists who are influenced significantly by it. Readers who are interested only in the critical tradition can learn how it is characterised in the following sections of the introduction, first in brief profiles about the domains and means of each thinker's critique, and then in relation to contemporary critical theory. There are also brief introductory sections to each chapter (under the heading '[Name of thinker] in the Critical Tradition'), which outline the relations between the thinkers in the critical tradition who are included in the volume. Those introductions can do no more than indicate the bare bones of the connections, which means that readers will have to look at the chapters on all the thinkers in whom they are interested in order to understand the intellectual relationships between them. Sometimes the chapters include more details on the specific points of connection raised in the introduction, but sometimes the brevity of the chapters precludes such detail, leaving the reader to configure rather more of the influence of thinkers on each other by comparing the concepts and themes discussed in the chapters. Table 1 below indicates the main connections between thinkers covered by this volume.

Readers primarily interested in the tradition of critique itself rather than in it as background to contemporary critical theory would probably find it useful to work through the book more or less in the order of contents, which is roughly chronological. There is a discernible line of influence of and engagement with the tradition from Kant through to Adorno and Horkheimer, which is why the chapter on them is placed before those on Husserl and Heidegger. Those two chapters and the one on Gadamer constitute a subsection about the phenomenological, existential and hermeneutic tradition. Any readers particularly interested in that philosophical tendency might find it helpful to read the chapter on Arendt along with them, possibly immediately after the chapter on Heidegger, with whom she has the strongest intellectual affinity. The chapters on Wittgenstein and Lévi-Strauss do not connect as easily with other chapters as is generally the case, but their place at the end of the volume allows for their less obvious relations with the preceding thinkers of the tradition to become more apparent. Having said

Table 1 The intellectual relations between thinkers in the critical tradition

Thinker	Intellectual relationship with
Kant	Hegel, Marx, Nietzsche, Weber, Adorno & Horkheimer, Husserl, Heidegger, Gadamer, Wittgenstein, Arendt
Hegel	Kant, Marx, Nietzsche, Lukács, Adorno, Husserl, Heidegger, Gadamer, Arendt
Marx	Hegel, Marx, Weber, Lukács, Adorno & Horkheimer, Arendt
Nietzsche	Kant, Hegel, Marx, Weber, Adorno & Horkheimer, Heidegger, Arendt
Weber	Kant, Nietzsche, Marx, Lukács, Adorno & Horkheimer
Freud	Nietzsche, Marx, Adorno & Horkheimer, Husserl, Heidegger, Arendt, Wittgenstein
Lukács	Hegel, Marx, Weber, Adorno & Horkheimer
Adorno & Horkheimer	Kant, Hegel, Marx, Nietzsche, Weber, Freud, Lukács, Heidegger
Husserl	Kant, Hegel, Adorno, Heidegger, Gadamer, Wittgenstein
Heidegger	Hegel, Nietzsche, Adorno, Husserl, Gadamer, Arendt
Gadamer	Kant, Hegel, Nietzsche, Husserl, Heidegger, Wittgenstein
Wittgenstein	Kant, Hegel, Marx, Nietzsche, Husserl, Gadamer
Arendt	Kant, Hegel, Marx, Nietzsche, Freud, Heidegger
Lévi-Strauss	Marx, Nietzsche, Freud, Heidegger

that, readers could also pick and choose in any order the thinkers in whom they are most interested, while referring to the chapter introductions. Those introductions will enable readers to get some sense of each thinker's place in the tradition.

This volume is also designed to be helpful to those readers who are being taught about or researching one or several contemporary critical theorists, but do not have enough knowledge of their precursors. Indeed the main motivation for publishing this volume was to meet the needs of students and researchers of contemporary

Table 2 Significant influence of thinkers in critical tradition on key contemporary critical theorists

Background thinker	Contemporary theorists
Kant	Deleuze, Foucault, Lyotard, Habermas, Rorty
Hegel	Lacan, Derrida, Lyotard, Habermas, Jameson, Taylor, Žižek
Marx	Barthes, Baudrillard, Bourdieu, Derrida, Foucault, Lyotard, Habermas, Jameson, Laclau & Mouffe, Spivak, Taylor, Žižek
Nietzsche	Deleuze & Guattari, Derrida, Foucault, Habermas, Irigaray, Rorty, Taylor
Weber	Bourdieu, Foucault, Habermas.
Freud	Deleuze & Guattari, Derrida, Foucault, Habermas, Irigaray, Kristeva, Lacan, Laclau & Mouffe, Lyotard, Rorty, Spivak, Taylor, Žižek
Lukács	Jameson, Laclau & Mouffe
Adorno & Horkheimer	Habermas, Jameson, Žižek
Husserl	Derrida, Habermas
Heidegger	Bourdieu, Derrida, Foucault, Irigaray, Rorty, Taylor
Gadamer	Derrida, Habermas, Rorty, Taylor
Wittgenstein	Habermas, Lyotard, Rorty
Arendt	Derrida, Habermas, Lyotard, Taylor
Lévi-Strauss	Barthes, Baudrillard, Bourdieu, Deleuze, Derrida, Foucault, Guattari, Kristeva, Lyotard

theorists who have not had the opportunity to study the intellectual background on which contemporary theory is based. The volume thus offers an overview of a representative sample of key thinkers in the critical tradition by providing introductory chapters on those key thinkers. Tables 2 and 3 below will be particularly helpful for those who want to know which background thinker is most relevant to which contemporary theorist, so that chapters can be read as needed. Table 2 shows the lines of influence of each of the thinkers included in this volume on contemporary theorists. Each of the chapters also concludes with a section which explains how the thinker in question has influenced the contemporary figures listed in the table. Table 3 shows which thinkers of the tradition of critique

Table 3 Key contemporary critical theorists and their main influences from the critical tradition

Contemporary theorist	Significant precursors
Barthes	Marx, Lévi-Strauss
Baudrillard	Marx, Lévi-Strauss
Bourdieu	Marx, Heidegger, Lévi-Strauss
Deleuze & Guattari	Kant, Marx, Nietzsche, Freud, Lévi-Strauss
Derrida	Hegel, Nietzsche, Husserl, Heidegger, Gadamer, Arendt, Lévi-Strauss
Foucault	Kant, Nietzsche, Marx, Weber, Freud, Heidegger, Lévi-Strauss
Habermas	Kant, Hegel, Nietzsche, Weber, Freud, Adorno & Horkheimer, Husserl, Heidegger, Gadamer, Wittgenstein, Arendt
Irigaray	Nietzsche, Freud, Heidegger
Jameson	Marx, Hegel, Lukács, Adorno
Kristeva	Freud, Lévi-Strauss
Lacan	Hegel, Freud, Lévi-Strauss
Laclau & Mouffe	Marx, Freud, Lukács
Lyotard	Kant, Hegel, Marx, Freud, Wittgenstein, Arendt, Lévi-Strauss
Rorty	Kant, Nietzsche, Freud, Heidegger, Gadamer, Wittgenstein
Spivak	Marx, Freud
Taylor	Hegel, Marx, Nietzsche, Weber, Freud, Heidegger, Gadamer, Wittgenstein, Arendt
Žižek	Hegel, Marx, Freud, Adorno

are relevant as intellectual background to a representative list of contemporary critical theorists.

The chapters are intended to provide simplified but not reductive accounts of the main themes, ideas and concepts of key figures in the tradition of critique. Each chapter includes a short introduction that provides biographical information about the thinkers and places them in their intellectual context. It should go without saying that each of the thinkers is more complex and their work more extensive than can be presented in a chapter. These chapters can do no more than offer the gist of what each thinker writes and means, which is why suggestions for further reading are given at the end of each chapter. The aim of the chapters is also to present the work of the thinkers in a fair and accurate way, which has left the authors of the chapters with little or no room to present their own interpretations. It should therefore not be assumed by readers that the chapter authors agree with the thinkers whose work they present. There has also not been much scope to present the main criticisms of the background thinkers other than when a later thinker develops his or her own ideas in contrast to an earlier thinker. More information about the standard criticisms of the thinkers in the volume can be found in the suggested further reading. Readers who are coming to this book as a result of an interest sparked by a contemporary theorist might be doing so because the contemporary theorist has directly criticised a precursor, such as Derrida on Lévi-Strauss. The book was written with such readers in mind, with the intention that an understanding of the critical tradition will enrich their appreciation of many contemporary theorists.

Domains and Means of the Tradition of Critique

Kant defines his mature work as critical philosophy, meaning that he offers critical analyses of the capacities and limitations of human mental powers or faculties. By focusing on critique, Kant suggests a way in which the thinkers who constitute the intellectual background to contemporary critical theory can be compared and contrasted. The following section characterises the thinkers included in this volume in terms of the domain of their critique, meaning both that which they subject to critique and the ends that critique is hoped or expected to achieve; and the means of critique, meaning their critical method and mode. These brief profiles of each thinker are also useful to readers who are unfamiliar with the tradition of critique, as they offer a very condensed overview of what the thinkers critiqued and how they went about it.

Kant's immediate targets of critique are in the philosophical domain, namely scepticism, rationalism and metaphysical speculation in general. But in broader terms, he is critical of 'immaturity', meaning unreflective reliance on intellectual traditions and authorities. His critical philosophical stance has social and political ramifications, namely that no authority should be considered legitimate if it cannot stand up to his mode of criticism. Kant's manner of critique could thus be characterised as one of legitimation, whether that be legitimation of scientific knowledge, moral principles, aesthetic judgements or political systems. His method of critique is transcendental, meaning that he both deduces and analyses what must be the case if humans have the knowledge, morality or aesthetic judgements that they do. He asks which sort of mental faculties humans must have as conditions of possibility for such understanding and judgement. Freedom of relation between human mental faculties and freedom for individuals to legislate for themselves are the underlying conditions of possibility for knowledge and morality, so that the legitimation of human freedom is a central aim of his philosophical critique.

The domain of **Hegel**'s critique is both philosophical and political in a direct way, yet cultural and aesthetic considerations are also central to his thought. Hegel is critical of Kant's attempt to reconcile the differences between the mental faculties, which Hegel takes to be a diremption of consciousness rather than a division of labour between the faculties. He extends his critique of the way consciousness is alienated from itself to a social and political critique of alienation in the modern world, in which the harmony of traditional community has been lost. Freedom, or the realisation of spirit, could only be attained by consciousness becoming conscious of itself and its role in the history of human activity, while social harmony could be achieved only through direction by the modern constitutional state. Hegel's method of critique is dialectical, meaning that it relates seemingly contradictory parts to a totality, which is understood teleologically, according to the end towards which world history develops. His manner of critique is historical, looking back over human activity to trace an underlying logic according to which the rational becomes real.

Marx's domain of critique is primarily socio-economic and political, but it also has a strong philosophical dimension in his criticism of Hegel's idealism. According to Hegel, consciousness determines social being, whereas Marx's historical materialism reverses the relationship. The list of Marx's critical targets is long: alienation of workers from the products of their work and from each other, the separation of mental and manual labour, the system of wage labour, exploitation and the extraction of surplus value, commodification of products and labour, bourgeois individualism; in brief, capitalism. His critique of capitalism also pitches him against versions of socialism which fail to recognise the revolutionary transformation required to end the capitalist mode of production, namely social democracy and utopian socialism. His critical methodology is historical materialism, which seeks material, generally economic explanations for developments in human history. Insofar as it takes the surface appearance of events and ideas to be less significant than deeper process underlying them, the manner of Marx's critique is hermeneutic. The tone of his work is often polemic, while in its emancipatory aim of a radically equal and free society in which humans control their own destiny, Marx's manner of critique is at times prophetic.

In contrast to Marx's critique of the socio-economic conditions of modernity, the domain of **Nietzsche**'s critique is primarily cultural, with a strong emphasis on the intellectual culture of which German philosophy is a part. He criticises Western civilisation for having led itself into a nihilistic crisis in which the grounds of belief required to sustain the will to power, or life, have been undermined. Nietzsche considers the character of his contemporaries to be mediocre and devoid of spirit. In place of the ideals and values of Western civilisation, such as scientific truth and universal moral principles, Nietzsche called for a transvaluation of all values. Yet, Nietzsche's critique is ambivalent, in that civilisation has also demystified the world to the point where those brave enough to do so can live happily with the thought that there is no order to the universe humans inhabit other than that which humans create for themselves. Nietzsche's critical method is genealogical, meaning a form of history which traces the way current conditions and ideas have solidified over time. His critical manner is both hermeneutic, looking below the conventional justifications of civilisation for messy contingencies, and iconoclastic, smashing the idols of modern culture and philosophy.

While **Weber** is, like Nietzsche, a cultural critic of modernity, his domain of critique is substantially socio-political. His critical analysis of modernity stresses its development into differentiated institutional social and value spheres as it becomes more complex, a process which has resulted in the disenchantment of the world in contrast to traditional, largely religious, holistic world-views. Although he was not a Marxist, one of the main targets of his critique is capitalism, which he regarded as a rationalised form of economics, just as the modern state and bureaucracy are a rationalised form of politics. The problem with modern rationalisation is the bifurcation between instrumental rationality and substantive, value-oriented rationality, with the former dominating modernity at the expense of the latter. Weber's critical method is genealogical, but in contrast to Nietzsche's speculative approach Weber bases his critique on extensive, often detailed, comparative historical work about European as well as non-Western civilisations. Weber hopes for some way of continuing ethical life under modern conditions, though his tone often suggests that is more of a hope than an expectation.

The domain of **Freud**'s critique appears different according to whether psychoanalysis is being considered as a therapy or a broader social diagnosis. As a therapist, Freud critically analyses psychic dysfunctions, neuroses and psychoses, with a view to understanding, curing or alleviating them. Looking to the more general significance of Freud's work, he is a critic of the rationalist account of self and society, in that he explains human behaviour in terms of unconscious motives and drives. His view that civilisation necessarily requires the repression of at least some libidinal drives also makes him a critic of utopians of all kinds. His critical method is the one he invented, namely psychoanalysis, which is also a hermeneutic method to uncover the unconscious motives for behaviour. He would certainly have liked to think of his methodology as rational and scientific, but whether or not it is remains a matter of dispute.

As he was a Marxist, much of the domain of **Lukács**' critique is the same as that of Marx. Lukács' concept of reification extends Marx's insights about commodity fetishism to explain the way in which capitalist relations of production and exchange reduce people to mere things, thereby alienating them from their consciousness. For Lukács, the key to social transformation is collective proletarian consciousness. His Hegelian and humanist interpretation of Marx put him at odds with Soviet 'scientific' Marxism, as reflected in his criticism of the Soviet imperialism under which he lived in post-war Eastern Europe. As a literary critic, Lukács also objected to certain literary trends which other Marxists of his time regarded as progressive, namely literary modernism and socialist realism. The former he finds too self-absorbed and the latter too didactic to project the utopian vision required to spark proletarian consciousness. His historical materialist methodology of ideology critique dialectically relates contradictory parts to a social totality, and thereby mediates between subjective consciousness and objective reality. When applied to realist novels, Lukács claims his approach both reveals a true picture of capitalism and testifies to the potential of creative, non-reified human relations. His literary criticism is thus central to his project of raising working-class consciousness.

Adorno's **and Horkheimer**'s domain of critique is socio-economic, philosophical, cultural and psychological. Philosophically, they criticise the dialectic of Enlightenment as an expression of the contradictions of capitalism, which result in an irrational rationalism. The rationalised control of the object world is extended to the domination of human affairs in the form of administrative reason, which leaves no room for the conduct of life according to substantive, ethical reason. The forms of individuality possible under such conditions are at best attenuated, and at worst produce authoritarian impulses that serve the most pathological embodiment of administrative reason witnessed in the Holocaust. They also develop a critique of the ideological forms of modern, mass society, particularly the commodification of culture as entertainment under the capitalist conditions of the culture industry. Their methodology is dialectical ideology critique, and is thus hermeneutic in the same sense as Marx's. There is a strain of utopian hope for a truly emancipated society running through their work, which, given their largely pessimistic diagnosis of modernity, has a messianic tone to it.

Husserl's domain of critique is predominantly philosophical, directed against the scientific mode of German philosophy which had become fashionable in his time in place of the critical tradition begun by Kant. In particular, Husserl criticised the subject/object dichotomy which had been a prominent issue in European philosophy since Descartes and which positivist science did nothing to resolve. His critical philosophical methodology is both phenomenological and transcendental, a way of attaining objective knowledge of the world through the active engagement of consciousness in the world while also bracketing out everyday assumptions about the world. His manner of philosophising is careful and rigorous, as befits his aim of establishing a new epistemological methodology.

Like his teacher Husserl, the domain of **Heidegger**'s critique is largely philosophical, his target being all of Western metaphysics since Plato which has forgotten the question of being, or, at its simplest, how strange it is that anything exists. In particular, he is critical of the focus of modern philosophy on subjectivity. For Heidegger these philosophical faults have deep social and cultural ramifications for modernity as a fallen state of existence, which is most clearly manifested in the technologisation of society and the subjection of humanity to calculation. His philosophical methodology is phenomenological but unlike Husserl his approach is both existential and hermeneutic, in that humans are thrown into a world whose horizons are inescapable, while the point of existence is to understand the message that the world presents to humans. Heidegger's mode of writing is notoriously opaque, perhaps so that reading his work requires the patience and hermeneutic effort that he believes modern humanity needs to become receptive to a different understanding of being, which is the aim of his work.

Gadamer's domain of critique is also mostly philosophical, and, as does Husserl, he targets scientific method and its prioritisation of objectivity at the expense of subjective understanding. He is also critical of Enlightened prejudices against tradition, which unlike Kant he wishes to retrieve rather than constantly critique. His methodology is hermeneutic, aiming for understanding which can be achieved by dialogic interaction between the historical, cultural horizons in the background of texts and readers. Dialogic understanding between people is also the wider, cultural impulse of Gadamer's work.

Wittgenstein is another thinker in the tradition of critique whose domain is primarily philosophical. Rather like Heidegger, he has objections to almost all preceding philosophy and metaphysics, which in his view has gone astray and created puzzles for itself by forgetting the ordinary language usage of philosophical terms. His intellectual aim is therapeutic, to free philosophical thought from the pictures of itself and the world by which it is trapped. Although in his early work his tone is often iconoclastic, dismissing previous philosophy as nonsense, in his therapeutic mode he tries to understand and explain the motives that lead philosophers to become captured by pictures.

Arendt returns us to a social and political domain of critique. Her famous targets are racism, imperialism and all other modern political phenomena that lead towards totalitarianism. More generally, she opposed all modern political forms that stood in the way of the expression of authentic human existence by obstructing political action in the public sphere. Arendt rehabilitates political activity in the tradition of critique in the face of a Marxist tendency to consider it epiphenomenal and Heidegger's view of it as inauthentic. Although she was also critical of theoretically rather than practically oriented political interventions, her analysis of modernity relies heavily on large philosophical concepts such as natality and plurality. At the same time, these general concepts are combined with insight gained from the study of particular historical events that typify the sorts of politics she condemns or endorses. Her underlying concern is that political engagement is enhanced so that freedom can be put into practice.

Lévi-Strauss' domain of critique might appear to be philosophical, in that his immediate targets are existentialism, phenomenology and all forms of subject-centred philosophy which he encountered during his intellectual formation. However, he regards philosophical humanism as simply the mythical or ideological expression of modern Western civilisation, rather than a paradigm of universal application. His semiological and structuralist analysis of non-Western cultures, inspired by the scientific methodology of linguistics, is intended to reveal universal cognitive features of the human mind beyond the specifications of individual experience or cultural norm. Moreover, his critique of Eurocentric and monoculturalist assumptions is accompanied by a call for a more universal humanism integrating the totality of cultural experience available to humankind.

Precursors and Contemporaries of Critical Theory

The intellectual tradition covered by the book could roughly be defined as the thought or theory which has had a significant impact on many theoretical innovations in today's humanities and social sciences. The thinkers included in the volume have been selected for their influence beyond the professional boundaries of philosophy. It is precisely because of that impact that so many non-philosophers from such a range of disciplines and interdisciplinary fields have an interest in the thinkers discussed in the volume, either for themselves or for their influence over subsequent theorists. As mentioned above, the most direct influences of the intellectual precursors of contemporary critical theory are indicated in Table 2.

The selection for the volume has been made with two considerations in mind, so that it provides adequate coverage both of a modern European critical intellectual tradition and of the intellectual background to contemporary critical theory. To some extent, the definition of the former has been made retroactively, in relation to the latter. Perhaps it is easiest to define contemporary critical theory in the same way that it is taught and written about in the Anglophone world, according to the names of generally acclaimed and acknowledged theorists. In that case, the 'contemporary' scene might include Lacan, Barthes, Eco, Derrida, Levinas, Kristeva, Cixous, Irigaray, Foucault, Deleuze, Guattari, Baudrillard, Lyotard, Habermas, Taylor, Bourdieu, Hall, Jameson, Laclau, Mouffe, Rorty, Said, Spivak, Vattimo and Žižek. It might certainly include others, but that is a good enough indication of the range of theorists mentioned in this volume who have been influenced by their precursors in the critical tradition.

There are clearly some intellectual distinctions that combine to form a more or less recognisable dividing line between the precursors and the contemporaries. Habermas is quite a different type of Frankfurt theorist to Adorno and Horkheimer, with more faith in the Enlightenment and Arendt's public sphere; Lacan's introduction of structuralist linguistics into psychoanalytic theory marks him off from Freud, whose Oedipal family Deleuze and Guattari rejected as the very source of hierarchy and domination; Barthes leaves behind in his later work his early, scientifically-oriented structuralist semiotics developed under the influence of Lévi-Strauss among others; Derrida deconstructs the structuralism of Lévi-Strauss as part of a poststructuralist trend; Foucault takes up Nietzsche's genealogical critique of modernity but attends to its effects on the weak rather than the strong; Baudrillard claims that Marx (not to mention Foucault) is out of date, though Laclau and Mouffe's post-Marxism is less dismissive, and Jameson awaits a pedagogic aesthetics of cognitive mapping for postmodern culture which neither Lukács nor Adorno could envisage. There is something 'post' about the contemporary figures in relation to their precursors, though neither of the terms 'postmodern' or 'poststructuralist' are adequate or even appropriate to characterise the distinction.

There are, however, some difficulties in any simple distinction between the critical tradition and contemporary theory, or between the latter and its background. First, the precursors of contemporary theory can be deployed to as much critical effect today as in their own time. Second, two of the background thinkers, Lévi-Strauss and Gadamer, are still living at the time of writing this volume, whereas some of those alleged to be more contemporary (Barthes, Lacan, Deleuze and Guattari, Foucault and Lyotard) are dead. Third, there is no convenient historical marker such as World War Two that demarcates a transition from one mode of theory to another, and indeed the active careers of several of the background thinkers bridge that war. The list does exclude anyone born after World War One began in 1914. Insofar as the long nineteenth century is said to have continued until then, and considering the enormous impact of that horrendous war on European culture, a case could be made for the tradition ending at the start of the twentieth century with those for whom that war was part of Europe's past rather than present. For that case to be justified, some careful work in the history of European ideas would have to be undertaken.

Another difficulty of categorising the precursors as the modern intellectual background in relation to the contemporaries is that the scope has to be restricted to prevent finite but considerable regress by beginning with Kant. Already by limiting the background to the modern period the selection rules out many ancient and medieval thinkers and ideas from whom contemporary theorists draw inspiration. For example, Foucault's earlier work is based on a familiarity with Renaissance as well as early modern thought, while his later work delves into Greek, Roman and early Christian thought and culture. Derrida's deconstruction of Plato is as instructive as his critique of Husserl or Freud, while both he and Levinas reach back to Talmudic sources. There are also early modern thinkers who are central to the concepts and themes of contemporary theorists. Rousseau is the central figure in Derrida's grammatology, as is Spinoza for Deleuze's concept of expression and Leibniz for his concept of the fold. Derrida and Foucault argued about Descartes, whose dualism of mind and matter continues to haunt contemporary theory as well as the critical tradition that preceded it. The volume, then, cannot begin at the very beginning without going back to the pre-Socratics, but Kant is as good a place as any to start a volume that delineates a critical tradition in modern European thought.

As well as the pre-modern and early modern thinkers who have had a significant impact on contemporary critical theorists, there are other figures in the critical tradition who would fit well in an enlarged list and a longer volume. More space could have been given to Western Marxism by including Gramsci, whose notion of ideological hegemony is crucial to cultural studies as well as post-Marxism. Chapters on Bloch and Brecht would have built up the argument about politics and aesthetics which so engaged Lukács and the Frankfurt School. That area would also be more rounded with chapters on the Freudo-Marxist Marcuse and the idiosyncratically Marxist cultural critic Benjamin. Weber's social and cultural analysis could be compared helpfully with the earlier critique of modernity by Simmel. More background could have been provided for contemporary French theorists such as Deleuze and Baudrillard by chapters on the earlier figures Bergson and Bataille. More of the structuralist and semiotic theories to which poststructuralism responds could have been presented if one or more of Bakhtin, Peirce, Jakobson or Saussure had been included. The coverage of phenomenology and existentialism could have been expanded with chapters on Merleau-Ponty, Sartre and Beauvoir, which in the last case would have the added virtue of including another woman in the volume.

It is inevitable that a book of this size is haunted by absences, just as any quest to understand all of the intellectual background of contemporary theory must remain incomplete. However, the selection of thinkers included from the modern critical tradition for this volume is intended to be sufficiently representative of different intellectual tendencies such as Marxism, phenomenology, hermeneutics, psychoanalysis and structuralism to provide enough background to gain a sound understanding of contemporary developments. It also includes enough of the key philosophical figures such as Kant, Hegel, Arendt and Wittgenstein, whose names or concepts may not define contemporary theoretical tendencies, but who have an enormous influence on contemporary theory.

The result of this mode of selection is a list which is almost entirely Germanophone except for Lévi-Strauss, male except for Arendt, and includes many thinkers with a Jewish background, though some of them would not define themselves as Jewish. The Germanophone emphasis reflects the intellectual predominance of German speakers in the period covered, in contrast to an earlier modern time in which the French and also the Scots appeared to be the philosophers of Enlightenment. The Germanophones were also the precursors of the Francophones who predominate in contemporary critical theory. As Vincent Descombes notes, post-war French philosophy was first dominated by the 'three H's', Hegel, Husserl and Heidegger until 1960, and thereafter by the three 'masters of suspicion', Marx, Nietzsche and Freud, thereby emphasising the degree of Germanophone influence on French thought.[1] The absence of women is explained by their relative lack of access to education, financial resources and academic positions, all of which Virginia Woolf famously summed up as '£500 a year and a room of her own' in her explanation of why there had not been a female Shakespeare.[2] A list of contemporary critical theorists would include more women, who, unlike Arendt, would also identify themselves as feminists. The thinkers included in the volume generally use the term 'man' in a way that is now considered sexist, either because it deliberately excludes women from humanity or because it uses a male-gendered term to refer to all of humanity. As there is not space in the book to explore the issue of sexism, the chapters often follow the thinkers' use of the term 'man' so that there is no attempt to disguise the possibility of sexism on the part of the thinkers who are discussed.

The relatively high proportion of thinkers with varying degrees of Jewish backgrounds (Marx, Freud, Husserl, Lukács, Adorno, Horkheimer, Wittgenstein, Arendt and Lévi-Strauss) can be explained in terms of what Arendt defined as the 'pariah' status of assimilated Jews in modernising Europe.[3] Assimilating European Jews were both insiders and outsiders of modern culture, especially Germanophone culture, and as such were placed for a time in particular social contexts in which the stresses and contradictions of modernity could be experienced and reflected upon. Such pariahs were the paradigmatic critical thinkers of their time. As is explained in the preceding section, the main characteristic of the tradition of critique which constitutes the background to contemporary critical theory is that it was critical of different aspects of modernity. Contemporary theorists continue that critique, even when they criticise it as postmodernity or in postmodern ways, so the tradition of critique continues.

Notes

1. Vincent Descombes, *Modern French Philosophy*, trans. L. Scott-Fox and J. M. Harding (Cambridge: Cambridge University Press, 1980), p. 3.
2. Virginia Woolf, *A Room of One's Own and Three Guineas* (London: Penguin, 1993), p. 3.
3. Hannah Arendt, *The Jew as Pariah: Jewish Identity and Politics in the Modern Age*, ed. Ron H. Feldman (New York: Grove Press, 1978).

2

Immanuel Kant (1724–1804)

Jon Simons

Kant in the Critical Tradition

Kant's critical philosophy is the most obvious starting point for the European philosophical tradition that constitutes the background of contemporary critical theory, in many ways setting the parameters for subsequent debate. Kant himself is significant as a philosopher who defends the principles of Enlightened reason against scepticism. He argues for the validity of the knowledge accrued by the natural sciences, but also for the possibility of reason legislating for both individual moral action and the constitutional structure of the state and its relations to other states. Kant's critical philosophy inspired as much criticism as admiration in the tradition of critique that followed him. Hegel criticised Kant's transcendent notion of reason and formalist morality, arguing instead for the immanence of reason and ethics to concrete practices and historical periods. For Hegel, as for Marx, teleological judgement about human progress can be made only retrospectively, depending on whether a social or political development actually contributes to the realisation of reason in human life.

One of Kant's most productive moves is his analytical distinction between different mental powers, especially theoretical understanding and reason. The former relies on scientific rationality to gain understanding of the natural world of objects which can then be mastered technologically, while the latter is a version of Kant's practical reason which deliberates about the ends and purposes of instrumental action. Kant's philosophical system aims at mediation between these two forms of reason, warning about the overextension of either into the domain of the other. Subsequent thinkers, especially Weber and the Frankfurt theorists, have reformulated that distinction as one between two different types of rationality. As a result, Kant's basic moral principles of respect for persons and autonomy underlie much of the substance of the critical tradition.

Kant also explains how humans can be understood from the perspectives of both scientific rationality, as natural objects, and moral reasoning, as free subjects. In spite of Kant's attempt to mediate these two incompatible perspectives, a good deal of critical thought has been dedicated to asserting the latter in face of the former, especially when the methods of the natural sciences have been deployed in the domain of the human sciences. Moreover, phenomenologists such as Husserl have elaborated ways of understanding the world which require the perspective of subjective consciousness. Hermeneuticists such as Gadamer have developed approaches to historical and social enquiry which stress ethically directed human action. Weber is a key figure in the interpretative turn in the social sciences that focuses on the meaning of action, which is echoed by the later Wittgenstein's attention to meaning rather than truth in language. While Kant's first critique aims to establish the validity of natural scientific knowledge, his philosophy, including the problems it fails to solve, has inspired critical thinkers to ground the knowledge gained by the human sciences.

Kant's sustained attention to aesthetics and judgement has also had its impact on the tradition of critique. According to Kant's tripartite division of what Weber calls value spheres, aesthetic production and appreciation do not serve the purposes of theoretical understanding and the moral reasoning. Accordingly, in a sense which is highlighted by modernist sensibilities, art is autotelic, meaning that it gives its end to itself. In a world dominated by instrumental reason and administration, certain forms of art can thus be valued by Adorno as a privileged area of freedom indicating utopian possibilities. Nietzsche regards artistic creativity as paradigmatic human action because neither God nor the nature of the universe determine human purposes. Rather, the human will imposes myths and metaphors on existence in order to give it a manageable form, but Kant refuses to acknowledge that only humans invest the world with purpose. Nietzsche's radical critique of Kantian reason speaks of the immaturity humans have displayed by attributing the limits they have imposed on the world to reason instead of admitting that they invented those limits. In Arendt's hands, by contrast, Kant's notion of undetermined judgement is closely linked to the sense of community that accompanies public expression of aesthetic taste, which in turn becomes the grounds for political community.

Introduction

Kant is the most influential of modern Western philosophers, whose mature work, which he called critical philosophy, continues to shape thought in general, including contemporary critical theory. He was born in Königsberg, Prussia, in 1724, where he lived all his life until his death in 1804. His Pietist (reformist Lutheran) family background, which stressed individual conscience and duty, left its mark on his moral philosophy. Kant remained a bachelor, leading a very regular life, which included entertaining for lunch a variety of guests he came across in what was then quite a cosmopolitan port city. Under the rule of Fredrick the Great (1740–86), Prussia enjoyed an air of Enlightenment and religious toleration, but under the rule of Fredrick William II he was bound to silence on his rationalist views on religion. Although Kant had republican sympathies, he was not one to confront political authority, keeping his criticism to his writing. Until his appointment as Professor of Metaphysics and Logic at the University of Königsberg in 1770, Kant's lectures and writing had been mostly about mathematics and physics, so it was quite late in life that his mature philosophy took off as an effort to establish the objectivity of the knowledge provided by the natural sciences.

In this chapter Kant's critical philosophy is presented as a system. His main works were his *Critique of Pure Reason* (1781), *Critique of Practical Reason* (1788) and *Critique of Judgement* (1790). In turn, they analyse the capacities and limits of human mental powers, called faculties, of theoretical or scientific understanding, moral reason and both aesthetic and teleological judgement (meaning judgement about ends or purposes). They are critical in that in each case Kant assesses how far our faculties can take us in answer to the questions: 'What can I know? What ought I to do? What may I hope?'[1] Theoretical understanding gives us empirically-based, objective knowledge of nature, as established by Newtonian mechanistic physics, but not of 'things in themselves' beyond our experience, or of metaphysical entities such as the soul or God. Reason gives us a universally binding moral law, obedience to which constitutes freedom. Each of the first two critiques is immensely significant in itself, but it is the third which systematises Kant's philosophy in that judgement mediates between understanding and reason, indicating a finality or purpose to the world according to which we can be both objects under the laws of nature and free subjects of the moral law.

The Rational Critique of Reason

Kant's *Critique of Pure Reason* is an answer to the question: what can we know?, but also a rebuttal of both Hume's empiricism and Leibniz's rationalism. Kant wished to avoid the contemporary philosophical orthodoxy of dogmatic rationalism represented by Leibniz and Wolff, according to which all true knowledge is derived from the exercise of reason, following innate principles which are known to be true independent of experience. Our subjective knowledge of objects is guaranteed by a divine harmony of the universe between ideas and things, which can be known by understanding the innate principles, and which in turn give us knowledge of metaphysical concepts such as the soul and God. Kant held that such metaphysical speculation was beyond the reach of human understanding, leading instead to a series of antinomies, meaning apparent philosophical paradoxes based on pairs of false assumptions. When pure reason proceeds on the basis of unempirical ideas, it is being used illegitimately.

At the same time, Kant did hold that if used legitimately, the ideas of reason lead to objective knowledge. According to Hume's philosophy, the only reliable knowledge we have comes from sense impressions, whereas what we consider to be valid scientific knowledge is really nothing more than a habit of thought which subjectively links experiences into regular successions. Although we believe we know that causal necessity requires the sun to rise tomorrow because it always has done so far, such habitual certainty that day always follows night is merely a projection of the human mind. Kant agrees with Hume that our human perspective on the world constitutes knowledge and that no knowledge is possible without experience, but does not accept Hume's sceptical conclusions which deny the possibility of objective knowledge, as given by common sense and natural science. Instead, he regards the cognitive power of understanding as a higher form of knowledge that is required to order experience but which goes beyond experience by establishing not only *a posteriori* knowledge, meaning what is known from experience, but also *a priori* knowledge, which is valid universally and necessarily, as under a law of nature.

In order to justify objective knowledge, Kant argues that it requires a synthesis of reason and experience, of that which we know *a priori* beyond experience and that which we know from experience. The main difficulty is in establishing the first part, which Kant asks as:

'How are synthetic propositions *a priori* possible?'[2] Synthetic propositions, or judgements, are distinguished from analytical or logical propositions. In the latter, the predicate concept is contained in the subject concepts, as in 'all bachelors are unmarried men'. Synthetic judgements tell us something about the world not given in the terms or concepts of the proposition, such as 'Kant was a bachelor'. But how can a proposition be both *a priori* and synthetic? Put very simply, Kant argues that we can know certain things by reasoning beyond experience, such as that every event has a cause, because such concepts are presupposed by or are conditions of possibility of experience and knowledge. Kant characterises his method for arriving at these conditions as transcendental deduction, because we must transcend our experience to deduce what makes it possible. These presuppositions come in two forms. First, space and time are *a priori* intuitions of perception, meaning that we can only experience objects as existing in space and time, though we cannot know space and time through our experience. Second, there are twelve *a priori* categories or concepts of understanding, which are present in our understanding before experience, such as the notion of causality, or that objects exist as substance. These concepts give form to our thoughts about experience in a way that makes our sense impressions intelligible to us. The link between sense-perceptions represented as intuitions in time and space and concepts, and hence between empirical experience and reason that transcends experience, is made by the imagination, which is another faculty that schematises by relating a diversity of sense-perceptions to concepts. The faculty of understanding legislates over reason and imagination to establish a determinate accord between the faculties.

Another aspect of the accord between our faculties is that it is presupposed by self-conscious experience. It is another precondition of knowledge that sense-intuitions must allow for the application of the categories, which also means that if the world is comprehensible it must appear to conform to the categories and their schematisation as laws of nature, such as Newtonian physics. This deduction of *a priori* principles is subjective rather than objective, because it refers to the perspective of human subjects. It is also the grounds for Kant's Copernican revolution, according to which the condition of possibility of objective knowledge is that physical objects must conform with our cognitive powers, not vice versa. Yet this does raise the problem that Kant seems to presuppose a similar harmony between *a priori* truths, or the ideas of reason, and the world, or between the capacities of the knower and the nature of the known, as the one asserted by dogmatic rationalists. His justification for the accord of the faculties with each other and the world does not come until his third *Critique*.

The knowledge gained by our cognitive faculties is one of phenomena, or physical objects as appearances, rather than noumena, or things in themselves. Kant does not mean that reality is hidden from us behind mere appearances, but that we cannot aspire to knowledge of the world which is conceived apart from the perspective of the knower. Nonetheless, our faculty of reason is inevitably drawn to overextend itself by using concepts unempirically, applying them to transcendental objects such as the soul and God that are knowable to thought alone. For example, we might assume that because we are aware of ourselves as consciousness that thinks and organises experience, we have knowledge of a substantial and unified self. Kants warns that the Cartesian *cogito* is a perspective that makes knowledge possible, not a known substance. The overextension of reason generates illusions when taken as descriptions of empirical reality, illusions which supply the falsely contrasted assumption of the antinomies of pure reason. For example, according to theoretical understanding, everything in the world is causally determined, which includes us as rational beings. On the other hand, we presuppose in our actions that we have free will. The apparent paradox disappears as in the first case moral agents are conceived as phenomena, from the perspective of theoretical understanding, and in the second case as noumena, from the perspective of reason. There is a gap between the two perspectives, but it is a mistake to conceive the moral agent as a physical object.

Kant also sees much value in reason's positing questions beyond theoretical understanding, such as: what caused the world to exist? First, it demonstrates the limits of our cognitive power, because we cannot answer the question. Second, by pushing us to think about the world as a totality, reason provides us with a regulative principle, or a correct hypothesis, according to which we think of the world as subject to universal and necessary laws. By presupposing a systematic unity of nature, reason symbolises the accord between the content of particular phenomena and the ideas of reason. Kant's interest is not only in establishing the illegitimacy of the use of reason beyond certain limits as a way to justify natural science and debunk metaphysical speculation, but also to establish the legitimacy of reason's interest beyond the phenomenal world.

Moral Reason

Kant's *Critique of Practical Reason* is so called because it is about the application of reason to action or practice. Our faculty of desire often operates according to natural causes such as instincts, desires or feelings, allowing our will to be determined by heteronomous, or external influences. In that case, reason is, as Hume put it, the slave of passion, for our cognitive powers are limited to figuring out instrumentally the best means to achieve our ends, not what our ends or goals ought to be. But humans are not merely objects governed by the laws of nature. The first *Critique* had already argued that knowledge presupposes a unified consciousness that thinks and transcendental freedom as cognitive deliberation, but under the legislation of theoretical understanding nothing could be known about the transcendental self which is not determined by the laws of nature. Practical reason, which is the higher form of our faculty of desire, is at work when we stop to reflect, asking ourselves, 'What ought I to do?' Practical reason is known itself through the exercise of freedom, which is the only idea of reason that has an objective reality, in human action. The central aim of the second *Critique* is to show that there are objective and universal principles of human action, in the form of a moral law. The moral law is synthetic *a priori* practical knowledge based on reason alone. Kant does not criticise practical reason for overstepping its proper limits, but he does critique the impure exercise of practical reason when heteronomous motives hold sway. In contrast, autonomy of the will is the ability to be governed by reason or to will an end of action for oneself. The faculty of understanding does play a role, in that it gives us the form of conformity to law as the form of freedom, as we can draw an analogy between the 'suprasensible' (meaning, non-empirical) realm of freedom and the 'sensible' (empirical) world of nature. Reason also adopts the notion of causality given by theoretical understanding, turning it into the notion of free causality. But it is the faculty of reason that legislates for practical reasoning.

The idea of freedom as obedience to a law one makes for oneself, or autonomy, came from Rousseau, who was a key influence on Kant. Autonomy is also a question of maturity, an ability to abstract away from one's personal desires, interests and tastes as well as the opinions of others. If one thinks as oneself only as a rational agent, as free and unconditioned, reason will compel one to embrace duty in the form of 'categorical imperatives', which are rules that all rational beings must obey without exception, in order to be true to their nature as autonomous beings. In this *Critique*, Kant does not have to prove that objective moral principles are true, but that they are what rational beings must think when they think about universal and necessary principles.

There are two basic formulations of the categorical imperative, the first of which is: 'Act only according to that maxim by which you can at the same time will that it should become universal law.'[3] Kant's rule can be considered as a formalisation of the golden rule: 'Do to others as you would have others do to you.' For example, one must always keep one's promises, because one cannot break them without undermining the very notion of a promise, and because one would want others to keep their promises. Kant's basic point is that if every rational being would follow the same maxim, that is proof that it is an exercise of autonomy, free from individual desires and appetites. The second formulation is called the practical imperative: 'Act so that you treat humanity, whether in your own person or in that of another, always as an end and never as a means only.'[4] This seems like a particular application of the first formulation in relation to human beings, commanding us to respect others as we would have them respect us, acknowledging our capacity for freedom and autonomy. Yet it also contains the extremely significant point that rational agents must be considered as ends in themselves, because pure practical reason is not conditioned or determined by anything other than itself. In other words, freedom is the goal of rational agents capable of freedom.

The notion of reason and freedom as ends in themselves also indicates a way out of the key problem for Kant's system. How can freedom be possible in a causally determined world? How can we humans be both noumena and phenomena? How can the practical knowledge we have of freedom be reconciled with the theoretical knowledge we have of nature? Kant admits that, as a result of his first two *Critiques*,

> an immense gulf is fixed between the domain of the concept of nature, the sensible, and the domain of the concept of freedom, the supersensible, so that no transition from the sensible to the supersensible ... is possible, just as if they were two different worlds.[5]

Kant's full answer to the problem comes in his third *Critique*, but in his discussion of practical reason he suggests that the realisation of moral good presupposes an accord between nature and freedom, such that the 'ought' of the categorical imperative implies that it can be fulfilled. That does not mean that we mere mortals are always virtuous, but that the possibility of a 'kingdom of ends' in which rational beings always act autonomously is given to us as an idea of reason. In the case of practical reasoning, reason does not overextend itself when it extrapolates from our practical knowledge of moral action. In this case, reason intimates a transcendental reality populated by immortal souls aiming for moral perfection, and created by God in a fashion that makes moral action in nature possible. The soul and God, which are postulates of practical reason, are also its conditions of possibility. This is another aspect of Kant's Copernican revolution: it is not the idea of God and the soul which provide us with morality, but the practice of freedom and morality which leads us to the idea of a divinely ordained world. The ideas of reason which lead to illusion from the perspective of theoretical understanding of nature are rescued in the second *Critique* as the basis for moral reasoning and freedom.

Aesthetic and Teleological Judgement

To complete his philosophical system by establishing a link between freedom and nature, Kant needs his third *Critique of Judgement*: 'the family of our higher cognitive powers also includes a mediating link between understanding and reason. This is judgement.'[6] In particular, this *Critique* focuses on reflective judgement of which there are two kinds, aesthetic and teleological, of which the first kind can be about either beauty or sublimity. As well as dealing with judgement, the third *Critique* also covers another faculty, namely the feeling of pleasure or displeasure which lies between our cognitive faculty and our faculty of desire. Just as each of those faculties has a higher form, respectively theoretical understanding and reason, so does feeling, in the form of judgement. Similarly, Kant is concerned to establish a synthetic *a priori* of aesthetic taste, or a justification for the possibility of aesthetic judgement.

The problem, characterised as the antinomy of taste, is that aesthetic judgement involves both feelings related directly to subjective experience, not conceptual thought, and judgement, for which we give reasons and claim universal assent. Aesthetic pleasure, claims Kant, presupposes that others ought to agree that 'this rose is beautiful', or that there is a subjectively universal 'common sense' of beauty. The point is not that we should all recognise the same property of beauty in objects, but that we can all share the same feeling. To feel beauty, Kant says we make a disinterested judgement, which means that our feeling of pleasure may not be empirically determined as sensory satisfaction or what feels agreeable to an individual, as in 'this rose smells beautiful'. Rather, we take delight in the accord of nature's beauty with our disinterested pleasure. Aesthetic judgement is free of all individual inclination in the same way that practical reasoning is, which is why we expect universal assent. Already we can see one way in which, for Kant, beauty is a symbol of the good, because we make aesthetic and moral judgements from the same disinterested position.

Also, we judge beauty without applying concepts, so that what we have in mind is not the concept of the rose but our intuition, or perception, of the rose. In aesthetic judgement imagination is freed from concepts, that is to say, from the task of bringing concepts to bear on experience, as when we understand, 'that red and green thing is a rose'. Moreover, aesthetic judgement entails a free, undetermined accord between the faculties. Judgements of beauty always concern singular perceptions, such as of the colour and shape of a red rose. Yet, the imagination still brings concepts to bear on experience, but in a free and undetermined way. Another way to put this is that the faculty of judgement has an indeterminate concept which serves as its *a priori* principle, in parallel to the principle of 'lawfulness', or the systematic unity of nature, for the faculty of understanding, and 'final purpose', or the realisation of freedom in the 'kingdom of ends' for the faculty of reason.

The principle of judgement is 'formal' or 'subjective purposiveness', which means nature's purposiveness for our power of judgement considered from the subjective perspective of humans. Nature lends itself to our judgement by manifesting regularity not only in its universal laws but also in its particular and contingent arrangements. We feel the pleasure of beauty when we apprehend how the shapes and hues of a rose harmonise into a whole, but at the same time we feel pleasure that nature produces beautiful forms that can be reflected in our imagination. Moreover, the harmonious forms in nature that we judge to be beautiful match both the lawfulness in nature that is presupposed by understanding, but also the accord between understanding and imagination which is a necessary condition of cognition. The pleasure felt in contemplating beauty is thus an awareness of the harmony of our faculties required for all cognition and judgement. We project the harmonious working of our faculties on to the empirical world, finding in it the order which our imagination apprehends in harmonious, aesthetic wholes. As all humans are assumed to share the same conditions of cognition, then even though aesthetic pleasure is particular and subjective, it is at the same time a pleasure that is shared with all rational beings.

For the most part, Kant considers beauty only in relation to nature, rather than art. He explains that pure judgements can be made only about free beauty in contrast to beauty that is fixed by the concept of a thing's purpose. All fine art involves the concept of a purpose, in that the artist has a purpose in creating it, though genius can animate fine art by creating a second nature. Kant thus prefers to focus on pure aesthetic judgements, but his focus on nature also fits his philosophical system better, because it allows him to argue that aesthetic judgement is universal because of its accord with nature's formal or subjective purposiveness. Judgements of beauty also relate to nature's real or objective purposiveness, which, according to Kant, should properly be the subject of teleological judgement. Nature's objective purposiveness is not its suitability for human cognition, but its end in itself or final purpose, which is beyond theoretical understanding as it pertains to the 'suprasensible' domain of freedom, not the 'sensible' empirical domain. The end which we judge teleologically is the realisation of freedom in the natural world, which presupposes that the world has a divinely ordained order that ultimately enables us to be free and autonomous. According to the teleological principle that freedom is humanity's purpose, it is the highest good. Aesthetic judgement mediates between the formal purposiveness of nature and its objective purposiveness because beauty consists in aesthetic harmony or unity which has no empirical purpose, and is characterised by Kant as 'purposiveness without a purpose'.[7] If something does not have a purpose for anything else and yet seems to have been designed, it leads us to the idea that the object has an end in itself.

The aesthetic idea of harmony and unity thus leads us to the idea that nature and humans have a 'suprasensible purpose', a purpose which is an end in itself. We cannot know the transcendental design of nature, but aesthetic judgement intimates it by enabling us to feel it. This intimation is similar to the way in which practical reason does not give us knowledge of freedom as the final purpose, but our practice of morality enlarges that idea of reason that there is a harmony between freedom and nature. Beauty symbolises good because it leads us by analogy to the same idea. The free and indeterminate harmony of faculties in aesthetic judgement leads to the idea of an undetermined accord between our faculties and nature, which in turn leads to the idea that there is an objective purposiveness to both that accord and the apparent design of nature, which is freedom.

The impossibility of knowing rather than feeling the purposive design of nature is brought very much to mind in judgements of the sublime. We experience the sublime when confronted with something immense, such as a mountain range, or something powerful, such as rolling waves on an ocean. The feeling of horror in the face of the sublime which Burke identified is explained by Kant as the failure of the imagination to apprehend it. The imagination is thus forced to acknowledge its limits in fulfilling the demand of reason to represent objects as wholes. There is also a subjective purposiveness to sublime judgement, in that the imagination learns of the immense power of reason. It is not nature itself which is sublime, but the power of the mind to present the idea of a suprasensible purpose which is inaccessible to the imagination. That suprasensible purpose is freedom, the idea of reason which is presupposed in our moral actions. Judgements of the sublime are universal because they are linked to awareness of the power of reason to legislate for itself and to posit a purpose for nature and man.

The idea of a final end or purpose that is determined by reason is a matter for teleological judgement. From the perspective of the first *Critique*, it may seem that such judgements about a final end, a purpose for which the universe was designed, belong to the realm of metaphysical speculation. That would be the case if they were taken as objectively known facts, rather than as necessary presuppositions about the systemacity and unity of nature. Kant argues that we need to use reason's idea of objective natural purpose in order to understand nature as an ordered, rule-governed system, which is different from understanding it in terms of causal relations, the latter being the only objective explanation of which theoretical understanding is capable. Such judgements are used regulatively, as maxims, to allow our faculties of understanding and reason to give us knowledge of nature by operating as if it has natural purposes. If nature is organised systematically and purposively, it leads us to think of an intentional cause beyond nature, a suprasensible cause of nature, meaning God as the supreme cause. Moreover, if nature has been created for a purpose, it must have a final purpose, which is to make it possible for man to cultivate virtue in pursuit of freedom under the moral law. Teleology thus becomes moral teleology, leading us to the same ideas as does pure practical reason. Neither can prove the existence of God, which would be metaphysical speculation, but each indicates that the idea of God is presupposed both by our theoretical understanding of nature as a systematic whole subject to the causal laws of nature, and by our reason, which give us practical cognition of an unconditioned domain of freedom beyond nature. Both understanding and reason have as their conditions of possibility something akin to an enormous yet unknowable hypothesis about the purpose of the 'sensible' natural domain and the 'suprasensible' domain of freedom. Aesthetic and teleological judgement mediates between nature and freedom by reflecting on the unity, wholeness and purposiveness of each domain, intimating that the moral purpose experienced in practical action is the unknown purpose that is felt aesthetically and presupposed theoretically. That is the complex if not convoluted argument that must be followed if judgement is to unite the three *Critiques* into a system, though there is dispute about whether Kant succeeds.

Kant and Contemporary Critical Theory

Kant's critical philosophy is more than ample fodder for criticism by contemporary theorists, though some find his philosophical method and system productive as much for its failures as its successes. As a leading Enlightenment philosopher, Kant is often attacked from various postmodern perspectives for the alleged transgressions of modern thought. Most notably, Rorty regards Kant as the arch-foundationalist philosopher, the architect of philosophy that attempts to ground valid claims to knowledge and to rule out invalid claims.[8] Bauman also picks up on Kant's terminology of reason as legislator, criticising him for asserting the authority of intellectuals to provide universal standards of truth, morality and taste in alliance with modern state rulers in a joint effort to establish modernity as a fundamentally ordered social and political system.[9] Yet, Kant brings reason before its own tribunal, disallowing illegitimate uses of it by debunking dogmatic rationalism. Kant is clearly concerned with the limits of theoretical understanding and the necessity of both moral reason and reflective judgement which cannot be grounded epistemologically. Kant's political theory of constitutional republicanism and world peace might best characterised as a framework to make morality and autonomy possible on a public scale, and is certainly not an attempt to apply a scientific understanding of causality in the natural world to society.

Kant is also criticised by some feminists for positing what they take to be male-centred norms and values of the self and reason as universal, a criticism which is reinforced by Kant's view that women are not capable of maturity in the sense of moral autonomy.[10] Gilligan's feminist 'ethic of care' is posited as a contrast to a Kantian 'ethics of justice', which, allegedly, is based on a model of moral development reflecting the experience of boys but not girls.[11] Kant is one of many male Enlightenment philosophers whose work is subject to a feminist debate about whether such bias is inherent to his philosophy, such that the notion of rational being cannot be applied to women, or whether his chauvinist opinions can be edited out to produce a gender-neutral philosophy.

Several other key contemporary theorists have critical relationships with Kant which begin from the premise that Kant's philosophy fails as a system to achieve grounding or validate judgements. Habermas follows the tripartite structure of Kant's critical philosophy by analysing the different bases for validity claims in three value spheres: cognitive-instrumental, moral-practical and aesthetic expressive. However, he rejects Kant's notion of transcendental reason, instead proposing a pragmatically based communicative reason which must be presupposed for communication through speech to be meaningful.[12] Lyotard focuses on what he takes to be Kant's impossible attempt to bridge theoretical understanding and practical reason through judgement, which he interprets as a particular instance of the impossibility of a universal discourse that rules over heterogeneous discourses or 'phrase regimes'. For Lyotard the incommensurable difference and agonistic contestation between discourses and social groups, rather than universality, is the principle of justice.[13] Lyotard also highlights Kant's aesthetic of the sublime as that which resists representation by totalising discourse.[14] If Lyotard has a postmodern Kant, Foucault's attitude is more ambivalent. On the one hand, he regards Kant's philosophy as the epitome of modern thought which is trapped in anthropological slumber, unable to extricate itself from fundamental antinomies such as between man's empirical existence and transcendent reason.[15] On the other hand, he credits Kant with an admirable philosophical ethos of critique of modernity as analysis and reflection on limits. But in a Nietzschean twist, Foucault historicises Kant's analysis of *a priori* conditions of knowledge, denying that they are universal and necessary and suggesting that limits be transgressed rather than regarded as necessary conditions.[16] Kant's influence on contemporary critical theory remains considerable, either as a target of criticism or as inspiration for critical philosophy.

Notes

1. Kant, *Pure Reason,* A: 805; B: 833. (The references follow the custom of giving the page numbers in the first and second German *Akademie* editions, which are given on each page of the English translation.)
2. Kant, *Prolegomena,* p. 23.
3. Kant, *Metaphysics of Morals,* p. 39.
4. Ibid., p. 47.
5. Kant, *Judgement,* p. 14.
6. Ibid., p. 16.
7. Ibid., p. 65.
8. Richard Rorty, *Philosophy and the Mirror of Nature* (Princeton: Princeton University Press, 1979), p. 5.
9. Zygmunt Bauman, *Intimations of Postmodernity* (London: Routledge, 1992), pp. 116–20.
10. Jane Flax, 'Postmodernism and Gender Relations in Feminist Theory', in Linda Nicholson (ed.), *Feminism/Postmodernism* (New York: Routledge, 1990), pp. 42–3; and Genevieve Lloyd, *The Man of Reason,* 2nd edn (London: Routledge, 1993), pp. 64–70.
11. Carol Gilligan, *In a Different Voice: Psychological Theory and Women's Development* (Cambridge, MA: Harvard University Press, 1982).
12. Jürgen Habermas, *The Theory of Communicative Action, Volume I,* trans. Thomas McCarthy (Boston: Beacon Press, 1984).
13. Jean-François Lyotard, *The Differend,* trans. Georges Van Den Abbeele (Minneapolis: Minnesota University Press, 1988).
14. Jean-François Lyotard, 'An Answer to the Question, What is the Postmodern?', in Julian Pefanis and Morgan Thomas (eds), *Postmodernism Explained* (Minneapolis: Minnesota University Press, 1993), pp. 1–16.
15. Michel Foucault, *The Order of Things,* unidentified collective (trans.) (New York: Vintage, 1973), pp. 303–43.
16. Michel Foucault, 'What is Enlightenment?', trans. Catherine Porter, in Paul Rabinow (ed.), *The Foucault Reader* (New York: Pantheon, 1984), pp. 32–50.

Major Works by Kant

Critique of Pure Reason, trans. Norman Kemp Smith (New York: St Martin's Press, 1965 [1st edn 1781; 2nd edn 1787]).

Prolegomena to any Future Metaphysics, trans. Peter Lucas (Manchester: Manchester University Press, 1953 [1783]). A condensed version of the first Critique.

Foundations of the Metaphysics of Morals, trans. Lewis White Beck (Indianapolis: Bobbs-Merrill, 1959 [1785]). Kant's easier version of his second Critique.

Critique of Practical Reason, trans. Lewis White Beck (New York: Macmillan, 1956 [1788]).

Critique of Judgement, trans. Werner Pluhar (Indianapolis: Hackett, 1987 [1790]).

Perpetual Peace and Other Essays, trans. Ted Humphrey (Indianapolis: Hackett, 1983). Shorter essays on moral, historical and political themes.

Suggestions for Further Reading

Appelbaum, David, *The Vision of Kant* (Rockport, MA: Element, 1995). Concise 50-page overview of Kant's philosophy and selections from his work.

Caygill, Howard, *Art of Judgement* (Oxford: Clarendon, 1989). Focuses on the political implications of the third Critique.

Deleuze, Gilles, *Kant's Critical Philosophy*, trans. Hugh Tomlinson and Barbara Habberjam (Minneapolis: University of Minnesota Press, 1984). A condensed essay which attempts to integrate Kant's three Critiques into an overall system by focusing on the faculties.

Guyer, Paul (ed.), *The Cambridge Companion to Kant* (Cambridge: Cambridge University Press, 1982). Useful but advanced collection of essays.

Hutchings, Kimberly, *Kant, Critique and Politics* (London: Routledge, 1996). Concise summary of Kant's critique, and chapters on Habermas, Arendt, Foucault, Lyotard and feminism read through the problematique of Kantian critique.

Körner, S., *Kant* (Harmondsworth: Penguin, 1955). Exposition of Kant's philosophy which has stood the test of time.

Scruton, Roger, *Kant* (Oxford: Oxford University Press, 1982). Brief and accessible account of Kant's work.

3

Georg Wilhelm Friedrich Hegel (1770–1831)

Matt F. Connell

Hegel in the Critical Tradition

Hegel is less convinced than Kant that Enlightened reason could solve humanity's problems. Whereas Kant enthuses about the rational ideals of the French Revolution, Hegel's enthusiasm is more measured. Influenced by the German Romantics, Hegel comes to the view that the rationalisation of reason into freedom is not a matter of abstract theorising but of the historical development of possibilities inherent in particular cultures. Thus he does not share an Enlightened disdain for traditional forms of life, which all contain at least the seeds of reason and freedom. Nor does he conceive of the individual self as abstracted from culture but as embedded in it, so that even individuality is a cultural achievement. In general, Hegel's philosophical as well as social and political orientations favour harmony rather than the divisions and distinctions evident in the complexity of modern society and the philosophical systems of his time.

Hegel's philosophical system can be understood as a response to Kant's critical philosophy, in particular the attempts by figures after Kant such as Fichte and Schelling to develop the method of 'transcendental idealism'. The key problem for those who came after Kant was to elaborate the basic categories of experience in a way that connected them both to each other and to the free, self-determined human subject. Hegel criticised Kant and his followers for considering such key issues as subjectivity from incomplete and undeveloped perspectives, as a result of which philosophy ended up with a series of dualisms or incompatible oppositions between terms such as freedom and determinism. Hegel's systematic concept of totality is conceived as a way of overcoming dualisms such as those addressed by Kant's antinomies, attempting to reach the whole of which terms such as nature and human action are parts. The perspective from which the whole can be perceived, so that free humans can be seen to be at home in a causally determined world, is that of the history of human experience. Rather than focusing on individual subjectivity and autonomy, Hegel regards the proper subject of philosophy to be humanity as a collectivity coming to self-consciousness. In a related contrast to Kant's moral philosophy, Hegel stresses the collective or institutional nature of ethical life in the family, civil society and the state, all of which ensure that duty does not conflict with individual free will. He considers Kant's moral law to be hopelessly abstract and formal, unable to guide action while insisting on an unrealistic devotion to duty. Hegel's understanding of the strained interaction of personality with modern social structure has some affinity to Freud's notion of ego alienation (though there is no evidence of a direct influence), as well as to subsequent Freudo-Marxist deployments of the dialectic to address the interaction.

Although Hegel's approach remains idealist, in that the subject of history is 'spirit' or *Geist*, his dialectical notion of totality became positively important for Marx's historical materialism, as discussed in the chapter on Marx. However, Hegelianism's reception in Western Marxism has been mixed. Whereas Lukács found the key to dialectical thought through Marx's appropriation of Hegel's notion of totality, Adorno rejected the totalitarian implication of Hegel's 'identity' thinking, seeking instead to rescue the more fluid side of his philosophy, as discussed in Chapters 8 and 9. Hegel thus appears in the tradition of critique as both an ally in the critique of modernity and as an advocate of modernity to be criticised.

Introduction

Hegel was born in Stuttgart in 1770, the same year as Beethoven, Wordsworth and Hölderlin. He absorbed the Greek and Roman classics alongside scientific ideas, immersed himself in the emerging literature of Goethe and Schiller, trained as a Lutheran pastor and engaged seriously with the German philosophical tradition, especially post-Kantian idealism. As a young man, he was an enthusiast for the Enlightenment and for the French Revolution, which were to modernise the fragmented and still semi-feudal Germany into which Hegel was born. He later developed a more tempered assessment of the limits of both. The atmosphere of artistic and philosophical ferment coupled with political upheaval and progress nevertheless had a profound impact on Hegel, who traced these developments through the production of a philosophy capable of demonstrating how they, and it, were the product of all prior forms of thought, a living expression of the whole spirit of the age.

This chapter concentrates on Hegel's first systematic book, the *Phenomenology of Spirit* (1807), which is an introduction to the scope and method of his whole project. Hegel's grandest of grand narratives is an exegesis of its own process of coming to be, dealing with the development of self-consciousness, society, religion and culture in an ambitious explication of the origin and goal of the free human spirit.

Hegel's Notions of Totality, Dialectic and Teleology

Hegel suggests one cannot understand any particular thing without understanding everything else as well: the totality. Yet philosophers are confronted with splits between alienated spheres of knowledge and experience: natural science, art, religion, politics and the various competing philosophies which try to order this fragmented *mélange*. Hegel's huge system uncovers interconnections which resolve contradictory spheres of experience by reaching the whole of which these are parts. Hegel's slippery concept of *Geist* (spirit or mind) links the disparate moments of historical existence together: 'past existence is the already acquired property of universal Spirit which constitutes the Substance of the individual'.[1] Spirit is at work behind our backs, propelling us on to the point where reason becomes conscious through a process of dialectical development and change which constitutes subjectivity in relation to the totality.

The notion of dialectics is now associated with Hegel above all others, but comes from German philosophy's long engagement with the Greeks, especially the neo-Platonists. In Plato's famous dialogues, clashes between Socrates and his hapless debating partners revealed the contradictions internal to various opposed philosophical notions, contradictions which were resolved by Socratic wisdom into a higher form of reason. In Kant, and especially Fichte, we find a similar triadic structure. A thesis (1) and its opposing antithesis (2) are transcended through a synthesis (3). Although Hegel does not make much use of these terms, dialectical triads dominate the structure of Hegel's philosophy, as all the a, b cs and 1, 2, 3s of the contents pages of the *Phenomenology* reveal. Each new synthesis emerges as the third term of a triad, becoming in turn the first term of a new one, in a spiralling process of development, which in the end comes full circle as the whole movement completes itself in a final shape of consciousness capable of expressing all the moments without contradiction.

Hegel's dialectic is teleological: the origin (*archē*) of the movement has its ultimate aim (*telos*) implicit within it, as a necessary part of its full expression, just as the aim of a spear is implicit in the cast that sets it in flight. The final resting place of reason is the necessary completion of its first wavering motions. The whole truth is the entire 'process of its own becoming, the circle that presupposes its end as its goal, having its end also as its beginning; and only by being worked out to its end, is it actual'.[2]

The aim of the *Phenomenology* is to follow the linear movement of the truth as it unfolds, with the eventual aim of escaping temporality by setting out its moments in a circle. The paradox is that because the self capable of this circular reflection via conceptual speculation has no other source than the unconscious moments that have led up to it, differentiated self-awareness must involve a surrender to the immanent motion of those moments, not a hasty transcendence of them. If we are to grasp the significance of an experience, state of consciousness or phase of history as it appears, we must first try to immerse ourselves within it. This immersion is what Hegel means by phenomenology, 'the Science of Knowing in the sphere of appearance'.[3]

As an exegesis both of the coming to be of this Science of Knowing and of the subjects who know it, the *Phenomenology* has to juggle several perspectives on the evolving states of being which lead up to itself. Hegel's text simultaneously tries to enter into the developing modes of being which it takes as its object, to understand the way each mode of being experiences its own objects and also to ascertain to what degree and in what way each state of being is conscious of its own workings. By reflecting on itself, Hegel's text completes the developments it explores, discovering its own dialectical method as the principal of their movement. To use the complex Hegelian terms, phenomenology may be carried out in the register of the *for-us*, but this is always an account of experience as it is *in-itself.* The moments of experience which Hegel presents are an ideal version of them, restricted initially to their own immanent unfolding, that being what is meant by the term *in-itself.* Of course, even in this restriction we, the readers, recognise the presence of a developed self-consciousness who has witnessed it *for-us*, which is a different perspective within the dialectical process. We may feel that this ideal observer has been smuggled in by conceptual trickery. But Hegel aims to show that this undifferentiated presence in the beginning of the completed end is the reality of unfolding spirit, not only a projection of the phenomenologist. He asks us, in his preface, to accept that this spirit will not stand as revealed in its actuality until the long passage through the whole process has been completed. *For-itself*, the experience has yet to catch up with us phenomenologists, and its subject does not comprehend that the inclusive medium for the movement of phenomena is the conceptual consciousness that allows the whole movement to become explicit *in-and-for-itself*. This shifts our focus from the moments which move on to the movement itself.

As in a piece of music by Beethoven, the early movements of the *Phenomenology* hint at things which are only fully developed later on, after many detours have brought spirit to the point where what is latent within it may become manifest. Hegel's recapitulation of the adventures of spirit periodically explicates its early episodes through an awareness of the later ones, jumping backwards and forwards through the history of philosophy and the experiences it seeks to articulate. The discontinuities and transitions that make real history so confusing are overcome by a mode of presentation which allows the phenomenologist to take advantage of the totality that only emerges at the end of the whole movement. Historical processes and conceptual ideas of them, which at first appear to be chaotic and erroneous, are an essential component of the ultimate truth, which 'includes the negative also, what would be called the false, if it could be regarded as something from which one might abstract'.[4] The categories 'true' and 'false' are therefore a form of intellectual myopia that fails to grasp the bigger picture in which the dichotomy is resolved in an ultimate unity. This is a good example of Hegel's key notion of a self-conscious dialectical *Aufhebung* of the estranged sides of a conceptual dichotomy. This is a 'sublation', 'supersession' or 'sublimation' (the nearest English translations of *Aufhebung*) of those sides which both destroys and conserves them as moments of a progressive process.

Some Dialectical Models from Hegel's *Phenomenology*

The idea of dialectical development is explicated below by using a tiny selection of models from the *Phenomenology*, which makes no attempt to take the whole road traversed by Hegel. Since a sketch of the whole would provide an illusion of completeness only by sacrificing the details which render the movement convincing, I look at a few stages of the journey in enough depth to capture the method by which Hegel propels himself, following his earlier signposts without covering all the ground which leads to their destination.

At the beginning of the *Phenomenology*, Hegel introduces the notions of teleological progression and dialectical completion through a botanical model drawn from Aristotle:

> The bud disappears in the bursting-forth of the blossom, and one might say that the former is refuted by the latter; similarly, when the fruit appears, the blossom is shown up in its turn as a false manifestation of the plant, and the fruit now emerges as the truth of it instead. These forms are not just distinguished from one another, they also supplant one another as mutually incompatible. Yet at the same time their fluid nature makes them moments of an organic unity in which they not only do not conflict, but in which each is as necessary as the other; and this mutual necessity alone constitutes the life of the whole.[5]

The whole life of the plant is not expressed by each stage in isolation, even though the flower is potential in the seed: the truth of it can only be expressed by a concept of the plant which can theoretically recapitulate all the phases of its development. Only the knowing human subject can step outside of time through a recollection of all the moments, negating the contradictions of the particulars and reconstructing the positive life of the whole, holding the separate stages together in a speculative idea which can articulate difference within its own unity. The novel property of human subjectivity is that it, unlike a plant, is potentially capable of rendering conscious *in-and-for-itself* the various stages of its own historical development, hinting at the *telos* of the identity of concept and object towards which spirit moves.

Hegel begins the odyssey of human consciousness with the basic experience of 'sense-certainty'. This is an initially undifferentiated state which takes its certainty from its sensuous experience of the world of objects. But the simple certainties of the senses have a habit of changing on their own, like the plant. The basic experience of what 'is' cannot avoid division into an 'I' and a 'thing' that lies before it. Sense-certainty tries to maintain its stability by focusing on 'this' thing which confronts it, but the solidity of the 'this' sunders into another duality: the 'now' and the 'here'. Hegel further disrupts the claim of sense-certainty to have grasped its essence in what is immediately in front of it, by focusing on the incomplete nature of each of these new moments.

If one writes down the certain truth that it is now daytime, by the time dusk falls that truth has fallen into darkness. The now persists, but becomes what it was not. 'Now' is not immediate, but mediated '*through* the fact that something else, viz. Day and Night, is *not*'.[6] So the simple 'now' has a negative character, indifferent to its particular content: the now is a universal. The contradictory antithesis of past and present is unified by the concept of an ever-recurring universal now that is the temporal stage for the subject's becoming. Likewise, the 'here' is a universal based on a negation of the particular 'this'. As one gazes around a house and garden, the simplicity of the 'here' persists whatever the object of one's glance: '"Here" itself does not vanish; on the contrary, it abides constant in the vanishing of the house, the tree, etc., and is indifferently house or tree.'[7]

In an inversion of the earlier positing of the object as ground, the certainty of sense tries to retain a moment of immediacy by shifting from the 'this', whose solidity has dissolved into the universals of 'here' and 'now', to the subject as the power that can hold them together in a unity: 'the vanishing of the single Now and Here that we mean is prevented by the fact that *I* hold them fast'.[8] But this subjectively inflected certainty suffers the same divisive fate as the previous objective ones:

> I, *this* 'I', see the tree and assert that 'Here' is a tree; but another 'I' sees the house and maintains that 'Here' is not a tree but a house instead. Both truths have the same authentication, viz. the immediacy of seeing, and the certainty and assurance that both have about their knowing; but the one truth vanishes in the other.[9]

The particular certainty of the senses has to complicate itself with the intersubjective idea of the I as a universal in order to express its truth. A sense-certainty such as 'this is a house', which seems immediate and solid, in fact deploys the universality of the here, the now, and the I – 'If you were sitting where I am now, you would see that this is a house.'

Neither the 'I' nor its 'this' (the subject and the object) can subsist alone:

> neither one nor the other is only *immediately* present in sense-certainty, but each is at the same time *mediated*: I have this certainty *through* something else, viz. the thing; and it, similarly, is in sense-certainty *through* something else, viz. through the 'I'.[10]

The truth of sense-certainty is not its perspective on either the subject or the object, but the fact that this perspective is insufficient and yields, instead of a concrete particular, a set of conceptual universals whose heart is the negative itself.

Showing how rarefied philosophical speculation about basic experience may be expressed in developed forms of culture, Hegel here makes one of his characteristic leaps by drawing on religious examples. The mysteries of Ceres, Bacchus and the Christian communion initiate consciousness into the knowledge that certainty in the objects of sense voids itself into nothing, through a transmutation and destruction of material substances that also profoundly transform the initiate himself. At a basic level even animals grasp this: 'they do not just stand idly in front of sensuous things as if these possessed intrinsic being, but, despairing of their reality, and completely assured of their nothingness, they fall to without ceremony and eat them up'.[11] This animalistic perspective introduces the notion of desire into Hegel's considerations. Any particular life can never be self-sufficient, must transform itself through the overcoming of otherness, and can only be comprehended as part of the totality of all the interacting negations of each transient living particularity. Hegel transposes this observation into a meditation on what happens when rather than an animal eating the object of its desire, we are faced with a confrontation between two humans who each desire the recognition of the other.

The dialectic of lord and bondsman[12] sets out an archetypal encounter between hostile subjects, who try to force the desired recognition out of each other. But the victor of a battle to the death is faced with a corpse who can recognise nothing: if the I destroys the other vital for self-consciousness, the I destroys itself, so the best way to obtain the recognition of the loser is to enslave them instead.

This arrangement affords the lord advantages in his relations with the objects of his desire, because now the bondsman can be used to procure and refine them, leaving the lord free to enjoy the fruit of the bondsman's labour without getting his own hands dirty. In accepting servitude before death, the bondsman admits his dependency, setting aside his potential for free action in a submission based on fear. However, the lord now faces the same problem as confronted him with the corpse, for he has reduced the bondsman to a dependant whose recognition is not worth having because it does not match up to the concept of self-consciousness. The truth of the lord is therefore 'the servile consciousness of the bondsman', who turns out to have the key to independence in what apparently encumbers him: his fear of the 'absolute Lord', death, and his productive labour for his earthly master.[13] The lord who directs the bondsman also serves the latter as a model of self-consciousness that the lord has denied himself. Fear has a potentially liberating effect for the enslaved consciousness, which

> has trembled in every fibre of its being, and everything solid and stable has been shaken to its foundations. But this pure universal movement, the absolute melting-away of everything stable, is the simple, essential nature of self-consciousness, absolute negativity, *pure being-for-self*, which consequently is *implicit* in this consciousness.[14]

But as with any idea which falls back upon itself, stoical self-reliance becomes a sceptical solipsism locked up within its own categories.

Emerging from this dialectic comes the realisation that an individual cannot properly recognise him- or herself without another subjectivity. Self-identity is constructed through a perception of the difference between self and other, but this distinction nevertheless falls within itself: I am different from the other, but because my difference from them is what defines me, the difference is also my identity. The lord's freedom from labour makes him the slave of the social relationship he has mastered by binding another, and the slave masters himself through the productive activity to which he is chained. The realisation that otherness belongs to the heart of the I is the dawn of an inclusive spirit, a reciprocal social dialectic in which each willingly recognises the freedom of the other, offering the validation each desires: the '"I" that is "We" and "We" that is "I"'.[15]

Here, Hegel's youthful enthusiasm for the French Revolutionary notion of freedom found its philosophical expression. Hegel explains why that utopian promise of freedom decayed into the horrors of the Terror. The gap between the abstract assertion of universal freedom and the cabal which actually took over the state was too wide, and the ethical life of the new republic could not provide the concrete freedom it promised. Freedom lacked the social means whereby it could properly actualise itself in forms of ethical life. The proliferating victims of the guillotine were scapegoats for this lack. Freedom from oppression cannot be achieved simply by slaughtering representatives of the old order: a new order must cultivate institutions that allow citizens the freedom to remake themselves and their world through particular forms of social activity. This historical process of remaking allows for the reintegration of alienated facets of existence, through the subject's development via the institution and then transformation of successive forms of self, society, culture and religion.

Like the social and psychological forms with which they are entwined, art, religion and philosophy pass through processes of externalisation and re-inwardisation, of alienation and reconciliation, gradually reaching beyond externalised picture-thoughts of beauty, God, and the good life towards a pure inward thought which renders art and religion philosophical and philosophy artistic and religious through the overarching idea of spirit's self-productive activity. In art, spirit externalises itself through representational forms such as sculpture, painting and architecture, and then develops the more inward forms of music, literature and poetry, which become conceptual in their final manifestations.

In religion, spirit initially takes on external shapes, polytheistically populating reality with spiritual entities. Judaic monotheism marks an antithetical abstract turn, but God is still alienated from his worshippers. With Christianity that alienation is superseded through a reciprocal dialectic between God and humanity. The unknowable Godhead externalises itself through Jesus' incarnation and returns back to itself through the Word which supersedes the division of the one into two through a third term, spirit, which now encompasses humanity. Hegel transfigures the picture-thoughts of these particular historical events into the universal essence of human subjectivity, which unconsciously makes the world that seems alien to it through its own spiritual activity before superseding the diremption by consciously discovering its own activity as the truth of what confronts it. The mysterious divinity who seems alien to humanity reveals the oneness of creation through the manifestation of minds unified with the spirit that birthed them, and which they themselves birth. Spirit is the mind of God coming to know itself as a concept.

In philosophical terms, which for Hegel are the purified culmination of artistic and religious ones, the core movement of his absolute idealism is the progressive revelation of the objective world as a property of the subject which gathers within itself that which has gone before it and that which lies outside it using conceptual thought. As we saw above with the dialectic of sense-certainty, Hegel uses the gulf between subject and object as the negative spur for an on-going development and critique of spirit.

Kant's unbridgeable gap between the knowing subject and the object known forgets that knowledge of a limit already transgresses it. Hegel's *Aufhebung* of subject and object completes that transgression, revealing that the alienated object had actually been the subject all along. This negation of the negative yields the positive of spirit's awareness of itself as spirit. Self-consciousness comprehends that since its own mental activity provides the unity of the object, the concept is itself always its real object. This comprehension is the sole locus for the disclosure of the totality. The knowing 'I' can see itself as a particular instantiation of the universal development.

The unity of the knowing subject yields the final shape of spirit, in which all being is 'absolutely mediated; it is a substantial content which is just as immediately the property of the "I", it is self-like or the Notion [Concept]'.[16] The unspoken logic of Hegel's text is that in the end, because the 'I' behind the *Phenomenology* is a particular one – Hegel's – his self-sacrifice to unfolding phenomena must become an unfolding of Hegel's own self-consciousness. In Kojève's words, Hegel,

> By understanding himself through the understanding of the *totality* of the anthropogenetic historical process [...] and by understanding this process through his understanding *of himself* [...] caused the completed whole of the universal real process to penetrate into his individual consciousness, and then he penetrated this consciousness. Thus this consciousness became just as total, as universal, as the process that it revealed by understanding itself; and this fully self-conscious consciousness *is* absolute Knowledge.[17]

Whilst this seems megalomaniacal, the point could hold for everyone: if sedimented processes of world historical spiritual development give rise to particular subjects, then a dive deep enough into subjectivity may yield the pearl of wider knowledge. Hegel hopes in the *Phenomenology* to have worked through the process of historical development to the point where he can begin to set out a philosophical system proper: a task which occupied the rest of his life, and which is perhaps best represented by his *Science of Logic* (1812–16).

From Hegel to Here

As the last great idealist, Hegel spurred on the competing modern materialisms which all sought to bring idealism back down to earth. From the sharp bump to Hegel's head delivered by the hard rock of scientific-analytical scepticism for any philosophy dealing with spirit, to the soft landing of Marxist respect for the granddaddy of dialectics, which gently sets him on his feet, a range of receptions have dealt differently with Hegel's impact.

One of Hegel's biggest impacts was on political and social theory. Hegel's *Philosophy of Right* (1821) celebrated enlightened capitalist modernity, but cautioned that it rode roughshod over ethically significant elements of the feudal tradition, such as the ideal of the politically neutral monarch or the sophisticated artisan identities supported by the guild system, as well as undermining the peasantry and creating instead an indigent rabble. His ideal of a reformed Prussian state which would balance monarchy, democracy and the various 'estates' of society in an earthly expression of a harmonious divine ideal has been interpreted in very contrasting ways. It has been taken as an archetype by various Right Hegelians, who valorise existing social forms as positive expressions of the totality, resisting the notion of thorough-going revolutionary change. Most recently, Fukuyama has portrayed capitalist democracy as the final social form, confirming Hegel's announcement of the beginning of the end of history, an end which will come with the universalisation of capitalism through globalisation.

In contrast, Left Hegelians use progressive elements of Hegel's theory to generate critiques of what they see as his political compromises. Hegel's ideal Prussia was never fully actualised, and his apologetic for the state was arguably targeted against those who sought to return to a more authoritarian tradition. Marx concurred with Hegel on the social devastation brought about by emergent capitalism's war of all against all, but suggested this could not be remedied by hanging on to vestiges of pre-modern social forms which were supposedly already validated as carriers of spirit. Marx opened up the closed Hegelian conception of history with the notion of a dialectical progression through capitalistic social forms, predicated on the development not of mere self-consciousness, but of a class consciousness forged in social struggle.

Hegel is crucial to any notion of humankind as produced through its own historical activity. From Feuerbach and Marx to Lukács, Sartre and the Frankfurt School, Left Hegelian thought refigures spirit as social labour. Ideas are reflections of economic and social relations rather than vice versa. Marx suggested that philosophy should stop walking around on its head and get its feet back on to the ground by becoming political and seeking to change those relations rather than merely interpreting them. In Hegelian Marxism, Hegel's notion of the totality counters economism by showing how the cultural superstructure is not only determined by the economic base, but also maintains that base. In a bad sense, ideas are still crucial expressions of the spirit of the age. They are ideologies, compensations for the alienated reversals of capitalist ethical life. These reversals endow what is dead with the semblance of life by allowing capital to be the agent of history, whilst also turning what is living – social labour – into a dead thing, a reified appendage of the economic structure caught in a false-consciousness which cannot find itself in the social product from which it is alienated. Ideologies transmute this reality into the image of a meritocracy of self-made citizens – a persistent fantasy which blocks its actual revolutionary realisation.

A psychological version of these theses on alienation and its ideological compensation has found its way into psychoanalysis. Whilst Freud claimed not to understand dialectics, his notions of projection and ego alienation closely match Hegel's meditations on those psycho-philosophical confusions in which the subject is alienated from its own processes: 'what seems to happen outside of it, to be an activity directed against it, is really its own doing'.[18] Lacan was influenced by his attendance (alongside many other French intellectuals) at Kojève's famous 1930s seminar on Hegel. Kojève's emphasis on Hegel's dialectic of desire and recognition proved important for Lacan's concept of identity formation through the 'mirror phase'. This early phase of child development involves the alienation of the nascent subject through the formation of an imaginary skin-bound ego based on the image of unity formed through the child's recognition of itself in a mirror or in its interactions with others who become a model for the self.

Similarly Hegelianised forms of psychoanalysis take a role in Freudo-Marxism, with a Freudian dialectic of desire acting as a materialist corrective to Hegel's spiritualisations, while a Marxian filter renders his dialectical method of use to political economy. The dialectic is deployed to show how personality interacts with social structure, either as the cement which keeps that structure together or the dynamite with which to blow it apart.

Hegel's impact on philosophy has been profound, despite analytical philosophy's almost complete dismissal of what it sees as the pseudo-problems of dialectical logic. Hegel is much more sympathetically received by the traditions of so-called continental philosophy: even when he is severely attacked, he is accorded his due measure of importance. For example, Adorno established a dialectical counterweight to what he called Hegel's 'identity thinking'.[19] Influenced by Nietzsche's playful disdain for the rigidities of dialectical logic, Adorno shows how Hegel's narcissistic philosophical subjectivism reduces all non-identical otherness to nothing by enthroning the human subject as an all-inclusive identity. For Adorno, this mirrors at the level of philosophy the imperialism of patriarchal-bourgeois modernity, which establishes itself through the colonisation of everything other to itself. Dialectic is an all-consuming prison house, but it cannot be simply thought away, because its closed form reflects an important truth: the problematic spirit of the age, capitalism. For Hegel, 'The True is the whole',[20] but for Adorno, 'The whole is the false'.[21] The unity of the totality is provided not by reason, but by an irrational expansion of administration. A free humanity would be free from dialectics, not bound to it.

Irigaray's philosophy of sexual difference criticises Hegel's concept of the free subject, which is a masculine public identity predicated on the positioning of woman as other: as nature or matter confined in the private realm. To fully realise each other, men and women must create a world in which sexual otherness is not collapsed in neuter conceptions of identity which mask a patriarchal bias, but is opened out and cultured. Neither sex is the truth of the whole.

Whereas figures like Adorno and Irigaray produce critiques of Hegel which remain within his dialectical orbit, postmodernist and poststructuralist intellectual currents want to escape Hegel's gravity altogether. 'Post' theory follows Nietzsche all the way by identifying forms of power and knowledge which decentre and deconstruct the supposedly unified Hegelian subject, as well as the Marxist dream of a transparently rational society. As in Goya's famous picture, Hegel's 'dream of reason' brings forth a monstrous nightmare, a rationalistic terrorism, a mistaken conception of life, which even in its atheistic versions crowns an abstract concept of reason or an image of a true society with the authority lost through the death of God, substituting one anthropocentric grand narrative for another. From this perspective, the social totalitarianism of Stalin or Mao is a political actualisation of the philosophical totalitarianism latent in all Hegelianisms.

These considerations are crucial to any reception of Hegel today, but as Rorty has pointed out, Hegel waits around the corner for the unwary. Dialectic is akin to judo: the force of an antithetical attacking argument may easily be turned against it. The *Phenomenology* passes through several stages akin to postmodernism in their resistance to the logic of the totality, but their radical scepticism always in the end collapses into some new sort of conceptual order. Attacks on existing notions of reason may be the stepping stone to new ones, not an annihilation of the concept of reason itself, and as a result various types of return to Hegel are still a recurrent feature of contemporary critical theory.

Two recent returns to Hegel are provided by Butler and Žižek, who in different ways demonstrate Hegel's survival of the postmodern attempt to surpass him. Both make varying uses of Lacan's critical reception of Hegel's dialectics of recognition. According to Žižek, it is Hegel rather than his poststructuralist critics who offers the strongest affirmation of difference and contingency by acknowledging a subjectivity that does not simply overcome contradiction but also accepts it as internal to every identity. Butler's theory of subject formation draws on Hegel alongside Nietzsche, Freud and Foucault in an effort to understand how consciousness, and psychic life generally, both generates and is generated by the social operations of power. Her use of dialectics to explicate the heterosexual othering of homosexuality has become important in queer theory, demonstrating how aspects of Hegel's legacy may now operate productively in a political arena radically different from his own.

Notes

1. Hegel, *Phenomenology*, p. 16. I would like to thank Alison Martin and Bill Hutson for the spirited stimulation provided by many discussions of Hegel.
2. Ibid., p. 10.
3. Ibid., p. 493.
4. Ibid., p. 27.
5. Ibid., p. 2.
6. Ibid., p. 60.
7. Ibid., p. 61.
8. Ibid.
9. Ibid.
10. Ibid., p. 59.
11. Ibid., p. 65.
12. Also often translated as 'master' and 'slave'.
13. Ibid., p. 117.
14. Ibid.
15. Ibid., p. 110.
16. Ibid., p. 21.

17. Kojève, *Introduction*, p. 35.
18. Hegel, *Phenomenology*, p. 21.
19. Theodor W. Adorno, *Negative Dialectics*, trans. E. B. Ashton (London: Routledge, 1990); *Hegel: Three Studies*, trans. S. W. Nicholsen (Cambridge, MA: MIT Press, 1993).
20. Hegel, *Phenomenology*, p. 11.
21. Theodor W. Adorno, *Minima Moralia*, trans. E. F. N. Jephcott (London and New York: Verso, 1994), p. 50.

Major Works by Hegel

Phenomenology of Spirit, trans. A. V. Miller (Oxford: Oxford University Press, 1977 [1807]).

Science of Logic, trans. A. V. Miller (London: Allen and Unwin, 1969 [1812–16]).

Philosophy of Right, ed. A. Wood, trans. H. B. Nisbet (Cambridge: Cambridge University Press, 1991 [1821]).

Encyclopaedia of the Philosophical Sciences [1830], in three volumes (Oxford: Oxford University Press): I: *Logic*, trans. W. Wallace (1975); II: *Philosophy of Nature*, trans. A. V. Miller (1970); III: *Philosophy of Mind*, trans. W. Wallace (1971).

Suggestions for Further Reading

Beiser, F. C. (ed.), *The Cambridge Companion to Hegel* (Cambridge: Cambridge University Press, 1993). Good essays on most aspects of Hegel and his reception, excellent bibliography.

Harris, H. S., *Hegel: Phenomenology and System* (Indianapolis: Hackett, 1995). Limpid, short and authoritative introduction.

Inwood, M., *A Hegel Dictionary* (Oxford: Blackwell, 1992). Scholarly guide to key concepts, with comprehensive referencing and a good bibliography.

Kojève, A., *Introduction to the Reading of Hegel*, ed. Allan Bloom, trans. J. H. Nichols (New York: Basic Books, 1969). Distillation of Kojève's influential seminar.

Marcuse, H., *Reason and Revolution: Hegel and the Rise of Social Theory*, 2nd edn (London: Routledge, Kegan and Paul, 1955). Exegesis of the development of Left Hegelian thought from the Frankfurt notable.

Marx, K., *Early Writings*, trans. G. Benton and R. Livingstone (Harmondsworth: Penguin, 1975). The key text for understanding Marx on Hegel.

Singer, P., *Hegel* (Oxford: Clarendon, 1983). Short, accessible primer.

Solomon, R. C., *In the Spirit of Hegel: A Study of G. W. F. Hegel's Phenomenology of Spirit* (Oxford: Oxford University Press, 1983). Detailed exegesis, energetically done.

Spencer, L., and Krauze, A., *Hegel for Beginners* (Cambridge: Icon Books, 1996). Clear overview, with good biographical and intellectual contextualisation.

Taylor, C., *Hegel* (Cambridge: Cambridge University Press, 1975). Comprehensive and widely respected.

4

Karl Marx (1818–83)

Simon Tormey

Marx in the Critical Tradition

Marx is one of the most profound critics of modernity, which he analyses under the concept of capitalism. Capitalism is the mode of production of modernity which undoes not only the preceding mode of production, feudalism, but also the social forms and cultural authorities of the time. Tradition is undermined not so much by the exercise of reason as by the dynamic of capitalism, which demands different social relations. But although capitalism frees people from feudal obligation and traditional authority, it forces them to submit to a new system of class domination, wage labour and the structural imperative of the accumulation of capital. Modernity promises universal emancipation, but for Marx the path to freedom lies neither through Kant's autonomy, or the mature exercise of reason, nor through Hegel's realisation of reason in the state. Only when the mode of production is organised rationally to fulfil the needs of all, rather than some, can humanity be free to rule its own history.

Marx developed his impressively comprehensive critique of capitalism by drawing on British political economy, French sociology and German philosophy. In particular, Marx developed his method of historical materialism through criticism of Hegel's idealism. Hegel characterises alienation as a split between the subject and object of history, between the knower and the known, which can be overcome when both are united in the Absolute Spirit or Mind that is fully self-conscious. Hegel also considers the reconciliation of subject and object to be the condition for political freedom, brought about by the modern state, which could realise freedom for all, universally, rather than the particular freedom of only some. Marx retains Hegel's historical perspective on the antinomies of freedom versus necessity, and subject versus object, but insists that Hegel has confused the causes of alienation with their effects. Inverting Hegel, according to Marx's dialectical materialism, it is being that determines consciousness, not consciousness that determines being. Alienation is to be found in practical human activity, that is, in the mode of production and hence cannot be overcome through self-consciousness or the political community of the state. Yet Marx remains faithful to Hegel's insight that humanity is a product of its own historical activity.

Marx's continuing influence on the tradition of critique is most obvious through the development of Marxism itself, which is represented in this volume by Western Marxism, in particular by one of its founders, Lukács, and by the Frankfurt School thinkers, Adorno and Horkheimer. Even while Marx was still alive but especially after his death, a somewhat doctrinaire or 'orthodox' version of Marx's work became widespread. Focusing especially on his later work and bearing the imprint of Marx's collaborator Engels, 'scientific socialism' has the ambition of explaining society as if it obeys natural laws of historical development. Capitalism must give way to communism as feudalism did to capitalism, while the proletariat will become conscious of itself as a class of universal significance by understanding (with the help of a 'vanguard' party) its role in transforming the capitalist mode of production. 'Superstructural' social, political and legal forms could be understood to be determined by the economic 'base', the mode of production. Western Marxism, in contrast, has tended to be more interested in Marx's earlier, philosophical works and in concepts such as alienation or commodity fetishism, which offer a great deal of insight into the subjective conditions of life under capitalism. Western Marxists focus on the cultural and social forms of capitalism which characterise the experiences of social classes, specialising in analyses of the ideologies that sustain capitalism in its varying social forms.

Introduction

One of the most important thinkers of the modern world, Karl Marx was born in Trier in 1818 and studied at the Universities of Bonn and Berlin before establishing his reputation as the most original of the so-called Young Hegelians. Over the next fifty years Marx produced a stream of books, articles, pamphlets and letters which established him as the most significant figure of the nascent international communist movement he had helped to create. During his own lifetime he established a reputation primarily as a vociferous critic of social democracy and utopian socialism, reflecting his active engagement with the politics of his day. It was only after his death in 1883 that his significance as a theorist really emerged, in part due to the efforts of his long-time friend and co-author Friedrich Engels, but also due to the impact of his ideas on debates concerning the future of working-class struggle.

Today Marx's influence within critical theory is mainly felt through the work of Western Marxists, particularly Lukács, Gramsci and the Frankfurt School, all of whom sought to develop Marx's suggestive analysis of culture and literary form into an account of the ideological basis of capitalism. This reception was in turn aided by the discovery in the twentieth century of two key works *The Economic and Philosophical Manuscripts of 1844* and the *Grundrisse*. More obviously humanistic in orientation than his economic writings, these works helped to establish Marx as a key source for thinking about the nature of alienation, reification and ideology in contemporary societies. They also served to stress the critical and emancipatory thrust of Marx's work at a time when it had effectively been held hostage by the guardians of 'official' Marxism in the Communist Bloc. For this reason communism's collapse has not, to the surprise of Marxism's many enemies, resulted in the decline of Marx's influence, but rather to continued reflection on his importance to the tradition of critical thought and action.

Alienation and Wage Labour

Marx's early work is usually described in chronological terms as the period from his doctorate on the philosophy of Epicurus, written in the late 1830s, to *The Communist Manifesto* of 1848, a period which includes, most notably, the 1844 *Manuscripts* and *The German Ideology* (1846). In philosophical terms it can be described as the period in which the focus of Marx's work is the development of a materialist account of human essence to challenge the otherwise dominant idealist accounts of Hegel and many of his immediate followers. Hegel insisted that freedom was inscribed in the modern. Modernity for Hegel is the epoch of 'universality', and that universality could be seen at its most striking in the pronouncements of the revolutions rippling through the contemporary world from the end of the eighteenth century onwards. Absolute Spirit was on the march and would soon obliterate local hierarchies and asymmetries. Unlike Hegel, however, Marx argued that there was a contradiction between the self-image of the modern (universally 'free' and 'equal') and the manner by which modern societies reproduce themselves. As Marx sees it, the paradox of modernity is that at the very moment when greatly increased productive potential seems to offer so much in terms of meeting human needs, it takes away so much in terms of increasing human misery. Thus Hegel may well have been right to describe the potential of modernity in such glowing terms, but the reality was not merely at odds with the potential, it stood in antagonism to it.

The paradox was not difficult to understand, for according to Marx one form of serfdom, feudalism, had merely given way to another, wage labour. Here, as argued in the *Manuscripts*, lay the key to understanding the widespread and pervasive alienation that characterised life in the most 'advanced' European societies. As Marx sees it, what defines existence and gives it meaning is sensuous practical activity. Humanity is the architect of the world; we apply ourselves to its creation and reproduction, and in doing so we give character to our own existence, to language and social life more generally. Wage labour, on the other hand, subordinates this activity and hence our existence to the end of creating profit. In working for another we in essence surrender control over ourselves, over the product of our work, over the relations we have with others and the world or nature more generally. Sensuous practical activity gives way to 'objectification', which in turn destroys the specifically 'human' in production, social relations and communal existence.

To discuss the manner in which alienation is reproduced through the system of wage labour is also to think of the world 'after' wage labour, which is what Marx does, albeit in a suggestive, philosophical way in the *Manuscripts*. Here we find that 'communism' stands in for or represents that which is non-alienated, non-hierarchical, non-dominating. In this sense the master term 'wage labour' is the key to unpacking Marx's views on the 'ought-to-be'. If it is the case that the essence of alienation can be found in the 'loss' of control over the terms and conditions of one's creative existence and, by extension, over the system of social reproduction, then logically communism, as the flip side of alienation, represents the recuperation of all that would otherwise be 'lost'. Though he says relatively little in the *Manuscripts* about either the form or the substance of 'communism', in a sense he does not need to. If wage labour represents the obstacle to individual, social and species development then it is clear that the abolition of wage labour to be replaced by the collective ownership of the means of production is the necessary basis of a politics dedicated to genuine emancipation. This would be a vision of emancipation sharply at odds with the manner in which Hegel and post-Hegelian radicals such as Bauer and Ruge conceived it, that is as 'political' emancipation. As Marx argues in early political works such as *On the Jewish Question* (1843–4), emancipation must rather be thought of as the transcendence of the entire system of social reproduction so that the causes of estrangement and alienation can be overcome. As the causes are located in the system of relations that maintains capitalism, it follows that it is capitalism itself – including the political architecture of 'rights', liberties and obligations characterising bourgeois civil society – that must be transcended. In this sense we can see that the radicalism of Marx's early work is 'humanistic' in character. Through an analysis of what wage labour denies humanity, Marx erects an ideal characterisation of what we need in order to recover our 'species essence'.

Historical Materialism and the Base/Superstructure Model

In the transitional works of the late 1840s and 1850s Marx introduces a crucial dimension into his discussion of what had been a discussion of a largely philosophical nature. This dimension is that of social and historical development, first analysed at any length in *The German Ideology*. Marx was sensitive to the limitations of philosophical 'idealism', which he criticises in the contemporaneous 'Theses on Feuerbach', and strove in effect to transpose the discourse on the 'essence' of an abstracted 'Man' into a discourse on the fate of ordinary men and women at the hands of superior forces, namely the ruling class. In the transitional works wage labour is thus characterised as the outcome of a historical process rather than as a relation to be rendered in philosophical terms. As Marx explains in *The German Ideology*, we need to see history as driven not by changes in the ideals and values of a given people, as Hegel had argued in *The Philosophy of History*, but in terms of changes in the material 'base' of human society. What ultimately drove the historical process, Marx argues, is the development of science and technology in turn feeding through into changes in the technology of production. As the mode of production changes, so too do the relations of production, so that, to paraphrase Marx, just as the 'handmill gives us feudalism', so 'steam power gives us capitalism'. This is to say that as the relations of production develop so too do the governing ideological, legal and political forms (the 'superstructure') needed to maintain a given mode of production. In other words, whereas Hegel posited changes in values and ideals as the motor force of history, Marx argued that the motor is objective 'material' processes. Ideas are effects, not causes of fundamental change. As he famously puts it in *The German Ideology*, 'it is not consciousness that determines social being, but rather social being that determines consciousness'.[1]

This, in highly abbreviated terms, is what characterises 'historical materialism' as an approach to social explanation: social life and phenomena are seen as effects of an underlying material structure and are to be studied in terms of that structure. Just how exactly the one 'determines' the other, how for example art and literature 'reflect' the underlying base, has been and remains the subject of intense debate. This is in turn a reflection perhaps of the relatively undertheorised character of Marx's analysis of 'determination', and, indeed, of ideology more generally in these transitional texts. Marx is less interested, certainly at this point, in such questions than in what they presage in terms of an understanding of social and historical development, and in terms of the future progress of the species. The sting in the tail of Marx's account of historical development was his conviction that just as capitalism and the bourgeoisie had driven out feudalism, so communism and the proletariat would drive out capitalism. An important corollary of Marx's account of capitalism is thus that revolution is not merely desirable, but inevitable. As Marx went on to make clear in the 'preface' to *The Critique of Political Economy* (1859), bourgeois relations

> are the last antagonistic form of the social process of production – antagonistic not in the sense of individual antagonism, but of one arising from the material conditions of life of the individuals; at the same time the productive forces developing in the womb of bourgeois society create the material conditions for the solution of that antagonism. This social formation brings, therefore, the prehistory of human society to a close.[2]

It is worth dwelling a moment on what Marx is claiming here, for if there is one aspect of Marx's method that has received overwhelming criticism by critical theorists hostile to Marxism (in particular postmodernists), it is undoubtedly its 'totalising' view of history, which in the 'preface' seems to be at its most acute. As the latter see it, Marx offers a teleological view of history, the effect of which is to rule out the contingency of human action and, by extension, the notion of the individual as an autonomous agent fully responsible for his or her acts. Feudalism gives forth capitalism, capitalism gives forth communism and along the way 'history' is surrendered to process and its subjects reduced to mere cogs in the machine.

Common though it is to equate, in this fashion, teleology with totalisation, such an interpretation discounts Marx's own view of *praxis*, which lays enormous emphasis on the contingency of human action, though it is a contingency he sees mediated by the historical circumstances in which it takes place. As he notes in an oft-quoted passage of *The Eighteenth Brumaire of Louis Napoleon*: 'Men make their own history, but they do not make it just as they please; they do not make it under circumstances directly encountered, given and transmitted from the past.'[3] As seems clear enough from the above, Marx does want to claim that capitalism is an unsustainable form of life; but this does not in itself commit him to the claim that the establishment of a communist society is inevitable. On the contrary, communism is clearly regarded by Marx as one possibility, albeit one which in his view history offers as the 'solution to the riddle of history'. Other futures are also available to humanity, though none are, in Marx's view, as desirable from the point of view of genuine human emancipation. This is because it is only communism that confronts the true source of misery and exploitation, which is the ownership by one person over the labour power, and thus creativity, of another. Communism is a necessity from the point of view of the progress of the species; but to say that one form of society is a necessity is not to say that history has been programmed in advance to ensure its realisation. Such a conclusion would make a nonsense of everything that Marx says about the vicissitudes of revolutionary action.

Capital and the Commodity Form

Marx's work from the 1850s onwards divides more neatly between the political and the economic. As regards the political works which include most notably *The Civil War in France* (1871) and the *Critique of the Gotha Programme* (1875), Marx's principal conclusions concerned the importance of class identity in social transformation, and by extension the importance of alliances between classes. What emerges in these works (as in the earlier analyses of the 1848 revolution) is an account of the intensely complex nature of class formation and thus of the highly contingent nature of revolutionary action. It is precisely the complex background against which political action takes place that necessitated an active and disciplined communist movement to ensure that the proletariat is not led down the road of compromise with those whose objective class interests clashed with their own. We also gain the impression that Marx believed the revolutions of the capitalist era would be radically different from the bourgeois revolutions of the eighteenth century. The latter were short, relatively bloodless affairs involving the displacement of a numerically small class, the aristocracy, by another, the bourgeoisie. The latter, on the other hand, were likely to be long and drawn out, necessitating the use of state power against a no doubt determined and well-organised opposition. The question of the role of the state was a source of antagonism between Marx and his anarchist colleagues in the First International such as Mikhail Bakunin, who, by contrast, argued for an immediate transition to a stateless society. It was also the source of much controversy between later Marxists as to the exact role and function of the state during the period of 'transition' between capitalism and communism, and indeed as to the exact role of the communist party in ensuring that the revolution produced the desired outcome. Whilst later 'revisionists' such as Eduard Bernstein and Karl Kautsky set great store by the developmental nature of Marx's analysis, which seemed to speak to an inevitable communist victory, revolutionary Marxists such as Lenin and Rosa Luxemburg emphasised the necessity for a more active radicalism to overthrow the existing order.

As for the economic works, the later Marx dedicated himself to the study of capitalism both in the concrete, as it had emerged in Europe, particularly Britain in the course of the eighteenth and nineteenth centuries, and also in the abstract as an 'ideal type' or model as explored most famously in the three volumes of *Capital* (1865–79). No matter how abstracted the models became, Marx was nevertheless always insistent that capitalism involved the exploitation of the propertyless majority by a minority of property owners, and thus that the long-term interests of humanity could only be realised through the transcendence of capitalism by a system of 'socialised' production. What intrigued Marx was, nevertheless, the precise mechanism by which capitalism kept itself in being and the nature of the crises that, even during his own lifetime, periodically beset capitalist societies. In this regard Marx argued that in essence capitalism produces its own crises and thus its own 'gravediggers', as he put it in the *Manifesto*. This is to say that crises are objective, structurally necessary features of the capitalist mode of production and could no more be prevented than could storms or floods. On the other hand, whether revolution would occur on the back of any given crisis was a subjective question whose resolution is a matter of *praxis* rather than theory, again underlining the need for communist organisation and agitation prior to revolution itself, and for the deployment of force against reactionary forces in the period immediately preceding it.

Marx's analysis of capitalism is a famously complex and technical one, particularly as it appears in the first nine chapters of *Capital*, volume I; but at its heart lies the same proposition that we find in the earlier work. Capitalist production contains a fundamental, yet unavoidable contradiction, the resolution of which necessitates capitalism's transcendence. Whilst the bourgeoisie is immensely successful at exploiting new markets, developing new products, refining ever newer systems of production, management and control, ultimately it is compelled by the very nature of market competition to extract the maximum possible 'surplus value' or profit from the proletariat. Capitalism is thus characterised both by the extreme 'overproduction' of goods and services reflecting the rapid advances in the technology of production which occurs under the bourgeoisie, and by the progressive 'immiseration' of the proletariat, which is the necessary long-term effect of capitalist competition. Capitalism, that is, produces an ever expanding array of products, but ultimately at the cost of denying those who would consume them the means of doing so. In describing capitalism in such a fashion Marx relies heavily on certain contentious propositions about the nature of capitalist production itself. Among the more significant are the 'labour theory of value', the utility of which is probably the most debated aspect of Marx's economic theory; and also the famous thesis concerning the 'tendency of the rate of profit to fall', which appears in volume III of *Capital* and which is taken as a statement of why Marx argues that ultimately capitalism is doomed.

It is, however, Marx's critique of the commodity form that is of greatest significance for debates in critical theory, as here he offers the basis for the advanced critique of bourgeois ideology begun in the earlier works. Marx's primary object of critique in the *Manuscripts* was, as we have noted, wage labour and in turn his primary objective was the recuperation of a 'lost' relation between individuals and their creativity. The earlier model of alienation was necessarily based on certain premises about 'human nature' or species existence which many of his contemporary critics have argued are ahistorical, asocial and 'essentialist'. The importance of

Capital, certainly as far as later structuralist or anti-humanist Marxists such as Althusser is concerned, is the development of a critique of alienation, reification and bourgeois ideology from the analysis of the product of wage labour rather than wage labour itself, thereby in turn escaping the pitfalls the latter associate with a humanistic approach.

Throughout his economic work Marx deploys a distinction between 'use value' and 'exchange value', or, in plainer terms, between those objects whose utility lies in their serving human needs and commodities whose primary function is to create profit. This is in contrast with 'bourgeois' economics, which tends, in Marx's view, to regard exchange value as the only meaningful way that value can be expressed. If, in this way of thinking, an object does not have a price it cannot be of 'value'. To Marx, however, the commodity is an object abstracted from the human and social relations that created it. An object for sale in a supermarket is just that: an object. What we do not see is the manner of its production, the social conditions that produced it and the relations which make its production possible. Because we do not see how or under what conditions it is created, a commodity can be imbued with 'magical' qualities which disguise and distort its use value. The more advanced an economy becomes, the more abstract the system of production and so the more 'fetishistic' the character of commodities. Under such conditions, commodities 'enchant' us; they persuade us that they offer us the solution to the general feeling of 'lack' induced by the harsh realities of capitalist life. A pair of shoes is a means of protecting our feet; but a pair of Nike Air Jordans is an iconic product of near-religious importance to the contemporary gaze.

In Marx's view such forms of enchantment are shallow and illusory. Commodity production represents the denial of human life through the subordination of everything that is specifically human to the logic of exchange value and profit maximisation. The result is that the world and the relationships that compose it become 'reified' or projected in terms of their utility for individuals. The only value that counts is instrumental value, and the only form that human existence can legitimately take becomes that of the ruthless 'utility maximiser' of bourgeois thought. As Marx persistently argued to the end of his life, it is only through the abolition of the commodity form via the creation of systems based on 'associated production' for use not exchange that the reified world of capitalist alienation can be overcome. It is for this reason that Marx was so hostile towards 'market' socialists and social democrats. Whilst, for example, the schemes of market socialists might reduce the degree to which the proletariat felt itself to be exploited, as long as production was based on the creation of commodities, then, on Marx's terms, human creativity would be sacrificed to profit.

Marx's analysis of the commodity has been and still is the subject of enormous discussion, holding as it does the key to the development of the critique of alienation and ideology in capitalist society and an understanding of the contribution of Western Marxists. This is particularly so in the case of Lukács, who developed the theory of reification, and the Frankfurt School, whose analysis of contemporary culture was strongly influenced by Marx's analysis of commodities. This area of Marx's work is still highly influential, offering, as it still does, critical tools for those seeking to analyse consumerism and the place of ideology in the maintenance of the liberal-capitalist status quo.

Marx's Legacy

It is clear that despite the regular announcements of the 'death' of Marx, his work remains an important resource for critical theory, even if the numbers of those seeking to maintain some form of 'orthodoxy' continue to decline. Although Marx's influence on critical theory is mediated through later developments of Marxism, neo-Marxism and post-Marxism, that influence extends through social and political theory, feminist theory, as well as literary, cultural and film theory. In social theory, for example, Marx's influence can be found in the later Frankfurt School, principally in the work of Jürgen Habermas, Albrecht Wellmer, Claus Offe and Axel Honneth. Habermas' attachment to the fundamental tenets of Marxism has been on the wane since his shift from a paradigm of production to communication in the 1980s, yet he still regards his work as a development of historical materialism rather than a wholesale rejection of it. Similarly the work of Pierre Bourdieu remains within the spirit of Marx's work, particularly in the manner of his attack on neo-liberalism and his desire to promote a politically engaged form of social critique. However, Marx is not without his critics in contemporary critical theory. Jean Baudrillard, for example, subjected Marx's understanding of the commodity form to searching critique in a number of works, including *The Mirror of Production*, *For a Critique of the Political Economy of the Sign* and *The*

System of Objects. Baudrillard argues that the only way to comprehend the commodity is as a 'sign' whose meaning is internal to the system of consumption in which it appears and is exchanged. An object has a value independent of the system of signs of which it is a part, because individuals only learn to assign value to objects through the pre-existing system into which they are socialised. The availability of a notion of value unmediated by exchange is thus a contradiction in terms, and the dream of a transparent world beyond the sign is a vain one. Yet, even whilst attacking Marx as he did vociferously in his work immediately following the events of 1968, it is quite reasonable to regard Baudrillard as working within the Marxian problematic. His early work can be regarded as the attempt to reorientate Marxism towards a 'consumption'- as opposed to 'production'-centred form of critique, rather than as a critique of Marxism as such.

Marxist literary, cultural and film theory has for the most part focused on the 'superstructural' expressions or symptoms of capitalism, both in terms of form and content. More often than not, such Marxist critics are interested in works and genres in which they can interpret the pathologies, contradictions and utopian hopes within capitalist society, rather than in works which directly express Marxist positions. Fredric Jameson has made important contributions to the theory of ideology (*The Political Unconscious*) and also to the analysis and critique of postmodernism (*Postmodernism, Or the Cultural Logic of Late Capitalism*). Similarly, Terry Eagleton has produced a flow of important works of literary criticism and cultural theory. The Marxist concept of ideology has been central to the development of the Birmingham school of British cultural studies, in which Stuart Hall is a key figure. In addition, Marxist theory is applied to the analysis of the conditions of production, circulation and consumption of culture, focusing attention on mass culture as an industry rather than as aesthetic expression.

In the field of political thought an important development in the past two decades has been the emergence of 'post-Marxism', whose very name speaks to the continuing relevance of Marx for the development of emancipatory critique. Post-Marxism is most immediately associated with the work of Ernesto Laclau and Chantal Mouffe, former students of Althusser, who in *Hegemony and Socialist Strategy* sought to initiate a break with the orthodox tenets of Marxism whilst at the same time retaining the radical thrust of Marx's critique of capitalism. Laclau and Mouffe's work has proved extremely important in placing the issue of Marx's legacy at the forefront of current debates concerning the future of left radical politics. The same is true for Jacques Derrida's work *Specters of Marx*, which argues for the continuing relevance of Marx's work in the face of neo-liberal triumphalism and the intellectual inertia associated with the emergence of postmodernism.

In political philosophy more generally Marxism is still an important resource for challenging the otherwise dominant liberal paradigm in normative analysis. Here the work of so-called analytical Marxists such as Jon Elster and John Roemer are worth mentioning, as is the work of G. A. Cohen, whose *Marx's Theory of History: A Defence* is probably the most substantial work of Marxist scholarship in recent decades. Alex Callinicos' regular counterblasts are an important reminder of a continuing Marxist opposition to dominant trends in social and political theory as, more generally, is the work of Ellen Meiksins Wood and Iris Marion Young.

Marx's work is still influential within feminist debates, though whether the relationship between Marxism and feminism can still be described as an 'unhappy marriage' as opposed to an acrimonious divorce is a matter of contention. For Marxist feminists, the problem was how to fit Marx's 'gender-blind' concepts of worker and capitalist into a theory of women's oppression. Roughly speaking, opinions remained divided as to whether sexism and capitalism form a unified system of oppression, capitalist patriarchy, which could be analysed by means of the same conceptual tools, or whether women were subject to a dual system of oppression. Recent social trends and movements have presented Marxist theory with similar challenges regarding its relevance to a variety of issues which defy easy analysis in terms of class divisions: anti-colonial liberation movements, racial and ethnic conflicts, sexual identity and environmental concerns. While critics of Marxism find its concepts and categories restrictive or misleading, its advocates rise to the challenge, developing Marxism as a living intellectual force.

Finally, an excellent example of the enrichment of Marxism by meeting its intellectual and circumstantial challenges is the work of Slavoj Žižek. A writer of astonishing dexterity, Žižek couples an unorthodox yet recognisably Marxist approach to a Lacanian-inspired psychoanalytic framework of analysis. Žižek's importance for the recomposition of Marxism is still uncertain, but what is less so is the profound impact his idiosyncratic yet uncompromisingly radical approach has had on those debates in which he has intervened. Among his most important works, certainly from the point of view of demonstrating the continuing relevance of Marx's work, are: *The Sublime Object of Ideology*, *The Ticklish Subject* and his interventions in the edited collection *Contingency, Hegemony, Universality: Dialogues on the Left*. Whatever limitations there might be for the application of Marx's own theory to contemporary issues, its adaptability sustains its relevance.

Notes

1. Marx and Engels, *The German Ideology*, p. 47.
2. Marx and Engels, 'Preface to a Critique of Political Economy', p. 182.
3. Karl Marx, 'The Eighteenth Brumaire of Louis Napoleon', p. 96.

Major Works by Marx

'On the Jewish Question' [1844] and 'The Economic and Philosophical Manuscripts of 1844' [1844] in *Karl Marx, Early Writings*, ed. and trans. Rodney Livingstone and Gregor Benton (Harmondsworth: Penguin, 1992).

The German Ideology, ed. C. J. Arthur (London: Lawrence and Wishart, 1974 [1846]).

'The Communist Manifesto' [1848]; 'The Class Struggles in France' [1850]; 'The Eighteenth Brumaire of Louis Napoleon' [1852]; 'Preface to a Critique of Political Economy' [1859]; 'The Civil War in France' [1871]; and 'The Critique of the Gotha Programme' [1875] in Karl Marx and Friedrich Engels, *Selected Works in One Volume* (London: Lawrence and Wishart, 1968).

Grundrisse: Foundations of a Critique of Political Economy, trans. Martin Nicolaus (Harmondsworth: Penguin, 1973 [1857–8]).

Capital, 3 vols (Harmondsworth: Penguin, 1990 [1865–79]).

Suggestions for Further Reading

Althusser, Louis, *For Marx*, trans. Ben Brewster (London: New Left Books, 1977). One of the most influential and controversial interpretations by a key structuralist Marxist thinker.

Anderson, Perry, *Considerations on Western Marxism* (London: Verso, 1979). Short, engaged account of the trajectory of Marxism in the twentieth century.

Avineri, Shlomo, *Marx's Social and Political Thought* (Cambridge: Cambridge University Press, 1971). Useful and even-handed analysis of the development of Marx's political and social theory.

Baudrillard, Jean, *Baudrillard: A Critical Reader*, ed. Douglas Kellner (Cambridge: Blackwell, 1994). Collection of some of Baudrillard's most important work.

Carver, Terrell, *The Postmodern Marx* (Manchester: Manchester University Press, 1998). Essays on the fate and relevance of Marx's ideas by a leading commentator.

Cohen, G. A., *Karl Marx's Theory of History: A Defence* (Oxford: Clarendon Press, 1979). Influential rereading of Marx by a leading 'analytical' Marxist.

Derrida, Jacques, *Specters of Marx: The State of the Debt, the Work of Mourning, and the New International*, trans. Peggy Kamuf (London: Routledge, 1994). Stunning intervention by the guru of deconstruction.

Howard, Dick, *The Marxian Legacy* (London: Macmillan, 1977). Overview of developments in Marxism over the course of the twentieth century.

Jameson, Fredric, *The Political Unconscious: Narrative as a Socially Symbolic Act* (London: Methuen, 1981). Brilliant application of the theory of ideology to literary forms.

Jameson, Fredric, *Postmodernism: Or, the Cultural Logic of Late Capitalism* (London: Verso, 1991). Dexterous reading of contemporary cultural forms.

Kellner, Douglas, *Critical Theory, Marxism and Modernity* (Cambridge: Polity, 1989). Useful overview of the development of the Frankfurt School.

Kolakowski, Leszek, *Main Currents of Marxism*, 3 vols (Oxford: Oxford University Press, 1978). Critical yet magisterial account of the development of the thought of Marx and his followers up to the New Left.

Laclau, Ernesto, and Mouffe, Chantal, *Hegemony and Socialist Strategy* (London: Verso, 1985). The book that launched 'post-Marxism'.

Lukács, György, *History and Class Consciousness*, trans. Rodney Livingstone (London: Merlin Press, 1971 [1923]). Brilliantly original essays by one of the founders of Western Marxism.

McClellan, David, *The Thought of Karl Marx* (London: Macmillan, 1971). Reliable short introduction to the life and principal ideas of Marx.

Žižek, Slavoj, *The Sublime Object of Ideology* (London: Verso, 1989). Lacan meets Marx.

Žižek, Slavoj, *The Ticklish Subject: The Absent Centre of Political Ontology* (London: Verso, 1999). Startling intervention in debates in contemporary political theory.

5

Friedrich Nietzsche (1844–1900)

Jon Simons

Nietzsche in the Critical Tradition

Nietzsche's implacable criticism of his time is directed against its culture and the types of character bred by that culture. Using the religious terms of Judaism and Christianity to characterise Western civilisation, Nietzsche traces its arrival at a nihilistic impasse in which there is little prospect of life-affirmation, which would require a transvaluation of all values. His fundamental project is to question the values of Enlightened modernity, such as its fascination with scientific truth, its quest for universal moral principles such as equality and its assumption that reason could set humanity free. Although he does not use the terms directly, Nietzsche in effect criticises the developing mass culture and politics of modernity. Yet, however disdainful Nietzsche may appear to be about the newspaper-reading 'last men' who populated *fin-de-siècle* Europe, he is deeply ambivalent about the modern culture in which he lives, always aware that he is also a product of that culture. So, his own propensity to reflect on how Western society came to hold the values that it does is characteristic of the Western tendency to undermine its values by reflecting on everything.

The German philosophy that preceded him was a symptom of the culture that Nietzsche criticises, so it is not surprising to find him gleefully smashing the ideas that had become established as idols. Key among these was the notion of the subject or self as a substance existing outside of history, the very subject presupposed by Kant's critical philosophy. Nietzsche did not develop his philosophy through sustained criticism of his predecessors, but every now and then he devotes a passage to ridiculing them, often targeting Kant's nihilistic preference for the real world of noumena over the apparent world of phenomena. Kant is also dismissed for asking the wrong question about knowledge: 'How is objective knowledge?' possible rather than 'Why is truth to be valued?' Nietzsche has no more respect for Kant's morality based on impersonal duty, which requires self-abnegation rather than the affirmation of self-chosen virtues. In general, Nietzsche berates Kant for believing that he has deduced rationally or 'discovered' the categories of understanding or the moral law when he has actually invented them. Kant thus denies the key human 'faculty' to create our world and the values by which we live.

Nietzsche objects to Hegel's attempt to reduce everything to one philosophical system, but the two thinkers share a historical approach to understanding the present as the product of previous human activity. Similarly, and in contrast to Kant, both thinkers conceive of individual subjects as embedded in their time and culture, rather than as abstracted from society. But Nietzsche can not take metaphysical comfort in Hegel's Absolute Idea as the realisation of reason, as it is another human myth. As for Marxism, that is yet another symptom of mediocre, levelling culture for Nietzsche, to be dismissed as an unexamined drive for equality. But Nietzsche criticises modernity from the point of view of culture, whereas Marx does so from that of the material conditions of culture. Notwithstanding the gap between their two predecessors' perspectives, Adorno and Horkheimer manage to draw on both, receiving Nietzsche in part via Weber, treating his work as a description of the crisis of modernity. Nietzsche's attempt to overcome the metaphysics of the subject was also an important source for Heidegger.

Introduction

Nietzsche is one of the most provocative figures of the Western philosophical tradition of critique. Born in Saxony in 1844, Nietzsche grew up in a Lutheran family and received a classical education. In 1869 he was appointed Professor of Philology at Basle University, but he already had severe doubts about the value of his discipline. After a brief spell as a medical orderly during the Franco-Prussian War in 1870, Nietzsche took the first of several sick leaves from the university in 1871, finally relinquishing his academic position in 1879. Throughout his sixteen creative years from 1872 to 1888, he continued to be dogged by the ill-health which he experienced as a child, and from which he sought respite in the Swiss Alps and the north of Italy. He led a lonely life, punctuated by a period of closeness to the composer Wagner and his circle from 1869 until his disillusion in 1876 and an unrequited love affair in 1882. After his final, complete mental breakdown in Turin in January 1889, Nietzsche was nursed by his sister Elisabeth until his death in 1900. Nietzsche's work is deliberately unsystematic, expressed in dramatic prose and occasionally poetry, often as aphorisms. His work was generally not well received by the academic or broader public during his writing career, but by the time of his death his reputation was spreading dramatically.

Taken as a whole, Nietzsche's work amounts to an astonishing critique of Western culture, from its Greek and Jewish origins, through its Christian development, and into its modern, secularised and scientific form. If Kant's task was the establishment and justification of values, Nietzsche's was the transvaluation of all values. Nietzsche figures himself as a philosopher who uses a hammer when asking questions, probing the hollowness of idols, of unquestioned beliefs and principles.[1] Kant's problem was to establish the validity of already agreed upon enlightened human judgements. But Nietzsche grasped that this human desire to be rational, this will to truth which he traced back through Western history to his present by means of genealogical critique, is an expression of the will to power, or affirmation of life. In his view, however, the truths and values of his time were the opposite of life enhancing, plunging culture into a crisis of nihilism in which all sense of purpose was being lost. Nietzsche's central concern is with the connection between cultural values and the sort of person that is bred by, or is the product of, Western culture. In Nietzsche's view, those being bred by modern culture, characterised by a will to scientific truth and levelling social values, were mundane and mediocre, a herd. In his affirmative mood, he tried to propose new values, 'beyond good and evil', to quote the title of one of his most significant books, which could breed a new kind of person, the *Übermensch* or Overman who could create his or her own values and purpose. This chapter traces in broad brushstrokes Nietzsche's critique of modern culture and his affirmation of an alternative culture.

Genealogical Critique

Nietzsche's idiosyncratic form of genealogical critique consists of a search for the lowly origins of apparently sublime ideals or values. However, genealogy is less a history of the past than a history of the present, meaning a credible account of how we became what we are today, how we came to hold the values which we have. Genealogy both explains the present as the consequence of the past and simultaneously evaluates it, its purpose being to overcome the values and personality types of the present.

Genealogy, Truth and Language

Genealogy is a mode of investigation that historicises all values and concepts, including that of truth. Nietzsche's particular target is metaphysical truth, or any kind of concept which is held to be true *a priori* and for all time, such as those defined by Kant. Rather than assuming that truth is an intrinsic value, that it is a human good, Nietzsche asks: why should we know? why should we pursue truth, why do humans have 'a will to truth'? Nietzsche is adamant that life should dominate knowledge and science, so that he evaluates truths not according to a transcendental epistemology that judges as if standing outside human life, but according to whether or not beliefs are life enhancing. The *a priori* truth that all events have causes is one of those 'judgments [that] must be *believed* to be true, for the sake of the preservation of creatures like us'.[2] Different types of truth, especially moral truths, preserve and promote different types of life or culture, which breed different types of person. As we shall see below, Nietzsche objects to the modern 'will to truth' that values truth above life, asserting instead that: 'The falseness of a judgment is for us not necessarily an objection to a judgment ... To recognize untruth as a condition of life ... a philosophy that risks this would by that token alone place itself beyond good and evil.'[3] The historical and scientific truths accepted in modern culture may not be intrinsically good if they lead to nihilism.

The underlying principle of Nietzsche's approach to knowledge is perspectivism, meaning that what is accepted as true varies according to different cultural perspectives. Genealogy teaches a fundamental lesson: that truths or values are not static and eternal, but are subject to the contingency of struggles over interpretation. Everything bears the marks of the history of interpretations because human history is a contest between different wills to power: 'everything which happens in the organic world is part of a process of *overpowering, mastering* and ... in turn, all overpowering and mastering is a reinterpretation'.[4] Famously, interpretation goes all the way down for Nietzsche, such that 'physics, too, is only an interpretation and exegesis of the world (to suit us, if I may say so!) and *not* a world-explanation'.[5] Perspectivism stands opposed to all claims to know the essence of any substance or project, because knowledge cannot exist beyond human purposes which both motivate the will to truth and shape it according to human perspective.

There are two different levels of perspective at work in Nietzsche's genealogy, the perspective of the will to power and those of particular cultures in history. His views of the latter are explained in his critical genealogy of modern culture, whereas the general human perspective corresponds with Nietzsche's functional and evolutionary account of consciousness and language. As a weak and vulnerable animal, the human species survived only because of its special genius, consciousness, that enabled individuals to find help and protection in society by first knowing and then communicating feelings and needs. '*Consciousness has developed under the pressure of the need for communication*,' which means also the development of language.[6] The knowledge of ourselves and the world around us that is vital for the survival of the species is possible only because there is also a medium, language, by which to communicate it.

Language develops as the tool by which we can render the world knowable, yet according to Nietzsche 'the total character of the world ... is chaos', lacking any order or form.[7] Language, however, enables humans to know the world by creating it in our own image. Each leaf is different, but by inventing the concept of 'leaf' and naming objects leaves we have the illusion of knowing about things and their essences. Afraid of the unknown, we 'know' it by rendering it familiar, which is commonly done by means of metaphor.

> What then is truth? A movable host of metaphors, metonymies, and anthropomorphisms: in short, a sum of human relations which have been poetically and rhetorically intensified, transferred, and embellished, and which, after long usage, seem to people to be fixed, canonical, and binding. Truths are illusions which we have forgotten are illusions; they are metaphors which have become worn out and have been drained of sensuous force.[8]

In order to become fixed as truths, metaphors had to become reified into concepts over time, during which their usefulness for the species was proved. Their truth status depends not on their correspondence with the order of the world, 'but on its age, on the degree to which it has been incorporated, on its character as a condition of life'.[9] In other words, certain truths, such as that substances endure, are so deeply engraved in modern culture that, as 'irrefutable errors',[10] they are presuppositions of all other enquiries and actions.

Such is Nietzsche's genealogical account of the status of historical and scientific truth, an account which he admits is another interpretation. Yet, although genealogy opens up the possibility of 'infinite interpretations',[11] Nietzsche's perspectivism is not a relativism that regards all interpretations as equally valid. Rather, interpretations are evaluated according to how life enhancing each is, and what sorts of person will be bred by a culture that accepts each interpretation as true, as a condition of life.

Genealogy and the Self

One of the idols subject to Nietzsche's philosophical hammer is the soul, or in more modern terms, the individual subject endowed with a conscience and a free will. When genealogical critique is applied to the notion of the self or the subject, then it, too, is exposed as another metaphysical illusion which has become a basic presupposition of modern culture. In particular, Nietzsche attacks the apparent certainty that there is an essential or unitary self that acts in, has feelings about and knows the world, yet is somehow distinct from its acts. As with all concepts, the 'subject' is a simplification of all the different actions and feelings of a person: '"The subject" is the fiction that many similar states in us are the effect of one substratum.'[12] Again, the cultural condition that explains how the fiction of the subject is considered to be true is language and faith that the world's structure is the same as the structure of grammar: 'language understands and misunderstands all action as conditioned by an actor, by a "subject" ... But no such substratum exists; there is no "being" behind doing ... "the doer" is merely a fiction imposed on the doing'.[13]

Knowing, willing, feeling are not done by the subject, but rather we have a sense of agency because of these activities. These activities are not necessarily coordinated, so Nietzsche hypothesises 'the subject as multiplicity'.[14] The subject is a consequence of all its engagements in the world and the metaphors deployed to understand it, as well as a product of its cultural breeding. Nietzsche's genealogy of the subject is a history about how humans came to have a conscience, to be moral beings accountable for their actions; how they became that peculiar animal who makes promises. Moral conscience literally had to be burnt into people's flesh. Cruel ancient punishments convinced people to pay their debts, or have a pound of flesh removed. People can be relied on now to hold themselves responsible for what they do because of the historical labour of culture which has refined humans. Rational individuals thus have a history, a genealogy, in which thoroughly immoral means were used to create men as moral animals.

> The breeding of an animal which is *entitled to make promises* – is this not the paradoxical task which nature sets itself with respect to man? ... it was by means of the morality of custom and the social strait jacket that man was really *made* calculable ... Things never proceeded without blood, torture, and victims, when man thought it necessary to forge a memory for himself.[15]

Just as modern subjectivity is a cultural achievement, so is 'free will' the consequence of the labour of self-overcoming, or the organisation of the 'complex of sensation and thinking' that constitutes the will. It is 'the expression for the complex state of delight of the person who exercises volition' as the commander of the various under-souls that make the 'commonwealth' of the individual body.[16] Rather than using the terms weak and strong willed, Nietzsche prefers the metaphor of government of the many drives and impulses in each person by one commanding impulse to indicate a free will. The achievement of 'style' through the command of a 'single taste' is the 'one thing needful', and yet it is a 'great and rare art'.[17] As we shall now see, according to Nietzsche's genealogy of modern culture, the types of characters it breeds are unlikely to overcome themselves by giving style to their characters.

Genealogy of Modern Culture

According to Nietzsche's genealogical critique of Western civilisation, modern culture appears ambivalently as the culmination of a two-thousand-year process of decline, in which a morality and civilisation which denigrates life and its enhancement have almost obliterated an alternative morality which affirms life; but also as period of incredible ingenuity in which the principle of life as will to power has been preserved within its opposite. Nietzsche posits a prehistory to Western civilisation in which culture breeds two distinct character types constituted entirely by custom, nobles and slaves, each with their own class morality. 'Good' referred to any attribute of the aristocrats or nobility. Rather than acting altruistically, the ancient aristocrats did whatever came naturally and unreflectively to them as those born to command, which generally involved treating everyone else with cruelty. Nietzsche named these nobles 'blond beasts', a term which was eagerly seized on by his anti-semitic sister Elisabeth and subsequent Nazi interpreters of Nietzsche as a reference to the natural superiority of the Aryan race. However, Nietzsche not only refers to the nobility of all peoples, but also has little interest in these unreflective people without a conscience.

Humans become interesting animals through slave morality, which is forced to be reflexive because slaves are unable to take revenge on the nobles. First, they ascribe guilt to the nobles by insisting that they could behave other than according to their nature. The powerful are now accountable for their actions and the harm they do to the weak, whereas the weak, who could not act against their oppressors anyway, are praised for refraining from violence. In a reactive self-definition, the weak become good because they are not like the nobles. Second, the slave morality also makes suffering meaningful by positing the existence of another 'real' world where goodness is rewarded in contrast to this world of mere appearances, in which the good suffer.

Belief that the good suffer in this world gives rise to a general sense of resentment, a term for which Nietzsche used the French word *ressentiment.* Resentment of the strength of the strong is a major human malaise for Nietzsche, a weakness which should be overcome. It is based on the assumption that if something is wrong, there must be someone to blame. 'Every suffering man instinctively seeks a cause for his suffering; more precisely a doer, more definitely, a *guilty* doer ... something living on which he can upon any pretext discharge his feelings.'[18] Someone else is always to blame for suffering. Bearing in mind that Nietzsche conceives of the self as multiple rather than unitary, resentment might best be regarded not as the quality of a particular group of people, but as an impulse in everyone, though Nietzsche does not allow for the resentment that is caused by socio-political oppression. Resentment is akin to an existential problem, because everyone suffers. The overcoming of resentment is thus an awesome task, as difficult to achieve as self-styling. Thinking about resentment as an aspect of the individual psyche can also be applied to the distinction between noble and slave moralities, which then appear not as social distinctions but as internal psychological tendencies, which also need to be governed if the self is to be given style.

Nietzsche credits the Jews with the revolt of slave morality, whereby, through a religious reinterpretation of Jewish history, the misfortunes of the Jewish people could be explained as the consequence of sin. Their suffering could be born as it was ascribed meaning and purpose in a theology of future redemption. Although conquest would generally destroy the culture of a people, the Jews saved their culture by transforming it, finding purpose in defeat. 'The Jews are the most remarkable nation of world history because faced with the question of being or not being, they preferred, with a perfectly uncanny conviction, being *at any price*.'[19] In his typically ambivalent way, Nietzsche both admires Jewish culture for its ingenuity in preserving itself, yet also characterises it as the most unnatural culture which has made the noble values of life-affirmation, such as 'well-constitutedness, power, beauty', seem evil.[20] His ambivalence is born of the paradox that the Jewish will to power was sustained by a culture that denied the affirmation of life.

Jewish culture is the immediate forerunner of the Christian ascetic ideal which has universalised the meaning for suffering. Christian culture does this by taking up the Platonic distinction between the everyday world of appearances and a more 'real' world of essences and ideals. So, it persuades people that, for example, although they are downtrodden and oppressed in daily life, in 'reality' all souls are equal before God and the meek will inherit the earth. Moreover, Christianity finesses the culture of resentment by redirecting the ascription of blame on to the one who suffers. Christian culture denigrates the struggles, contingency and dynamism of life, of will to power, and prefers eternal stasis, or life after death.

The Platonic search for meaning underneath appearance develops as a will to truth in Christianity, especially as truth about oneself. With the advent of modernity the ascetic ideal is transformed into science, such as the search for immutable laws of nature underlying the contingent acts of nature, floods, drought, or famine, from which humanity suffers. Given that the truth is always somewhere else, somewhere deeper, the will to truth develops into an ethos of sceptical critique, which, by Nietzsche's time, has turned back upon its own premises. Science and rationality – the Enlightenment itself – eroded religious faith, which provided meaning to life. The will to truth is a sublimated will to power, in that it is a will to render life meaningful, yet has the paradoxical effect of undermining that meaning and encouraging nihilism. The ascetic ideal is paradoxically a will to power that preserves human life, yet it is a reactive will to power that denigrates will to power and the abundance of life. In Nietzsche's words:

> *the ascetic ideal offered mankind a meaning* ... any meaning is better than no meaning ... *the will itself was saved.* We can no longer conceal from ourselves what this willing directed by the ascetic ideal expresses in its entirety: this hatred of humanity ... a will to *nothingness,* an aversion to life ... but which is and remains none the less a *will* ... man would rather will *nothingness* than *not* will at all.[21]

Yet when the will to truth is turned back on itself, when it becomes conscious of itself, it discovers that there is no transcendental ground to the value of truth. The will to truth is serving no purpose other than itself, yet the truths it discovers are based on habits of the intellect and faith in grammar, rather than correspondence to reality. Nietzsche acknowledges his own indebtedness as a genealogist to the will to truth and ascetic ideal which has led to nihilism. Paradoxically again, the ascetic ideal has born a mode of enquiry and evaluation that attacks the ascetic ideal.

Nihilism and Affirmation

Nihilism occurs in two basic contrasting forms in modern culture, where the structures of concepts that produce meaning break down. 'The death of God' is the modern nihilistic crisis because once scientific rationality has undermined faith, there is no foundation to human values and morals. 'God' here means also reason, or categorical imperatives, or universal morality. Recognition of the absence of God is recognition that humans have no proper place in the order of the universe, because there is no such order. Having believed for two thousand years that essences lie behind reality, and that there must be an absolute guarantee of goodness and moral value, modern man is left without any values or any meaning. Nihilism as the crisis of modernity is nihilism in the form of paralysis, which is clearly a *fin-de-siècle* sense of despair. Educated for two millennia that there is a clear distinction between essence and appearance, good and evil, modern man is helpless and paralysed to discover that essence is a fiction, that good originates in evil. Having believed for so long that truth and values must be discovered, and having discovered that they do not exist as things in themselves, modern man finds himself with no truths, no values, no meaning, and is thus devoid of purpose.

What modern man is left with is the habit of two thousand years of resentment, denigration of life and slave morality. Modern man, who for Nietzsche is the 'last man', can only take comfort in various decadent 'democratic' ideologies: individualism, socialism and nationalism. All these are for Nietzsche forms of levelling, the pursuit of petty or false ideals, which express resentment of all that which is exceptional and remarkable.

> the *levellers* – ... What they would like to strive for with all their powers is the universal green-pasture happiness of the herd, with security, lack of danger, comfort, and an easier life for everyone.[22]

Nietzsche's expressions of disdain for democratic culture and the characters of modern mass society should not be glossed over. They might be understood to refer to impulses within each person, or as a call for democracy to aim for the highest common factor rather than the lowest common denominator. Such expressions could also be taken as evidence for interpretations of Nietzsche as an aristocratic or élitist philosopher with little concern for the majority.

Yet, from another perspective modern nihilism may be seen as the possibility for self-overcoming, for humans to create their own purposes rather than to seek them beyond this world. In other words, could we get by without God, without idols, without foundations for the truths we hold and the values we uphold? Yes, says Nietzsche, if only we dare to be noble in spirit, but what enables him to be not only a nay-sayer, but a yeah-sayer? According to the logic of his genealogical approach, a new type of character could only be bred if new cultural conditions emerge that can do the work of culture, just as in the past culture had made man an animal with a conscience.

Nietzsche's teaching of eternal recurrence is the thought that, he hopes, can be the cultural condition for breeding a new, reflexive and noble person. Far from being a cosmological doctrine about cyclical history, it is a way of overcoming resentment by living according to a regulative ideal. The dynamism of human life, with its moments of suffering as well as joy, of pain as well as pleasure, means that to affirm life requires not merely the love of fate, which could be passive, but an active pursuit of a destiny one has set for oneself. As the past cannot be changed, one must take responsibility for oneself from the present moment for the future so that all moments of a life can be affirmed as part of an existence lived according to a particular style, which is to be valued for its own sake. It is

> the ideal of the most high-spirited, alive, and world-affirming human being who has not only come to terms and learned to get along with whatever was and is, but who wants to have *what was and is* repeated into all eternity.[23]

Eternal recurrence is a teaching about 'the general economy of the whole' – that life as a whole consists of irreconcilable opposites, like good and evil. Eternal return is thus a teaching to overcome negative nihilism, the sense of meaningless and absurdity of existence.

Eternal recurrence is also closely linked to the art of creating a style for oneself, which indicates that for Nietzsche art is paradigmatic human action.

> The drive toward the formation of metaphors is the fundamental human drive ... It seeks a new realm and a new channel for its activity, and it finds this in myth and in art generally ... an ardent desire to refashion the world.[24]

Aesthetic action overcomes nihilism by giving shape and meaning to life, inventing truths to hold to and values to uphold, which are acknowledged as inventions. Art is the human activity in which humans take responsibility for their world and their values.

The character type who can bear the thought of eternal recurrence is the *Übermensch* or Overman, whose coming is announced by Zarathustra, the fictional teacher of Nietzsche's affirmative thought. Zarathustra teaches, to an unappreciative audience, that the life-affirming Overmen have to be strong and noble enough to be fully autonomous, fully self-legislative in the absence of a law. '*Genuine philosophers ... are commanders and legislators* ... Their "knowing" is *creating*, their creating is a legislation, their will to truth is – *will to power*.'[25] Nietzsche offers two types of Overman in recent history. One is the great leader, such as Napoleon, who is supposed to create the cultural conditions in which eternal recurrence becomes the basis of culture. Yet the actions of such a leader who treats the world as raw material for his artistic creation can hardly encourage the 'herd' to become responsible for their own destiny or artists of their own lives. Nietzsche's other type is precisely the artist of the self, such as Goethe, who can serve as an example to other individuals. Neither of these models goes very far in explaining how a new culture will breed a whole race of Overmen. Nietzsche seems to expect a lot from people, as he did from himself, and indeed he saw that one would have to be more than human to remain sane and be a cheerful nihilist. But on the other hand:

> How much is still possible! So *learn* to laugh beyond yourselves! Lift up your hearts, you fine dancers, high! higher! and do not forget to laugh well![26]

Nietzsche and Contemporary Critical Theory

Nietzsche's influence over contemporary critical theory cannot be underestimated. For some, such as Habermas, that influence is deleterious, because Nietzsche seduces his followers away from the Enlightenment project and into irrationalism. Rather than using critique to refine and develop the grounds for rational understanding, Nietzsche contradicts himself by using the resources of rational critique against reason, thereby unwittingly proving the value of rationality. Habermas also objects to Nietzsche's aestheticism; that is to say, his relation to the human world as if it is a work of art, to be treated as plastic material without reference to the constraints of cognitive or moral rationality.

In the French post-war intellectual scene, especially after 1960, Nietzsche was one of the three 'masters of suspicion' crowned by Ricoeur, who along with Freud and Marx, exerted enormous sway. The affinities between Nietzsche and Foucault are particularly striking. First, Foucault adopts Nietzsche's genealogy for his own histories of the modern subject, leading to the view that the modern will to power is exercised as a will to truth in the form of the human sciences. Moreover, his work follows similar themes such as the role of punishment in constituting the subject, the reactive self-definition of the normal in contrast to the sick, and the affirmative project of the stylisation of life. However, Foucault was concerned with the practical conditions for the constitution of subjects, not only the cultural ones, and also aimed to write from the perspective of the oppressed rather than the powerful.

Nietzsche was also a key figure for Deleuze, for whom he, rather than Kant, is the first truly critical philosopher. As a materialist, Deleuze draws on Nietzsche's insistence on a thoroughly this-worldly philosophy. He also interprets the distinction between the moralities of nobility and resentment in terms of the relation between the active and reactive forces that are central to his theory. Nietzsche is the inspiration for a philosophy of difference according to which active forces could assert themselves without reacting against other forces, while reactive forces are unable to bear the thought of eternal recurrence. Nietzsche is also one of the many figures whom Derrida finds useful as an illustrator of deconstruction. Nietzsche deconstructs the distinction between truth and untruth, good and bad, by showing in his genealogies how the positive term emerges from the negative one. Nietzsche is also an ally in Derrida's critique of the metaphysics of presence, as he both undermines metaphysics in general and attacks the notion that an essential being lies behind actions. Part of Derrida's project is also to highlight the importance of metaphor for philosophy, which echoes Nietzsche's understanding of the relation between metaphor and truth as well as the hold that faith in grammar has on philosophy.

Nietzsche sought not only to criticise philosophy but also to show the possibility of a new type of thinking that could flourish without transcendental or metaphysical grounding. In that sense, Nietzsche is an arch-postmodern philosopher in the eyes of non-foundationalist philosophers such as Rorty and Vattimo. Nietzsche is helpful for Rorty's project of debunking the correspondence theory of truth, according to which descriptions of the world are true insofar as they reflect reality, whereas for Rorty they are interpretations whose usefulness depends on the purposes to which they are to be put. But Rorty does not think that Nietzsche is at all useful politically, because the stylisation of the self should be a purely private activity which is actually made possible not by a transformation of democratic culture but by the institutions of liberal democracy that Nietzsche disparaged.

It is testimony to the richness, or ambiguity, of Nietzsche's thought that he can also be treated as a resource for radical democratic theory by North American postmodernists such as Connolly. He proposes an ethics of the cultivation of difference in which the resentment provoked by identities other than our own, compounded by the ascription of evil to those others for our suffering, is undone by genealogical reflection that shows all identities to be contingent. However, the surplus resentment caused by oppression and inequality would have to be removed in order to stop the projection on to others of existential resentment about the finitude of human life. Perhaps even more remarkably given the apparently misogynistic remarks that pepper his work, Nietzsche has been taken up in feminist theory because of his thoroughgoing anti-essentialism, which Derrida argues applies as much to the concept of 'woman' as any other. Misogynist or patriarchal discourse cannot tell the truth about 'woman' because there is no essence of which to tell the truth. Butler also deploys Nietzsche's anti-essentialism in her queer theory to argue that the subject is produced by its actions rather than a producer of its actions. So, even as crucial an attribute of the subject as gender must be repeatedly performed, which opens gender up to the possibility of being performed subversively, against the grain of normative heterosexuality. Perhaps rather than end with an image of Nietzsche as a looming presence in contemporary critical theory, we can picture his philosophical laughter and dance in the guise of a drag queen.

Notes

1. See Nietzsche, *Twilight of the Idols*, Foreword.
2. Nietzsche, *Beyond Good and Evil*, I, § 11. References to Nietzsche's works are normally given by part and section of his books.
3. Ibid., I, § 4.
4. Nietzsche, *The Genealogy of Morals*, II, § 12.
5. Nietzsche, *Beyond Good and Evil*, I, § 14.
6. Nietzsche, *The Gay Science*, § 354.
7. Ibid., § 109.
8. Nietzsche, 'On Truth and Lies in a Non-moral sense', in *Philosophy and Truth: Selections from Nietzsche's Notebooks of the Early 1870s*, ed. and trans. Daniel Brezeale (New Jersey: Humanities Press, 1979), § 1, p. 84.
9. Nietzsche, *Gay Science*, § 110.
10. Ibid., § 265.
11. Ibid., § 374.
12. Nietzsche, *Will to Power*, § 485.
13. Nietzsche, *Genealogy of Morals*, I, § 12.
14. Nietzsche, *Will to Power*, § 490.
15. Nietzsche, *Genealogy of Morals*, II, § 1, 2 and 3.
16. Nietzsche, *Beyond Good and Evil*, I, § 19.
17. Nietzsche, *Gay Science*, § 290.
18. Nietzsche, *Genealogy of Morals*, III, § 15.
19. Nietzsche, *Anti-Christ*, § 24.
20. Ibid.
21. Nietzsche, *Genealogy of Morals*, III, § 28.
22. Nietzsche, *Beyond Good and Evil*, II, § 44.
23. Ibid., III, § 56.
24. Nietzsche, 'On Truth and Lies in a Non-moral sense', § 2.
25. Nietzsche, *Beyond Good and Evil*, VI, § 211.
26. Nietzsche, *Thus Spoke Zarathustra*, IV, §20.

Major Works by Nietzsche

Beyond Good and Evil, trans. Walter Kaufman (New York: Vintage, 1966 [1886]).

The Gay Science, trans. Walter Kaufman (New York: Vintage, 1974 [1887]).

On the Genealogy of Morals, trans. Douglas Smith (Oxford: Oxford University Press, 1996 [1887]).

Human, All to Human, trans. Marion Faber and Stephen Lehman (Lincoln: University of Nebraska Press, 1984 [1878]).

Thus Spoke Zarathustra, trans. R. J. Hollingdale (London: Penguin, 1961 [1883–92]).

Twilight of the Idols and *The Anti-Christ*, trans. R. J. Hollingdale (London: Penguin, 1968 [Written 1888, published respectively in 1889 and 1895]).

The Will to Power, trans. Walter Kaufman and R. J. Hollingdale (New York: Vintage, 1968 [Notes written 1883–8, published 1901]).

Suggestions for Further Reading

Allison, David B. (ed.), *The New Nietzsche* (Cambridge, MA: MIT Press, 1985). A valuable collection of essays representing a 'French' reception of Nietzsche.

Ansell-Pearson, Keith, *An Introduction to Nietzsche as Political Thinker* (Cambridge: Cambridge University Press, 1994). Incisive explanation of Nietzsche's key concepts in the context of political theory.

Deleuze, Gilles, *Nietzsche and Philosophy*, trans. Hugh Tomlinson (London: Athlone, 1983). Central text in the poststructuralist appropriation of Nietzsche.

Nehamas, Alexander, *Nietzsche: Life as Literature* (Cambridge, MA: Harvard University Press, 1985). Marvellous interpretation of Nietzsche's work as the styling of his own life.

Owen, David, *Maturity and Modernity: Nietzsche, Weber, Foucault and the Ambivalence of Reason* (London: Routledge, 1997). Excellent study of the continuities and contrasts between the three thinkers.

Staten, Henry, *Nietzsche's Voice* (Ithaca, NY: Cornell University Press, 1990). Stunning analysis of Nietzsche's texts influenced by deconstruction.

6

Max Weber (1864–1920)

John Ellis and Jon Simons

Weber in the Critical Tradition

Weber's place in the background to contemporary critical theory is established because throughout his work he criticises modernity as a disenchanted cultural formation dominated by capitalism and state bureaucracy. Moreover, he interacts directly with other figures in the critical tradition. From Kant, he takes the basic distinctions between forms of reason which underlie Kant's critical philosophy, which he treats as the difference between instrumental and substantive rationality. As Weber and subsequently the Frankfurt School theorists argued, the institutionalisation of instrumental reason in administration and economy tends to treat humans as objects, in direct contradiction to Kant's categorical imperative. Weber explores the rational basis of different value spheres and shows how the generic term 'rationality' is contextualised in each through different forms of institutionalisation. This project is given a radical twist by the influences he draws from Nietzsche: primarily, an apprehension of the *fin-de-siècle* sense of nihilism, which is a consequence of secularisation, and a disturbed awareness that there are no ultimate foundations for social values. For Weber, these insights give rise to a sombre awareness of the dangers attendant upon a world that has lost all meaning. Weber's historical approach to sociology also adopts Nietzschean genealogy. He tells the history of the present by tracing the conflicting interpretations of life (in this case religious interpretations), so that he explains the fate of modern man (whom he also refers to as the 'last men') as the outcome of the secularised reinterpretation of the Protestant interpretation of life.

Weber's work clearly contrasts with Marx's historical materialism or Marxist economic determinism, especially the reductive form of it that was current in Weber's time, one which relied on a base/superstructure model of society. Weber not only focused on the cultural conditions of capitalism, but also on the legal, military and bureaucratic, as well as economic institutions of modernity, all of which might be considered 'superstructural'. The sweep of his analysis of societal rationalisation has been extremely influential and provocative. One immediate effect was a problematisation of the kind of utopian notions of post-revolutionary socialism espoused by certain contemporary Marxists (such as Lukács and Bloch), who imagined a post-revolutionary state in which the proletariat could escape the 'iron cage'.

More generally, Weber's pessimistic analysis of the development of Western rationality has been fundamental to the whole project of the Frankfurt School, for whom his critique of instrumental rationality and his vision of the 'iron cage' of administration were crucial. Weber's analysis of the purely formal nature of instrumental rationality provides the basis for the distinction between instrumental or administrative reason and substantive reason, which follows from Kant's distinction between the faculties of understanding and reason. There are also direct and obvious links between Weber's ambiguous judgement of modern rationality and the 'dialectic of Enlightenment' of Horkheimer and Adorno, as well as links with Adorno's later notion of identity logic. This critique of instrumental rationality also provides the basis (when mediated with Marx's analyses of the commodity) for Lukács' concept of reification and for his analysis of the formal rationality of the commodity form. Although he was by no means a radical himself, Weber's penetrating analysis of modernity has contributed to some of the most radical episodes in the tradition of critique.

Introduction

Max Weber is one of the three 'founding fathers' of modern social theory, along with Marx and Durkheim. Born in 1864, he grew up in the bosom of the establishment under the German Empire, remaining loyal to the rather élitist tradition of German liberal nationalism. Germany at this time emerged as one of the world's leading industrial and military powers, although it still had an archaic social structure. That combination gave rise to social and political struggles, which, after Weber's death, led to the collapse of democracy in Germany and the establishment of the Third Reich. Whilst Weber could not be expected to foresee these developments, his work would come to seem remarkably prescient to a post-Holocaust generation.

Weber's reputation as an original and powerful thinker is remarkable given that it is not easy to reconstruct his opus from his extant work, the majority of his output being essays. He completed some major projects, but these were on rather arcane topics: detailed analyses of German agrarian society; a vast project on the sociology of the world's major religions; a typology of the forms of political authority. Yet, through such work, Weber established a tradition of historical, comparative macrosociology, which is global in scale, yet aims to relate processes of change at the key levels of state and politics, culture, economy and personality. Weber was a key figure in the development of 'interpretive' sociology – basically an approach to the study of society which aims to grasp the meaning underlying social action rather than seeing it only in positivist terms as behaviour. The distinction crucial for the hermeneutic tradition arises in the paradoxical attempt to subject humanity to scientific enquiry. Hermeneutics recognises the distinction between human being as subject who searches for meaning and human being as object that is the site and occasion of meaning.

Weber's work is on the whole a pessimistic critique of modernity, as expressed by some of his most famous formulations: that it is the fate of modern man to live in an 'iron cage' of bureaucratic domination in a disenchanted world which has lost its meaning, a world dominated by an essentially 'irrational' form of rationality, in which man must serve a plurality of clashing gods and demons, a world marked by a fundamental sense of loss and fragmentation. The whole discussion is subtended by his analysis of the particular form of 'rationality' which characterises occidental modernisation. Weber uses the terms 'rationalism' and 'rationality' in different senses. First of all, there is the very specific sense of rationality as 'scientific-technological rationalism', that is, the capacity to control the world through calculation and know-how, exemplified by modern science. However, in a more general sense 'rationality' refers to any process aimed at the systematisation of meaning, a process which Weber sees as a consequence of an inner compulsion not only to understand the world as a meaningful whole but also to take a consistent and unified stance towards it. Weber also uses the terms 'rationalism' and 'rationality' to refer to the consequences of the institutionalisation of configurations of meaning and interest in cultural and social forms, such that it provides the basis for a practical rational orientation towards the world. Weber constructs a typology and genealogy of 'rationality' in history that does not simply take the dominant form of rationality in the West as the standard for what is rational, the basis for this project being his comparative analysis of the world-views of the major religions. Finally, Weber famously distinguishes between purposive or means–ends rationality (*Zweckrationalität*), which is also known as instrumental reason, and means choosing the most effective means to achieve given ends, and value rationality (*Wertrationalität*), which is also known as substantive rationality, meaning action oriented to achieve ends conceived in terms of ultimate values.

Weber's Sociology of Religion

Weber's sociology of religion begins from the assumption that each religion is a holistic interpretation of the world which serves to provide human life with meaning, explaining the daily suffering and social inequality in the world as part of a divine or cosmic purpose, and enabling individuals to relate themselves to God or the cosmic entity. The most fundamental distinction is that between the monistic, magical world-view of the 'primitive' tribe and the dualist, theocentric world-views of later world religions. Primitive religion does not posit a fundamental distinction between the concrete daily life of the creaturely world and the divine cosmological order. People remain close to their gods and to their divine purposes, there being no division between empirical knowledge and world interpretation, between magic science and magic ethics. The decisive development in this magical world-view is the idea that the divine world has established the laws for human conduct and now watches over their observance. This elaboration leads to a dualist view of a world divided between the divine and the creaturely. It thus becomes conceivable that the two spheres operate in relative autonomy according to their own laws, satisfying the need for calculability in the world while issuing in a separation of cognition (science) and interpretation (ethics). In a further twist the divine and the creaturely oppose each other, causing a tension which can be attenuated in three possible ways, namely: flight from the world; world adjustment; and world mastery.

Weber's typology of ethico-religious rationalism contains a coherent model of cultural differentiation and, as such, a historical theory of stages of rationalisation classified according to the degree to which each world-image is systematised and the extent of its magical content. Within this typology the most important distinctions are between oriental and occidental rationalism, and between ancient and modern occidental rationalism. These distinctions betray a major theme of Weber's sociology of religion: the attempt to grasp why it was only Protestantism which gave rise to the specific Western development of rationality, associated with modern science and capitalism, even though other religions demonstrably enjoyed the capacity for rationalisation. Weber characterises Protestantism as a particular variant of a common Judeo-Christian religious world-view, with specific ways of dealing with the theocratic dualist tension. First is the belief in an omnipotent, personal God as Creator – in contrast with, for example, the oriental, impersonal, non-created cosmos. This belief provides the rationalised grounds for a scientific understanding of the world by positing that the created world obeys God's laws, and thus behaves in a regular and calculable manner. Second, the Judeo-Christian world-view is characterised by the peculiar conception of the self as tool of the divine will – rather than, for example, as a vessel to be filled by the cosmic spirit – a conception that imposes a practical imperative in relation to the creaturely world. Third, the Judeo-Christian religion defines salvation in terms of world rejection – rather than the world-affirmation of a religion such as Confucianism – a rejection which implies the injunction to take up ascetic work and to struggle against the creaturely in order to render oneself worthy of salvation.

This ethically rationalised world-view is exemplified in the paradigm of the monastic life: the ascetic, disciplined life of prayer, study and maybe some good work, in which the self is developed as the bearer of conscience and ethical autonomy, in a space physically separated from the profane creaturely world. Only with the Reformation, and particularly with the emergence of the Calvinists sects, does this ethical world-view turn resolutely away from the option of 'flight from the world'. Instead laypeople must direct the whole of their lives and selves to striving for salvation through a worldly calling – a vocation or project in the world which is a means to discipline and control the self and to take control of the creaturely. Calvinism combines the imperative of salvation through world control with the demand that action be directed into a unified system in which the moral conduct of the average person was subjected to a consistent method for conduct as a whole. The dynamic which fuels this worldly striving derives from the unbearable tensions and anxieties which follow from the belief in predestination, which assured believers that they were either irredeemably damned in hell or members of that elect few who were saved, without knowing which. The only discernible hope was that the visible success of zealously fulfilling one's worldly calling might serve as a sign of one's status among the elect. This one residual hope depends upon the believer's actions becoming objectified in a systematic and methodical project in the world, which is dedicated to achieving certain goals in an objective or calculable way. The Calvinist does not turn to the world out of any love for the world because of the efficacy of 'good works', or from any desire for worldly comforts. Rather, disciplined work on the self in a worldly calling becomes the 'technical means, not of purchasing salvation, but of getting rid of the fear of damnation'.[1] Believers can never know their status with certainty and are, therefore, never free of the religious compulsion to exert a rational, methodical control over their total conduct and perfect the ethical integration of their personality. Weber draws out the affinities between this 'economising' religious ethic and the 'spirit' of capitalism as exemplified in capitalist accounting, showing how the religious ethic came to invest 'economising' itself with a moral significance. The Protestant ethic enjoins a sublimation of immediate gratification in an indefinite project of stewardship which is homologous with the moral habitus of entrepreneurship.

The Rationalisation of Society

Weber shows how there is an inevitable tendency within all theocratic religions for the religious and the lay realms to rationalise themselves consistently according to their own laws. This development is particularly fateful in the case of the Protestant, for whom the religious postulate to prove oneself in a calling becomes part of a self-defeating dynamic of secularisation. The devalued creaturely world now forces those who seek to control it to recognise its own laws and to seek control through them. This injunction ties rationality to 'objectification', framing thought within an efficient, means–ends calculation which enables the conscious or planned manipulation of external objects. The development of capitalism is bound up with the working out of the same kind of purposive-rational or instrumental orientation towards action. Standardisation and routinisation of life-activity aim at the control of the conditions of existence through objective calculation. Weber traces the impact of this kind of rationality and the forms of rationalisation it imposes upon modern society into the differentiation of two quite autonomous systems: the capitalist economy and the modern state. In both spheres, the means of operation (production in the economy; administration and warfare in the case of the state) are separated from the 'operative' and placed in the hands of the rationally calculating entrepreneur or political leader. Under these conditions, everyone is obliged to behave in a purposive-rational manner.

The way in which Weber defines the specific characteristics of a capitalist economy combines elements drawn from both the 'base' and the 'superstructure' of society, to use Marxist terms. They include the use of rational accounting; the organisation of 'free' labour; the application of scientific knowledge to enhance efficiency; and orientation towards profit and future accumulation. The abstract nature of economic terms is exemplified by the fundamental concept of 'utility', which does not refer to any concrete human needs. The economy is dominated by the rationality of 'technique', involving an instrumental calculation which assumes a given end and is oriented exclusively to an efficient choice between alternative means to it.

When Weber characterises the capitalist economy as 'rational' he uses the word in a rather limited and specific sense, namely, to refer to formal rationality, meaning that the economy is grounded upon a rational and reliable calculation of alternatives. However, there is no necessary reason why the resulting patterns of economising need be rational in any substantive sense, that is, from the standpoint of any specific social interest or value other than an increase in the calculability of economic action itself. In a formal sense, the economic system may indeed operate in a fully rational manner and yet fail to distribute society's worldly goods in a manner that conforms with, say, the ideals of justice or equality. The 'rationality' of capitalism says nothing about the ends to be pursued, which may be entirely 'irrational' in substantive terms.

The development of the modern rational state follows analogous processes of restructuring around the norms of technical and administrative efficiency and is, like the economy, characterised by its impersonality and its bureaucratic mode of action, which represents the triumph of purposive-rational technique in public life. Like the Protestant in his calling, agents of the state must act without personal predilection but only in accordance with impersonal duty, meaning the regulations of the modern power system. The modern rational state has a number of specific characteristics: it wields a monopoly of the legitimate use of force within its confines;

it has a monopoly on legislation and operates on the basis of the rule of law; domination is exercised by a bureaucratic administration of specialised and trained officials. However, our previous caveat applies: notwithstanding the demonstrable efficiency of the modern bureaucratic state, it can only be described as 'rational' in a purely formal sense. In terms of substantive rationality, the state pursues goals which are 'irrational', as the justice it dispenses unavoidably collides with the 'ethic of brotherliness' which is at the heart of the Protestant religious world-view. Furthermore, in its administrative action the modern rational state is condemned to a kind of alienation and unaccountability. Bureaucracy develops the more perfectly it is 'dehumanised', that is, the more completely it succeeds in eliminating any of those personal, irrational, or emotional elements which escape calculation. The kind of rationalised action fostered by the state (as well as the economy) constitutes a series of intensifying and continuing assaults on the socio-cultural world by means-specific instrumentalities. There is an ineluctable tendency to deal with all social problems by means of abstract and generalisable models, rather than in terms of their context, history, intrinsic nature, or unique character. Everywhere there is a convergence around norms of efficient management and standardisation. This inhumane rationality increasingly comes to frame the limits within which social orders, institutions and individuals may develop. New techniques of control and administration weigh on individual actors who experience the dissonance of modern life between the 'rationalised' social orders (exemplified in the modern division of labour and bureaucracy), which are becoming more and more complex, and their own ability to grasp this complexity. Individuals find themselves powerless before a proliferating discipline that increasingly undermines those cultural forms that previously generated practices of self-shaping and obliterates the significance of 'charismatic' or individually differentiated action.

In Weber's famous phrase, modern man comes to be trapped in an 'iron cage' of bureaucracy and sterile rationalisation, in which the dominant forms of rationality seem to manufacture a bureaucratic self and to obliterate precisely those sources of 'creativity' and 'initiative' which might work to counteract this development.[2] The paradoxical development of societal rationalisation thus begins with a promise of world domination but ends with the forces of rationalisation coming back to discipline and master the self, through the pressure of material needs and social order, undermining any original preconditions that may have engendered initiative and empowered the self.

The Rationalisation of Culture

Given the alienating and abstract instrumentalities generated by societal rationalisation, are there no resources within 'culture' that could attenuate the alienating effects of the 'iron cage', perhaps some source of human creativity to challenge the sterile bureaucratic self? Weber's analysis of the rationalisation of modern culture offers little grounds for optimism. For the Calvinist sects the value of methodical action in the world was underwritten by divine meaning and the goal of salvation, but in the modern context the injunction to rationalise the conduct of life becomes dominated less by ethical reason and increasingly by the central cultural feature of modernity – modern science and scientific method – which comes to definitively replace ethics as the leading exemplar of 'rationality'. Whereas Protestantism had championed the rationalism of world mastery in the name of God, scientific rationalism now propagates it in the name of man. The rationalisation of values in the service of religious ethics could, with the weakening of faith, generate entirely secular techniques and codes for shaping and legitimating the self. Crucial here would be philosophies of utilitarianism and, particularly in the German context, the Kantian conception of moral law and personality, with its ethos of self-cultivation. Weber shows how this process of secularisation plays out in the rationalisation of the sphere of culture, a development characterised by a differentiation of cultural phenomena into quite different spheres of value. Each sphere becomes autonomous, pursuing its own inner logic without regard for any holistic world-view. Weber, following Kant's division between his three critiques, identifies three principal 'life-orders': the pursuit of 'truth' (now primarily associated with the institution of science); the ethical-legal sphere; and the aesthetic sphere of art.

Science represents a particular form of rationality which is adequate to an understanding of the natural world. Scientific truth is accumulated as grounded empirical knowledge by devising logical and mathematical models of phenomena, which are constantly and continually tested by experiment. Science aims at a rational cognition of a world understood as an external object, framing the world in a form appropriate to instrumental manipulation. The type of consciousness appropriate to this sphere is cognitive-instrumental, that is, it takes the attitude that to know the world is to act on it and one seeks to know in order to act on it. Science is, notwithstanding its demonstrable successes, a 'rational' activity merely in the formal sense. It is able to determine the appropriate means to attain a given goal rationally but is quite unable to answer the question of why this goal should be pursued, or, indeed, why science itself should exist. Science is not a form of 'value rationality', as it cannot comment upon norms or goals and has no resources to justify the ends of science, art, or politics.

The development of modern science is exemplary of the autonomous rationalisation of value spheres which characterises modern culture as a whole. Yet, its demonstrably successful specialisation also renders it totally incapable of playing the part previously played by the religious world-view of providing a holistic meaning for life. Science cannot provide such a meaning because its bracketing of the 'objective' nature of phenomena means it can only ever provide a partial synthesis, never a holistic meaning, which, within the realm of science, is (like the 'ends' of capitalism) forever deferred because it is 'chained to the course of progress' and 'asks to be surpassed'.[3] Furthermore, it is a major theme of Weber's work that science inevitably works towards a 'disenchantment' of the cosmos and any notion of holistic meaning. Like all critique, science brings to bear a corrosive, relentless glare of suspicion on all claims to meaningfulness on the principle that there are no mysterious incalculable forces that come into play in the cosmos, but only the kind of mechanistic meaning that one can control by calculation. The Protestant world-view and its ethos of brotherliness are consigned to the realm of the 'irrational'. Science cannot become a resource for meaning in life because the rigorous and self-reflexive methods of empirical science tend to corrode the very assumption that the world could have an ethical meaning.

However, and this goes to the heart of the 'fate' of modern man, the disenchanted, impersonalised, rationalised world continues to pose the problem of meaning. The mind has a persistent metaphysical need to comprehend the world and to develop a unified attitude towards it. Weber is adamant that salvation religion can no longer play any role in constructing such a meaning as it is incapable of dealing with the disenchantment of science. But he is equally adamant that the attempt to make science fit this role, as in an ideology of scientism, is a contravention of its own autonomous rationality, representing a relapse, in Weber's typology, into a new kind of monism. Science which interprets itself monistically is, for Weber, a mystification, not enlightenment.

Weber finds the same logic (secularisation and the development of autonomous standards) at work in the realm of the law and ethics. The Protestant sects had espoused a universalist ethics of conviction grounded in the injunctions of God, but the rational principles lose their connection to their religious origins. As the law becomes formalised, its principles are increasingly systematised under the direction of professional jurists in courts and universities. The grounds of law and morality cease to be derived from the cosmos, as in the tradition of natural law (from which the modern European tradition is descended). Instead, laws are considered valid on purely procedural lines: the law must be enacted by the appropriate authorities (parliament, the judiciary, and so on), applied to appropriate cases and enforced by neutral, specialised office holders. The development of a rational legal system is considered by Weber to be one of the key factors in the difference between the East and the West that explains the modernisation and the development of capitalism. He argues that the development of the kind of rational accounting which underlies capitalism requires an unambiguous and clear legal system that would be free of irrational administrative arbitrariness and which could guarantee the legally binding character of contracts.

Yet, modern law and ethics are rational merely in the formal sense of the term. It is again part of the 'fate' of modernity that the gains (in terms of equity, fairness and universality of the law), which derive from the autonomous rationalisation of the ethical sphere, are achieved at the expense of a substantive sense of 'justice', which might answer the desire for meaning in the absence of a religious world-view. As Weber argues, the desire for a substantive justice oriented towards some concrete instance and person will 'invariably collide with the formalism and the rule-bound and cool "matter-of-factness" of bureaucratic administration'.[4] It is Weber's pessimistic judgement that in the context of modernity, the articulation of substantive justice would presuppose a genuine prophecy, which cannot occur, given the technical and social conditions of rational culture.

The third value sphere to emerge in the modern rationalisation of culture is the aesthetic sphere of art. Protestantism had stressed individual subjectivity and its ethical expression through work. Modern culture retains this stress, but in the sphere of art it becomes detached from the methodical conduct of life, just as it had previously become independent of its function as religious adornment and performance. As an autonomous sphere it has its own aesthetic values to pursue, that is, beauty and the authentic expression of subjectivity. Weber's analysis shows how, with the development of societal rationalisation and its abstract and alienating orders, there is a complementary growth of a radical subjectivism, meaning a peculiar sensitivity to human feelings and psychological truths, and a belief in the authenticity of emotion and the public power of 'personality' and personal style. The aesthetic sphere becomes the principle means of flight from the 'iron cage', taking on the functions of an 'inner-worldly salvation' by promising a kind of redemption, but one which is fundamentally inefficacious or inauthentic, as it becomes absorbed into an escapist 'culture of feeling'.

Thus, the modern rationalisation of the aesthetic sphere signals a flight into the 'irrationality' of emotionalism or 'charisma', a flight from the dominant, alienating forms of rationality, whose instrumental orientations devalue personal and humane forms of sociopolitical relationships in favour of the abstract, impersonal relations of the modern rational state. Radical subjectivity is constructed as the negation of the alienating impersonality of a rationalised society, in which culture emerges as either 'protest' or 'adaptation'. Art becomes a counter-cultural sphere, the bohemian realm of 'alternative' values and lifestyles, which gains its defining posture in opposition to the 'system'. Weber notes the tendency to substitute values from one cultural sphere for those of another, and, in particular, the trend to 'transform judgements of moral intent into judgements of taste ("in poor taste" instead of "reprehensible")', the intention and consequence of which is to bolster the claims for a radical subjectivity, as 'the inaccessibility of appeal from aesthetic judgement excludes discussion'.[5] Weber thus holds out little hope that the realm of art can provide an authentic way out of the 'iron cage', one which is not merely an illusory 'flight from reality'.

Modern culture, differentiated into autonomous 'spheres of value', each embodied in its own concrete institutional settings (the scientific enterprise; the legal system; the artistic enterprise or community), entails a fundamental antagonism, primarily between the methodical conduct of public life and private bohemianism. Weber's pessimistic analysis draws a picture of modernity in which it is the 'fate' of humanity to be torn between serving different and incompatible gods, none of which is capable of providing modern life with meaning. None of the three spheres has the metaphysical sweep even to justify its own existence, and yet, as we have already seen, this does not lessen the human compulsion to seek for a unified meaning. It is the ironic 'fate' of the modern individual to be released to his or her own resources for action and knowledge by a culture incapable of asserting any objectively valid meaning and, under these circumstances, the principle forms of 'flight' are merely inauthentic rationalisations of the ethic of brotherliness lost along with the religious world-view.

The Fate of Modern Man

Weber's vision of the modern world would seem to be unrelentingly pessimistic. Modern life is rationalised, driven by purposive-rational or instrumental orientations, divided into opposed life-orders and value spheres, without genuinely prophetic truths, yet wracked by endless searches for absolute experience and spiritual wholeness. But this pessimistic vision does not amount to a rejection of the modern legacy. Weber's position is fundamentally ambivalent. Weber is highly representative of his time, when any simple faith in Enlightenment progress had become problematic, especially in the wake of World War One. In its initial, optimistic and charismatic phase, Enlightenment reason posed as a holistic alternative to a religious world-view, not least because it promised to eliminate the human suffering and injustice which is at the heart of the religious ethic of brotherliness. This narrative provides the basis for an optimistic view of infinite human progress as a process of perfection of human intelligence and an accumulation of knowledge, which can be used to overcome the obstacles placed in humanity's path by nature. The same rational understanding which was demonstrably being used to master the natural world could also be used to promote social progress, first by dispersing the mist of prejudice and superstition, and then by understanding the laws of human behaviour so that the government could be rationalised as social engineering. According to an alternative narrative, the practical effect of the triumph of Reason is to eliminate everything that is humanly meaningful from the cosmos, which, reconceived as a Newtonian machine, becomes a Frankenstein monster that is increasingly out of control and at odds with human values.

Weber's work straddles these two narratives and has given rise, as a consequence, to quite disparate readings. Talcott Parsons' reading stresses the first narrative, judging modern societies to be the most rational that have ever existed, offering the greatest potential for autonomy. In contrast, Herbert Marcuse stresses the second narrative, seeing the extension of modern rational control as the ineluctable erosion of human freedom and initiative, and as the development of the most 'irrational' of societies.[6] As Weber is at pains to stress, although Reason (in the form of science) has become the predominant cultural logic, as the Enlightenment narrative predicted, it is not science that holds sway over human destiny, but 'fate'. Modern individuals, thrown upon their own resources, are torn apart by the 'war of the Gods' which rule their lifes, that is, the disparate and conflicting values thrown up by the differentiated life-orders. The economy is run for profit, politics is pursued to possess the power of the state, and art is for those seeking 'experience'. In this situation, there is an hegemony of abstract, objective intellect released on the world in its many forms: in politics bureaucratisation as 'mind objectified'; in science the victory of specialised and fragmented knowledge over holistic meaning; in the aesthetic the triumph of 'technique' and 'subjectivism'; in economic life the dominion of a human type formed by specialisation and a vocational ideal 'that prowls about in our lives like the ghost of dead religious beliefs', driven by an irrational pursuit of wealth.[7]

Weber is sceptical of any ready answers to these problems, being primarily concerned in his own writings with elaborating a principled ethical stance in the face of the existential challenge facing modern man. Weber delineates two contrasting responses to this ethical challenge, deriving from the old opposition between world-adjustment and world-flight: the 'ethic of conviction' and the 'ethic of responsibility'. The latter, which represents a resolute acceptance of the tragic realities of a disenchanted world, is guided by the outcome of an action, in sharp contrast to the former, which adopts a posture of world-rejection and is guided primarily by the act's intrinsic value. Weber's primary target here are theoretical positions that do little more than contrive some tolerable rationalisation of the ethic of brotherliness without its religious grounding. Weber finds that tendency alarming given modern subjectivist culture's predilection for 'charisma' and 'style', a predilection which perhaps found its apotheosis within a few years of Weber's death in the meticulous and zealous genocides perpetrated by the Nazis.

Weber and Contemporary Critical Theory

The influence of Weber in contemporary critical theory reflects his ambivalence towards modernity. On the one hand, his work plays a crucial role in the theory of Jürgen Habermas, where it provides the basis for his differentiation of reason into three value spheres, each with its own structure of consciousness, validity claims and institutional settings, as well as his critique of the rationalisation of the life-world. Habermas reconstructs Weber's scattered account of the rationalisation of culture and society, arguing that his pessimism is a consequence of his failure to acknowledge the possibilities for universally applicable reason that are inherent in communicative action. Like Parsons, who is another source for Habermas' social theory, he focuses on the rational achievements and potential of modern society. Whereas Weber could find no normative grounds to replace those of the religious ethics of brotherliness, Habermas finds them in communicative reason.

On the other hand, commentators have found significant affinities between Weber and Foucault, although there is no evidence of direct influence. The grounds for such connections would lie in a continuity from Nietzsche through Weber to Foucault, all of whom can be regarded as genealogical critics. Like Weber, Foucault is concerned with the institutional as well as cultural conditions of social rationalisation in modernity that produce disciplined individuals. Unlike Habermas, Foucault follows Weber in historicising rationality as a fragmented rather than unified notion. Yet, Foucault focuses not on the state but on the micro-institutions of modernity, such as prisons and families. His critique of science is directed not at the overweening pretensions of an ideology of scientism, but at the 'dubious' human sciences which are thoroughly imbricated with techniques of government. It is an indication of the richness of Weber's critique of modernity that it is identified with such disparate accounts of the modern world.

Notes

1. Weber, *Protestant Ethic*, p. 115.
2. Ibid., p. 181.
3. Weber, 'Science as a Vocation', p. 138.
4. Weber, 'Bureaucracy', pp. 220–1.
5. Weber, 'Religious Rejections of the World', p. 342.
6. Talcott Parsons, *Societies: Evolutionary and Comparative Perspectives* (New

Jersey: Prentice Hall, 1971); Herbert Marcuse, *One-Dimensional Man* (Boston: Beacon Press, 1964).

7. Weber, *Protestant Ethic*, p. 182.

Major Works by Weber

'Science as a Vocation' [1918]; 'Politics as a Vocation' [1918]; 'Bureaucracy' [1922]; 'Religious Rejections of the World and their Directions' [1922] *From Max Weber*, trans. and ed. H. H. Gerth and C. Wright Mills (London: Routledge and Kegan Paul, 1948).

The Protestant Ethic and the Spirit of Capitalism, trans. Talcott Parsons (London: Allen and Unwin, 1930 [1920]).

The Sociology of Religion, trans. Ephraim Fischcoff (London: Methuen, 1965 [1922]).

The Theory of Social and Economic Organisation, trans. A. R. Henderson, ed. Talcott Parsons (Glencoe, IL: Free Press, 1947 [1922]).

Suggestions for Further Reading

Bendix, R., *Max Weber: An Intellectual Portrait*. An authoritative secondary text.

Habermas, Jürgen, *The Theory of Communicative Rationality; Vol. 1, Reason and the Rationalization of Society* (Boston: Beacon Press, 1984). Systematic reconstruction of Weber's scattered account of the rationalisation of society and culture.

Lash, Scott, and Whimster, Sam (eds), *Max Weber, Rationality and Modernity* (London: Allen and Unwin, 1987). Interesting collection of more contemporary essays about Weber, including some about Foucault's relation to his work.

Owen, David, *Maturity and Modernity: Nietzsche, Weber, Foucault and the Ambivalence of Reason* (London: Routledge, 1997). Excellent study of the continuities and contrasts between the three thinkers.

Parkin, Frank, *Max Weber* (London: Routledge, 1982). A handy beginner's guide, which appears in the 'Key Sociologists' series.

Roth, Guenther, and Schlucter, Wolfgang, *Max Weber's Vision of History: Ethics and Methods* (London: University of California Press, 1979).

Scaff, Lawrence, *Fleeing the Iron Cage* (London: University of California Press, 1989).

7

Sigmund Freud (1856–1939)

Richard H. King

Freud in the Critical Tradition

At the centre of Freud's remarkable achievement is that he tried, and largely succeeded in, expanding the meaning and range of the concept of mind or psyche as such. In that sense, he saw himself as challenging the conventional philosophical wisdom that all thinking that counts is conscious and that the mind is to be understood as the seat of rationality. Freud had no deep grounding in philosophy but was educated generally in classical and German literature and culture (which also entailed considerable knowledge of Shakespeare) and trained specifically in the biological sciences. Yet, though the form of Freud's work is intended to be scientific, he is often regarded as an enemy of Enlightened rationalism, not only by those who question his scientific credentials but also by those who focus on the content of his work on the unconscious motivations of human behaviour.

Freud has been grouped with Marx and Nietzsche as part of the core of the modernist tradition of the 'hermeneutics of suspicion'. According to this general stance, what is obvious on the surface is less fundamental than what lies hidden underneath, which in Freud's case is the work of the drives and of the unconscious parts of the psyche. With Freud this also implied that early childhood experience, mostly forgotten, was basic in shaping and explaining our adult selves. Thus we do not always, or even often, know the 'real' or original motivation for our thoughts, feelings or actions. This in turn put Freud at odds with the phenomenological-existentialist tradition of Husserl, Heidegger and Sartre. Although this tradition shared with Freud and psychoanalysis a focus on subjective experience, they rejected the idea of the unconscious or the assumption that we are determined by biological and/or early childhood experiences. In their view, such presuppositions tended to place humans into the same category as animals and to deny to humans their freedom of choice and hence responsibility for their actions. The phenomenological-existentialist tradition followed Kant in stressing the centrality of human freedom to any definition of human being. Also trained in this tradition, Arendt saw the psychoanalytic preoccupation with private and hidden impulses as representing the modern de-emphasis upon the authenticity of public speech and action.

Freud's association with Marx as a master of suspicion was given substance by the Freudo-Marxist attempt to explain the interaction between individual personality and social structure. Freud and psychoanalysis were used to provide Marxism with a theory of subjectivity, while Marxism was used to provide a framework for Freud's limited social theory. In particular, different views emerged about the extent to which any society, in contrast to capitalist society, requires repression of unconscious drives. Wilhelm Reich proposed a utopian vision of a completely non-repressive society, whereas Herbert Marcuse distinguished between the repression of erotic and libidinal desires required for civilisation under conditions of scarcity, and the surplus repression under technologically advanced capitalism in which socio-political constraints prevent the possible confluence of Freudian reality and pleasure principles. As is explained in the chapter on Adorno and Horkheimer, both of those thinkers also developed versions of Freudo-Marxism. For Horkheimer, Freud and Marx could be combined to show the pathologies of personality and family which were both brought about by capitalist conditions and sustained them. But, for Adorno, ultimately the two cannot be unified because, under capitalism, society and self remain sundered apart.

Introduction

There are, it seems, an almost inexhaustible numbers of ways to situate Sigmund Freud and to evaluate his significance for modern thought. Born in Moravia, he lived and worked most of his life in Vienna, interrupted by studies in Paris in the 1880s, occasional trips abroad, and then exile from the Nazis in London, where he died. By his death, and even more after World War Two, his status was such that he was, in W. H. Auden's words, 'no more a person/now but a whole climate of opinion'. The influence of psychoanalysis has been as profound as it has been controversial, not only as a way of alleviating psychological distress but also as it has shaped modern pedagogy and child-rearing practices, not to mention its impact on modernist painting and writing. Almost from the beginning, Freud's psychoanalytic movement spawned schismatics and heretics, from the spiritualising efforts of the Swiss psychiatrist C. G. Jung to the sexual radicalism of Wilhelm Reich. For the first half of the century, Freud's influence was greatest in two, quite different, parts of the Western world: German-speaking Central Europe (Berlin, Vienna, Budapest, Zürich) and the United States, first in New England (where philosopher William James welcomed Freud on his first visit to America in 1909) and later in New York City.

After the mid-century, psychoanalysis gradually made headway in France and Britain, with far-flung outposts such as Buenos Aires emerging as a hotbed of psychoanalytic culture by the latter years of the century. Academic disciplines, particularly in the social sciences and humanities, incorporated many of the crucial ideas spawned by the movement and its heretics. By the 1960s, particularly in the United States, psychoanalysis was the crucial catalyst in what sociologist Philip Rieff has called the 'triumph of the therapeutic'. What Rieff meant, among other things, was that the language of self-description and evaluation among the educated middle classes was marked by the replacement of a moral vocabulary (right and wrong; good and bad) with non-judgemental therapeutic terminology (healthy and neurotic; self-fulfilling and repressive). Since the 1960s the psychoanalytic movement has continually fragmented and last rites are perennially being pronounced over the corpus of Freud's theory and therapy. Still, his influence remains surprisingly strong down to the present.

In what follows, I begin by suggesting some of the ways Freud can be situated intellectually and historically. I will then set forth the central tenets of his theory, with an emphasis upon its changing nature rather than upon its fixed and static quality. Finally, I want to look at some of the ways of relating Freud to contemporary developments in the human sciences and the study of literature and culture.

Situating Freud

To understand Freud's project is to explore the interrelation between Freud as the 'discoverer' of the unconscious, of the crucial part dreams play as the 'royal road to the unconscious', of infantile (bi-)sexuality and of the centrality of repression in individual and group life; as the 'inventor' of a theoretical edifice whose purpose is to cure disturbed patients; and as the 'founder' of an international movement still extant today. Another would be to take a cue from philosopher Paul Ricoeur and nominate Freud, along with Karl Marx and Friedrich Nietzsche, as one of the three great formulators of the 'hermeneutics of suspicion', the cast of mind underpinning modernist thought and culture. This basic interpretive stance seeks to dismantle or demythologise existing values and institutions in the name of something more basic or fundamental, in Freud's case the power of the drives. Others see Freud as working in the tradition of modern biological science, closer in spirit to Charles Darwin than to Nietzsche, an assessment that Freud would have happily seconded, while another line of thought considers Freud as a kind of visionary, one whose entire corpus is what the critic Harold Bloom might call a 'strong poem', that is, an imaginative achievement of the highest order. Finally, Freud has been called a charlatan, the purveyor of pseudo-scientific propositions and ineffectual therapeutic nostrums for the alienated (and idle) bourgeoisie of his time and since. In the barbed words of Freud's Viennese contemporary Karl Kraus, 'psychoanalysis is that mental illness for which it regards itself as therapy'.[1]

There are other ways to grasp something of the complexity of Freud's thought. First, Freud was a genuine bourgeois paterfamilias of the German-speaking, Central European, Jewish sort. Thus his attitudes on sex and gender roles were thoroughly conventional, though he provided the intellectual dynamite to explode those conventional positions. He was never an observing Jew, but the marginal status of Jews in the Austro-Hungarian Empire in the era of a waning Roman Catholic culture and rising political anti-semitism, along with his Enlightenment-derived hostility to religion, meant that Freud also possessed an ironic distance on mainspring bourgeois, gentile culture.

In more strictly academic-intellectual terms, Freud was trained in the natural and biological sciences, in medicine and neurology in particular. Thus, the positivist dream of formulating scientific laws of mental functioning exerted a great influence on Freud. At the same time, Freud, like many post-emancipation Jews, had a thorough grounding in classical German *Bildung* (educational formation), including heavy doses of German Romantic poetry and thought. It was a tradition that began with the languages, thought and literature of classical antiquity, came up through Shakespeare, and then worshipped at the shrine of the greats of modern German thought, including Goethe and Schiller, Kant and Schopenhauer and, of course, Nietzsche, although Freud always (unconvincingly) denied the latter's influence. If Freud the positivist sought to explain human behaviour in scientific terms, the humanist Freud sought to understand individual (and group) thought and action. A final large source of Freud's thought was Freud himself. For, Freud's first 'big' book, and arguably still his greatest, *The Interpretation of Dreams* (1900), had its source in Freud's own self-analysis. Overall, Freud's thought was a fruitful, though not untroubled, combination of the spirit of science and the spirit of the humanities, of theoretical enquiry with therapeutic practice.

The Many Faces of Psychoanalysis

Psychoanalysis is, first, a theory of therapy, which is neither a purely cognitive process of self-understanding nor a quasi-hypnotic state in which the analyst cures by suggestion. In fact, Freud rejected the use of hypnosis because, among other reasons, he wanted the patient to assume conscious responsibility for his or her cure. What brings the patient to analysis is a pattern of dysfunction and unhappiness, often expressed through the bodily symptoms. Or as Freud and Breuer famously stated: 'Hysterics suffer mainly from reminiscences.'[2] The cure lies not in a direct fulfilment of repressed desires. That would be what analysts refer to as 'acting out'. Rather, the task is to understand and then transcend the desires, since the original desire to be one's parent of the same sex and to have one's parent of the opposite sex can never be fulfilled.

Freud soon discovered that patients offered 'resistance' to being cured, but that, paradoxically, the source of resistance and the key to cure were the same thing, what he called 'transference'.[3] By this he meant that patients often comport themselves towards their analyst in the way that they had related to significant others in their earlier life, for example parents or siblings, figures of authority and objects of desire. In the transference relationship, the neurotic patterns of thought and behaviour are raised to awareness, brought from the past into the present analytic situation, and, through the process of 'free association', 'worked through' there. Ideally, the result is the transformation, through verbal articulation, of neurotic thoughts and actions into memories. The title of an essay of 1914 concisely sums up the process as 'recollection, repetition and working through'. But as the inclusion of the term 'working through' suggests, the process involves overcoming or 'abreacting' powerful emotions, often unconscious ones. Over the course of his professional life, Freud was to modify his early optimism about the 'talking cure' and came to feel that the most one could hope for from psychoanalysis was the ability to cope with, not to be completely cured of, neurotic symptoms. Freud also considered psychoanalysis appropriate only for neurotic patients. Neurotics still had contact with reality, while, for psychotic patients, the problem was not too much, but too little, repression; and, more importantly, their loss of reality made it impossible for them even to establish a transference relationship with the analyst.

But Freud's theoretical centrepiece was a theory of the psyche, sometimes called his 'metapsychology'. The ways he 'modelled' or depicted psychic structure and functioning were extremely diverse. Overall, Freud developed four dominant models of mental life: the dynamic, the economic, the topographical-structural and the developmental. For instance, the dynamic model stresses the psychic conflict between individual impulses and the dictates of reality. The conflict between the reality and pleasure principles was one way Freud had of articulating this dynamic model of mental functioning. Central to the dynamic model is the instinctual dualism Freud retained throughout his life, though he changed its terms at least once. In his first version Freud pitted the sexual drives against the ego or survival drives, the urge to perpetuate the race against the urge for individual survival.

But in the 1910s, Freud came to question this model on two grounds. First, the ego instincts, insofar as survival involved self-preservation, were hard to distinguish from the libidinal nature of the sexual drives. Here Freud's concept of narcissism pushed him towards an instinctual monism rather than dualism. But, Freud discovered that the dreams of shell-shocked soldiers recurred quite often to their traumatic memories rather than avoiding them. This seemed to undermine his fundamental assumption that dreaming was a form of 'wish-fulfilment'. Put another way: if dreams are attempts at wish-fulfilment, there might be a fundamental wish to suffer pain, even to die, and this seemed to contradict the pleasure principle. In his speculative essay *Beyond the Pleasure Principle* (1919), Freud recast his instinct theory by reaffirming its dualistic nature. But now he grouped the sexual and ego instincts together as Eros and grouped the drive to suffer or to inflict pain, even to cease existing, together as Thanatos or the death drive. The drives, which he once described as biological-materialistic impulses, now were quasi-cosmic, almost metaphysical, forces or tendencies.

A second, less well-known model of the psyche is Freud's 'economic' model. The term economic refers to the nature of the psyche when it is conceived of as disposing over a fixed quantity of libidinal energy (supplied by the drives). The economic model enabled Freud to talk about the way that objects are 'cathected' (or invested) with psychic or erotic importance. Fetishised objects are a familiar example of the way a particular object takes on an erotic charge, contrary to its normal usage or appearance. One of the main differences Freud drew between 'primary' and 'secondary' process (roughly conscious and unconscious) thinking was that in the unconscious there is a great mobility of cathexis. This means that various representations in the psyche are invested with unstable erotic attention, while in conscious thinking, a certain constancy is maintained.

Another particularly important example of Freud's use of the economic (or energy) model is his explanation of mourning-work. When someone loses a loved one or an object of great devotion or even a cause, mourning-work is the process whereby the libidinal cathexis, namely, love, devotion and dedication, to that 'object' is gradually withdrawn and redirected elsewhere. In depression ('melancholia'), this process is extended and intensified, because there has been a narcissistic identification of the self with the lost loved object. Thus, when the object is lost, part of the self is lost as well. Resenting this abandonment, the self directs aggression against itself. Though derived from a materialist model of psychic functioning, Freud used the economic model, particularly in his great essays 'On Narcissism' (1914) and 'Mourning and Melancholia' (1917), to explore the origins of the self with a power and subtlety rarely matched in modern thought.

Freud's topographical-structural model of the psyche has become much more familiar over the years. As with the instinct theory, Freud shifted his terminology in mid-career and thereby changed the meaning of certain key terms, such as the 'unconscious'. The basic idea of the unconscious in Freud's theory is not just that things are not present to consciousness; it is that they cannot be brought back to consciousness through an act of moral or epistemological will. It is not that I forget something; it is that I forget that I forget it. It is the role of dream-analysis and 'free association' to provide access to the unconscious parts of the mind. But it is important to note that the term unconscious can either be used as an adjective (X's 'unconscious desires') or as a noun (the 'unconscious' is unknown territory). In Freud's topographical model of the mind, the Unconscious (now capitalised) is a system with its own rules of functioning. For instance, there is no sense of time in the Unconscious; nor does the law of contradiction or negation work there. It is represented as a chaotic realm of forces and energies, images and symbols all mixed up together. Between it and the Pre-conscious lies a firm boundary of censorship, while between the Pre-conscious and Consciousness lies a more permeable and more easily transgressed line. In developing the Unconscious as a system, Freud was able to create a site for the stages and mechanisms of dreaming. Based on an infantile wish (usually sexual), the dream is linked up with dream thoughts in the present as they are triggered off by the day's events and are transformed by the dream work (such as condensation, displacement, symbolisation and considerations of representability) into the manifest dream. Obviously, the system Unconscious is highly structured and rule-governed rather than chaotic. It is this aspect of the Unconscious that Jacques Lacan is thinking of when he asserts that the Unconscious is 'neither primordial or instinctual'.[4]

But by the early 1920s, Freud's topographical model had become a 'structural' model. This new model retained the three-storey structure, but was now divided into the Id/Ego/Super-Ego. The Id (the It) is the realm of drive representations and repressed materials; the Ego (the I) is the part of the psyche that mediates between inside and outside; and the Super-Ego (the Over I) is the source of values and ideals and by implication enables the making of moral judgements. Three major changes had been made in the topographical model. First, the Unconscious as a system has disappeared. Now, portions of each of the three psychic agencies are unconscious. The Unconscious (a noun) has, as it were, become unconscious (an adjective) again; where it was once a system, it is now a quality. The second significant development is that the Ego now disposes over the 'defence mechanisms', which are unconsciously deployed to protect the self from external and internal threats. Desire can be repressed or it can be sublimated; aggression can be redirected against the self or projected outwards against the world. And so on. Finally, Freud sees the Super-Ego, fuelled by aggressive impulses, as acting very directly against the Id and the Ego. In lay terms, only a fine line separates moral scrupulosity from moral masochism.

Largely unconscious in its workings, the Super-Ego constitutes the cultural dimension of the self, but can itself be destructive of the self. All this is a reminder that Freud's patients, at least the original ones, entered analysis not because they lacked a fixed moral compass, but because their moral standards were so rigid that they were incapable of love or work or action.

Freud also spoke of the mind in developmental terms, as an entity in which the functions and structures of the psyche emerge gradually, though never automatically, over time. Freud's developmental model, focusing primarily on the individual's affective rather than cognitive or moral development, presupposes a primal unity between organism and the world. A sense of separation from the world leads to the gradual development of sexuality through stages of libidinal investment in parts of the body (the oral, anal and genital regions). For Freud, the by no means unproblematic development of normality depends upon the concentration of sexual pleasure in the genitals. With the development of heterosexual object choice and the move from self-love to the capacity to love others, the other parts of the body lose most of their erotogenic capacity.

It is in this developmental context that Freud's idea of the Oedipal Complex must be placed. The concept refers to what happens at the early childhood stage (from the age of four to five years) when children realise that they must give up the parent of the opposite sex as their sexual object choice. In little boys, Freud attributed this renunciation to castration anxiety, a fear of losing a vital part of his body if the young boy fails to sacrifice his desire to reality. This was the way that the nuclear family of Western culture inculcated the incest taboo in individuals. Yet, since nothing is ever lost to the psyche, Freud assumes that later object choices, be they objects of desire or of identification, are attempts to rediscover our original objects of desire and identification. Desire, then, cannot be understood apart from loss; loss in turn cannot be understood without mourning.

Despite his conventional way of life, Freud was far from unambiguous about sexual normality.[5] He assumes that human beings have sexual desires (roughly defined as organ pleasure) from the very beginning and that those desires can be satisfied by either sex. In non-technical terms, sexual choice has nothing intrinsic to do with the gender of the desired person. At the same time, Freud's first drive theory suggests that sexual choice is intrinsically connected with the (impersonal) urge to reproduce, something that obviously does require that the object of desire be someone of the opposite sex. Overall, there is a contradiction at the heart of Freud's theory of sexuality, which reflects a contradiction at the heart of human sexuality itself.

Finally, psychoanalytic theory is a theory of society and culture. From the beginning, conservative critics of Freud would charge him with undermining the foundations of civilised society by allegedly authorising free sexuality, while radical Freudians have sought repeatedly to combine Freud and Marx, so as to formulate a vision of a non-repressive society in which all forms of repression, public and private, were somehow fundamentally linked and abolished. Yet Freud confounded the dreams of both camps. Though Freud was personally and even therapeutically sympathetic to a freer sexual life for his patients and for the culture, he nevertheless insisted, as already mentioned, that we could never achieve our original object choices. This is another way of saying that cultural life must inevitably involve 'repression' and 'sublimation' of fundamental desires. Freud's mature social theory, as summed up in *Civilization and its Discontents* (1930) posits an inexorable conflict between the individual's instincts and society's requirements and also between the instincts themselves within each individual. In the case of the former, the family is the original and basic social institution. What is 'learned' by each individual when he or she gives up their original object of desire (namely, the parent of the opposite sex) is deferral of instinctual gratification. This is the template of all future renunciations, most of them accomplished unconsciously. Similarly, Freud also noted in *Civilization and its Discontents* that the demands of nature, expressed in and through our bodies, also require giving up or repressing certain urges.

Freud's most perspicuous account of his theory of culture as renunciation and substitution can be found in the 'fort-da' episode in *Beyond the Pleasure Principle*. There, Freud relates how he observed a little boy trying to come to terms with the fact that his mother inevitably must absent herself from him. He does so by throwing away a spool on the end of a string and then reeling it back in. All the while, the little boy repeats the phrase: 'Gone ... There' ('*fort-da*' in German). Thus this game is an attempt, through re-enactment, to give up his mother. By substituting an object for her, he tries to take control over the whole process through re-presenting it to himself. With this, he becomes a cultural being, as it were.[6] Freud's assumption generally is that we are 'uncomfortable in culture', a literal translation of the German title of *Civilization and its Discontents.*

Even more complexly, Freud's dualistic drive theory, whether in its first or second form, suggested that individuals were divided within themselves and that one sort of urge, for instance, erotic desire, might come into conflict or be combined with its opposite, aggression, even hate, towards another. More generally, the assumption in Freud's late thought of a conflict, whether individual, collective or cosmological, between Eros and Thanatos meant that he had no room in his social thought for utopian visions of social harmony and erotic fulfilment. So, though Freud refused to perpetuate the virtues of a highly repressive society, he also scotched the hopes of Freudian radicals such as Wilhelm Reich that there could be such a thing as a non-repressive society.

This only begins to touch on the various ways Freud and his followers sought to explain everything from the origins of human society and religion to the functions of literature, sculpture and painting. Freud's work as an analyst of collective life also engaged with crucial issues raised by the emergence of mass political psychology, and the phenomenon of individual and group prejudice, especially anti-semitism. Underlying all his work with groups is the assumption that group choices are rarely, if ever, rational and are often 'about' something other than what is ostensibly at issue. In broadest terms, Freud's theory always assumes that individual analysis is implicitly social and cultural commentary. As he once observed, individual psychology is already social and collective.

Freud and Contemporary Thought

Freud has been appropriated in many ways in contemporary thinking about crucial topics such as memory, the nature and construction of the self, gender and literary analysis, only some of which can be addressed here. The debates about the status of psychoanalysis, whether its claims have truth-value and whether it works as such, remain highly contentious, particularly in contemporary Anglophone philosophy of science.

One heated debate in recent years has concerned the nature of memory in psychoanalytic theory and practice. Jeffrey M. Masson challenged one of the keystones of Freud's theory, namely his claim that his patients' reports of early childhood seduction (read 'sexual abuse') were fantasies. Masson's contrary claim was that Freud covered up the existence of large amounts of child abuse. In the 1990s, literary and cultural critic Frederick Crews charged that psychoanalysis bore primary responsibility for the baleful idea that, since no memory is ever lost to the unconscious, all present testimony of child abuse should be accepted at face value. In other words, testimony coming from the patient's (or witness') unconscious should be unimpeachable.

Both critics oversimplified Freud. First, Freud never denied that some reports of sexual abuse were true; rather, reports had to be investigated very closely and actual abuse was not usually the only cause of the patient's problems. On the other hand, Crews seemed to neglect Freud's claim that, though nothing is ever forgotten in the unconscious, the memories retrieved from there are often highly distorted. They are what he called 'screen memories'. Freud's concept of memory is considerably more complex and interesting than his critics, from either direction, will grant. By extension, memory in its collective forms is just as problematic and just as crucial to handle with care.

Another dimension of recent psychoanalytic work with memory has been the idea that the self is constructed through (self-)narration. On this view, it is the task of analysis to help the patient discover and then reconstruct his or her story, thereby constructing a meaningful sense of self. Interestingly, a close reading of Freud discloses that he was not always so confident that the effort to find out the truth of the past would be successful. Lacking empirical confirmation, the patient and analyst together often make use of what Freud calls 'constructions' to bridge gaps and fill lacunae in the patient's story. The best that can be hoped for is that the patient will be finished with analysis when he or she is satisfied with the story reconstructed from the past. On a somewhat parallel track, Jacques Lacan's most influential, and creative, work was his early post-World War Two account of the formation of the self or subject. In the famous 'mirror stage' version of self-formation, Lacan attributes the initial formation of the self to a perhaps unavoidable misrecognition. The desperate attempt of the helpless infant self to gain control of his or her world by asserting self-control is partially successful but at the cost of creating a defensive, even paranoid self-structure. Indeed, for Lacan, the adult self still embodies this paranoid attitude. It is for this reason, among others, that Lacan's version of psychoanalytic theory has been seen as a main source of talk about the 'decentered self'.[7] One implication of Lacan's work is that to attempt to reconstruct a self based on a coherent narrative of the past is a defensive, even paranoiac, move.

Not surprisingly, feminist thought has had to come to terms with Freud, even when it most obviously rejected him. Early formulations of feminist thought after World War Two, such as Betty Friedan's *The Feminine Mystique* (1962) and Kate Millett's *Sexual Politics* (1969) attacked Freud as one of the contemporary architects of the ideology of patriarchy. Both Francophone and Anglophone feminism found their arch-villain in Freud and what was obviously a prime example of 'phallocentricism'. Had not Freud announced that 'anatomy is destiny'? Was it not the young boy, not the young girl, as the model he had in mind when he developed his theory of affective and sexual development? Yet by the mid-1970s, Freud was not without his defenders among feminists. Particularly in her *Psychoanalysis and Feminism* (1974), Juliet Mitchell defends Freud on two fronts. First, when Freud delineates the psychology of woman and her place in society and culture, he is not prescribing the way things should be but describing the way things in fact are. Neither women's alleged 'penis envy' nor the view that anatomy is destiny are meant to imply some sort of biological determinism. Rather, according to Mitchell, such concepts and phrases reflect the nature of social and cultural reality in Freud's and in our own time. Nor, claimed Mitchell, did Millett and Friedan get Freud's point about the unconscious. It was not that men, for instance, set out intentionally, generation after generation, to establish patriarchy and to oppress women. Rather they themselves were born into institutional structures, which are internalised in the unconscious as 'the way things are', and assume gendered positions as part of their social, not biological, roles. This explains the perpetuation not only of individual male attitudes but also cultural stereotypes and archetypes held by both sexes. In the broadest sense, Freud's was not a theory of intentions so much as it was a theory of structures and positions.

At a less polemical level, one of the major innovations in recent decades in both French and Anglophone feminist psychoanalytic thought has been a shift in focus to pre-Oedipal stages of development (in Freudian terms) to explain the origins and early development of gender differences and to re-emphasise the body in the development of the self.[8] In particular Nancy Chodorow has drawn upon object-relations theory to help formulate descriptive and normative accounts of early gender development. Carol Gilligan's work on the differences in ethical styles between young men and women has called attention to the way the developmental model of the self has been largely been a male model of development. In addition the object-relations approach emphasises, more than Freud did, the interpersonal, interactive model of self-development and has radically de-emphasised the role of the drives in individual psychology. Still, Freud remains a vital force in feminist psychoanalytical thinking, even when he serves as a whipping boy or as a springboard for the development of new positions.

Finally, Freud's influence on textual interpretation, especially of literature and film, has been profound. But in recent years, a shift in emphasis has modified the nature of that interpretive effort quite significantly. Under the influence of French structuralist and poststructuralist thought in particular, the position of psychoanalysis as a key theoretical discourse with priority over literary texts has been called into question. Rather, literature can, as it were, 'read' psychoanalysis in literary and rhetorical terms. The interpretive move can and should go both ways. Because, as Shoshana Felman has observed, there are 'no natural boundaries' between psychoanalysis and literature, it should now be possible to establish a 'real dialogue' between them.[9] Indeed, the new psychoanalytic way of reading calls into question all sorts of boundaries.

Beyond this shift in the relative importance of psychoanalytic theory for literature, what a psychoanalytic reading of a text looks like has changed considerably. Originally, one of the (un)appealing things about psychoanalytic theory for literary interpretation was that it seemed to be, first, a ready-made decoding machine, a way to discover and to interpret symbols; and, second, it promised a less moralistic, more intellectually powerful way of describing character and character development, particularly in the novel. As a result, pre-1960s psychoanalytic literary criticism tended to allegorise texts and their characters and thus provided a pat and predictable interpretive schema for bringing literature into line. It was also very much concerned with psychoanalysing the author and his or her intentions for the text. For all of the Freudian emphasis on the unconscious and the irrational, the relationship between author and text seemed to be relatively unproblematic, at least for the reader, if not for the author him- or herself.

But what developed under the Lacanian influence, as well as that of poststructuralism generally, was a focus on the relational aspects of a literary text and a de-emphasis of the author. Not how did the author come to write the novel, but how does the reader 'read' the text and how is the reader 'read' by the text became central questions. Something like a transference relationship is seen as a central part of the reader–text relationship. The diffuse and pervasive workings of desire within the text and between text and reader also receive new emphasis. Individual characters and their characteristics are de-emphasised, while the relationship among various characters, their positionality vis-à-vis one another, assumes greater importance. Overall, these developments amount to saying that recent psychoanalytic textual criticism is more concerned with how than what a story means and focuses on how a story presents its complexities and complications, not with how it resolves them. This in turn implies that literary interpretation itself has become a problematic enterprise. As Felman asserts, 'Criticism ... here consists not of a statement, but of a performance of the story of the text; its function is not constative but performative.'[10] Once again, interpretation is at the mercy of the text, re-enacting its conundrums and complexities, rather than explaining them.

At times the recent literary rereadings of psychoanalysis can seem pretty far from the original Freud in letter and in even in spirit. But if we have learned anything from recent theories of interpretation, there is not such a thing as an origin, no such man as the real Freud, no such thing as a fixed interpretation. Though we can imagine Freud the proto-scientist and conventional humanist disagreeing with this line of thought, we should also remember that one of Freud's last essays was entitled 'Analysis – Terminable and Interminable'.

Notes

1. Karl Kraus, *Half-Truths and One-and-a-Half Truths* (Montreal: Engendra Press, 1976), p. 77.
2. Sigmund Freud and Josef Breuer, *Studies on Hysteria*, Pelican Freud Library, vol. 3, ed. Angela Richards, trans. James and Alix Strachey (London: Penguin Books, 1974 [1895]), p. 42.
3. See Freud, 'Fragments of an Analysis of a Case of Hysteria' (1905), in *Case Histories I*, Pelican Freud Library, vol. 8, ed. Angela Richards, trans. James and Alix Strachey (London: Penguin Books, 1977).
4. Jacques Lacan, 'The Agency of the Letter in the Unconscious', in *Écrits: A Selection*, trans. Alan Sheridan (New York: W. W. Norton and Company, Inc., 1977), p. 170.
5. Juliet Mitchell emphasises this point in *Psychoanalysis and Feminism* (New York: Pantheon, 1974).

6. Sigmund Freud, *Beyond the Pleasure Principle* (1919) in *On Metapsychology*, pp. 283–7.
7. Lacan, 'The Mirror Stage', in *Écrits*, pp. 1–7.
8. See Meredith Skura, 'Psychoanalytic Criticism', in *Redrawing Boundaries: The Transformation of English and American Studies*, ed. Stephen Greenblatt and Giles Gunn (New York: MLA, 1992), pp. 349–73.
9. Shoshana Felman, 'To Open the Question', *Yale French Studies*, 55/56, 1977, p. 9; p. 6.
10. Ibid., p. 114.

Major Works by Freud

The Interpretation of Dreams, Pelican Freud Library, vol. 4, ed. Angela Richards, trans. James Strachey (London: Penguin Books, 1976 [1900]).

On Metapsychology: The Theory of Psychoanalysis, Pelican Freud Library, vol. 11, ed. Albert Dickson, trans. James Strachey (London: Penguin Books, 1984).

Civilization, Society and Religion, Pelican Freud Library, vol. 12, ed. Albert Dickson, trans. James Strachey (London: Penguin Books, 1981).

Suggestions for Further Reading

Crews, Frederick, *Memory Wars* (London: Granta Books, 1997). A polemical but in many ways effective attack on Freud and his followers.

Felman, Shoshana (ed.), *Yale French Studies*, 'Literature and Psychoanalysis: The Question of Reading: Otherwise', 55/56 (1977). One pioneering source for the new psychoanalytic literary criticism.

La Planche, J., and Pontalis, J-B., *The Language of Psychoanalysis* (London: Karnac Books, 1988). Remains indispensable as a dictionary of psychoanalytic terminology.

Mitchell, Juliet, *Psychoanalysis and Feminism* (New York: Pantheon Books, 1974).

Ricoeur, Paul, *Freud and Philosophy* (New Haven: Yale University Press, 1977). Still one of the most important philosophical engagements with Freud's work.

Rieff, Philip, *Freud: The Mind of the Moralist*, 3rd edn (Chicago, IL: University of Chicago Press, 1979). The best intellectual history of Freud's thought.

Schafer, Roy, *Retelling a Life: Narration and Dialogue in Psychoanalysis* (New York: Basic Books, 1992).

Schorske, Carl, *Fin-de-Siècle Vienna: Politics and Culture* (New York: Vintage Books, 1980). A rich account of Freud's intellectual and cultural milieu.

8

Georg Lukács (1885–1971)

Stuart Sim

Lukács in the Critical Tradition

Lukács was immersed in the critical tradition that constitutes the background to contemporary critical theory through the influence of various intellectual movements of the time, such as neo-Kantianism. Nietzsche was also an early influence, although one he turned violently against in later life. While at university he studied under the key social theorists Georg Simmel and Max Weber. The latter's critique of instrumental rationality provided the basis (when mediated with Marx's analyses of the commodity) for Lukács' analysis of the formal rationality of the commodity form. Hegel was the major influence of his early career, providing him with the crucial methods of thinking in terms of totality and dialectically when analysing the relations between literary form and historical process. The substance of the analysis, however, was derived from Lukács' Hegelian reading of Marx, who was Lukács' main political inspiration. Lukács understood that Marx's appropriation of Hegel's notion of totality undermined the supposedly Marxist theory of economic determinism. Rather than there being a simple relation of economic base determining the superstructure, all aspects of culture, society and economy have to be understood in relation as a totality. Marx had recognised that, under the distorted conditions of capitalism, commodity fetishism turns objects and capital into apparently living beings, while on the other hand human labour becomes another commodity. Lukács understood that the effect of commodity fetishism on human activity and consciousness is to render humans into mere objects or things, in a process that he refers to as reification. The subject which must become conscious of itself as the true agent of human history is the proletariat, which at the same time is the exploited object of capitalism. This identification of human emancipation with the reconciliation of subject and object is not only Hegelian, but also reflects the moral problem left over from Kant.

Lukács' unorthodox reading of Marx, as well as his adaptations from Weber, endeared him to the Frankfurt School, in particular to Adorno and Horkheimer. Both in his own right and through his influence on the Frankfurt School, Lukács is a founding figure of Western Marxism, which is a tendency in Marxism that breaks with the orthodoxy of economic determinism, thereby attaching much more importance to the political and cultural forms of capitalism and its opposition. However, Lukács upheld the Leninist view that the communist party incarnates the ideal interests of the proletariat, which was a political doctrine at odds with the philosophical flavour of Western Marxism. Lukács also disagreed with his contemporaries about the most appropriate literary forms for encouraging the development of revolutionary consciousness, which in his view develop in the proletariat. Lukács favoured nineteenth-century realist novels that showed historical processes at work, whereas Brecht preferred work with a direct political message (such as his own theatre) and Adorno argued for the negative hints of utopian alternatives to capitalism that could be read off the unconventional forms of modernist art. Lukács' Marxist critique is thus one that takes aesthetics as seriously as politics.

Introduction

Over the course of a writing career spanning more than sixty years, Georg Lukács made major contributions to the development of critical theory. His writings encompass philosophy, literary theory and literary criticism, and in each case Lukács left an important legacy that continues to inform debate through into our own century. Early Marxist philosophical works, most notably the controversial study *History and Class Consciousness* (1923), were seminal in the development of the Frankfurt School, and, working out from there, of what came to be called 'Western Marxism'. Earlier works of literary aesthetics, such as *The Theory of the Novel* (1916), have exerted an influence over several generations of theorists, including Lucien Goldmann and, in our own day, Fredric Jameson. Lukács' critical writings from the 1930s through to the 1960s established the concept of critical realism, which represented a less doctrinaire form of the socialist realist aesthetic then in vogue in Marxist circles. In the course of constructing a critical realist position, Lukács came into conflict with the modernist tradition, both inside and outside

Marxism; his arguments with Bertolt Brecht, for example, revealed some critical fault lines within Marxist thought in general. The anti-modernist stance, particularly as outlined in *The Meaning of Contemporary Realism* (1958), also establishes some links with post-modernist thought, which is similarly critical of the modernist ethos; although Lukács himself would most likely have agreed with his American disciple Jameson that postmodernism constituted the 'cultural logic of late capitalism' and should be opposed by Marxists.[1] We shall go on to explore the nature of Lukács' legacy to critical theory after considering his place in the development of Marxist thought.

Lukács and Marxism

Although he is undoubtedly one of the most important thinkers produced by the Marxist tradition, Lukács was never a very orthodox Marxist. For much of his life he was in conflict with the Marxist establishment, whether in his native Hungary, or in the Soviet Union, where he lived from 1933 to 1945. His first important writings, *Soul and Form* (1911) and *The Theory of the Novel* (1916), took their inspiration from Hegel rather than Marx (Nietzsche and Kant had been even earlier influences), although by the end of World War One Lukács was a confirmed communist. He was active in the revolution that founded the Hungarian Soviet Republic of 1919, and served as Deputy Commissar for Education in the revolutionary government before being forced to flee to Austria when the counter-revolution was successful. His first major work of Marxist theory, *History and Class Consciousness* (1923), fell foul of the Comintern for its Hegelian leanings, and Lukács was forced to recant in order to continue his career within the communist movement. A later plan calling for collaboration with the social democratic elements in Hungarian politics, the 'Blum Theses' of 1928–9 (Blum being Lukács' communist party codename), brought such severe criticism down on Lukács' head that he dropped out of active politics altogether. Then, as a theorist of literary realism writing in the Soviet Union during Stalin's reign, Lukács had a particularly uneasy relationship with official Marxism. He despised socialist realism, considering it to be a mechanistic and unsophisticated theory that cramped artistic expression, but was forced to pay lip service to it while Stalin lived. In late career, Lukács accepted a role in the revolutionary government formed after the Hungarian uprising of

1956, only to be sent into exile in Romania for a spell when the Russians invaded and crushed the rebellion.

Lukács did make periodic attempts to ingratiate himself with official Marxism. *Lenin: A Study on the Unity of his Thought* (1924), written in the aftermath of the Comintern's condemnation of *History and Class Consciousness,* praised its subject, by then raised to a place in the Marxist pantheon next to Marx and Engels themselves, as '*the only theoretician equal to Marx* yet produced by the struggle for the liberation of the proletariat'.[2] *The Young Hegel* (1948), for which Lukács was awarded a doctorate by the Soviet Academy of Arts and Sciences in 1938, identified proto-Marxist tendencies in the early Hegel, particularly when writing on political and economic matters, that made him seem a logical source for Marx to use in the construction of dialectical materialist philosophy. Lukács' objective was to overcome the suspicion of Hegel in official Marxist circles (where he was generally viewed as a hopelessly abstract metaphysician and political reactionary), and by doing so to protect his own heavily Hegelian-influenced thought from attack. For all his efforts, however, Lukács never quite overcame Marxist orthodoxy on this matter. Orthodox Marxism from the Russian Revolution onwards has been marked by a socio-political bias, whereas the Western Marxist school that Lukács helped to found has been more philosophically oriented, thus more receptive to the Hegelian legacy in Marxism. Western Marxism, which has been accused by its critics of having an academic bias, primarily concerns itself with the philosophical problems that Marxism poses – the nature of the social totality, the dialectic, materialism, or the Marxist aesthetic, for example.

The Theory of the Novel

The Hegelian strain in Lukács' thought is particularly evident in the pre-communist study *The Theory of the Novel.* Written during World War One, the work traces the development of literary forms through history from the classical epic down to the modern novel. It establishes a life-long obsession with the relationship between literary form and historical process that Lukács pursued in a series of related studies. In this book, Lukács posits a dialectical process whereby the epic gradually is displaced by the novel, the latter becoming the form which best captures the complexity and fragmented nature of modern existence. Hegel's conception of world history, as a series of stages where new forms of social organisation emerge out of the conflicts and contradictions of the old (see *The Philosophy of History*, for example), is clearly the model here. World history is seen to have an underlying logic to its development that means we can comprehend it as a total process. Whether drawing on Hegel or Marx, all Lukács' enquiries are based on that assumption.

Whereas the epic pictures an organic world where heroes seek out their destiny, the novel for Lukács speaks of cultural dislocation: 'The novel is the epic of an age in which the extensive totality of life has become a problem, yet which still thinks in terms of totality.'[3] Lukács later came to believe that we can resurrect that organic totality through the application of Marxist theory in the political realm. Marxism enables us to understand the totality of the socio-historical process, with its various class struggles, that has led to our current situation, where radical change is possible. Early in his career, however, Lukács regarded the novel as a symptom of a world experiencing a large-scale crisis in its system of values, which it does not know how to resolve. Novel characters are confronted by the impossibility of unifying their inner and outer lives in the manner of epic heroes (whose sense of destiny sustains them through adversity), and live in a state of personal insecurity and anxiety. Authors respond to the problems set us by the modern world with novels of abstract idealism or romantic disillusionment. Either their characters struggle to reconcile their inner and outer lives, as is done to comic effect in *Don Quixote*, for example, or they retreat from that unequal struggle into a private world of their own – as happens in Flaubert's narratives. Lukács is critical of those authors who take the disillusionment route, although in this pre-Marxist phase of his thought he can offer little in the way of an alternative. The romantic idealists are no more successful in his view at resolving the overriding dilemma of modern existence: our desire for an organic world which can never be recovered.

Lukács' Hegelian-inspired reading of the novel as the form which expresses the rise of bourgeois culture, with all its attendant problems, is one that was developed by a host of other commentators, both Marxist and non-Marxist, over the course of the twentieth century.[4] Perhaps its most direct influence can be seen in the work of Goldmann, whose theory of genetic structuralism is heavily indebted to *The Theory of the Novel*'s conception of the social totality. Genetic structuralism treats literature as articulating the world-views of influential social groupings at particular points in history. In his study *The Hidden God: A Study of Tragic Vision in the 'Pensées' of Pascal and the Tragedies of Racine*, Goldmann identifies parallels, or 'homoloies' as he refers to them, between Pascal and Racine and the extreme wing of the Jansenist movement within the Catholic Church of the period. The writings of Pascal and Racine are taken to be more precise renderings of the 'vague and confused' thought of their extreme Jansenist contemporaries.[5] Literary texts are conceived to be in dialectical interaction with their society, helping to reshape its ideology to encompass the beliefs of the groups they represent. There was, Goldmann argued, a continuous process going on, whereby the old social totality was being challenged and a new social totality was being created in its place.

Goldman's *Towards a Sociology of the Novel* went on to examine the relationship between novels and their social environment, positing homologies between, for example, the twentieth-century novel and the rise of monopoly capitalism – as in the work of André Malraux. It was the genetic structuralist's task to identify whose interest within the social totality (that is, general culture) of their time particular novels were expressing, with Goldmann having essentially the same view of historical process as Lukács.

History and Class Consciousness

History and Class Consciousness is the product of a thinker still convinced of the creative potential of Marxist thought. The most striking thing about the work, looked at in historical perspective, is its non-dogmatic approach to Marxist theory, as Lukács was fully prepared to be critical of the latter's premises where necessary. He claims that Marxism is a method rather than a body of doctrine, and that its principles are all but incidental to its success as a theory:

> Let us assume for the sake of argument that recent research has disproved once and for all every one of Marx's individual theses. Even if this were to be proved, every serious 'orthodox' Marxist would still be able to accept all such modern findings without reservation and hence dismiss all of Marx's theses *in toto* – without having to renounce his orthodoxy for a single moment ... orthodoxy refers exclusively to *method*.[6]

The orthodox did not agree with this thought experiment, and, as the Comintern were soon to verify, treated Lukács' attempted revision as heretical. Soviet Marxism in this period was in the process of hardening into a doctrine which could not be questioned by its adherents, and Lukács was out of step with a development that was to become even more pronounced with the rise to power of Stalin. Lukács' fear was that Marxism was turning into a determinist theory, where the ultimate triumph of the proletariat was assumed to be inevitable. Lukács argues strongly against this mind-set in *History and Class Consciousness*, insisting that the theory could neither foretell the future nor guarantee the success of its followers' actions; but that was not what a communist party in the first flush of political success wanted to hear, and Lukács was accordingly censured.

If it failed to impress official Marxism, however, the non-doctrinaire quality of Lukács' thought went on to become a distinguishing feature of Western Marxism. As late as the 1968 *événements* in Paris, Lukács was regarded as a model of how to interpret Marx creatively and anti-deterministically; although Lukács himself, chastened by his treatment at the hands of the Comintern, had long since disowned *History and Class Consciousness* and was distinctly unhappy at its reappropriation by student revolutionaries.

History and Class Consciousness regards the growth of proletarian class consciousness as the key to bringing about the downfall of capitalism. The proletariat is for Lukács the class which is most conscious of being exploited by the capitalist system. It is both the subject and the object of capitalism, exploited by a system which depends on that exploitation for its continued operation. The proletariat is therefore historically destined to challenge its exploiters once its consciousness has developed enough to recognise its identical subject–object status (which is not to say that its success is then assured; Lukács is no determinist about such things). Only the proletariat has this potential to alter the course of world history, to achieve – with the help of the communist party – 'the unity of its theory and practice, the point at which the economic necessity of its struggle for liberation changes dialectically into freedom'.[7]

Lukács appears to allow for a dynamic relationship between the party and the proletariat, and insists that the proletariat cannot be coerced into revolution against its will: it can only be led 'into battle in pursuit of a goal to which it itself aspires'.[8] This alone is enough to make him suspect in the eyes of the Soviet establishment, where the party is already beginning to assume dictatorial powers. The fact that Lukács was also very critical of Engels at several points throughout *History and Class Consciousness* did not help his case with the Soviet authorities either. Engels had already attained canonical status, and to query his analytical findings was, to the orthodox, to query the foundations of the Marxist scheme itself. More to the point, those authorities considered the conception of the proletariat as the identical subject-object of history to be Hegelian rather than Marxist. For Hegel, the individual had freedom at the level of being a subject, and this freedom enabled him or her to act upon, and in principle change, the objective world. To become an identical subject–object was to have the power to alter the course of history. The shift from being exploited to being aware of the nature of one's exploitation is, in Hegelian terms, a shift from quantity to quality, and thus indicative of the attainment of a higher form of knowledge which could threaten the existence of the capitalist system itself. It is a highly abstract argument, however, very much in the Hegelian mould, and as such it provoked the ire of a Comintern more concerned with the practical political issues of establishing a new social order. Lukács, in the Comintern's opinion, was guilty of the sin of 'old Hegelianism', making him a danger to the integrity of Marxist theory.

Despite Lukács' recantation, *History and Class Consciousness* soon had a circle of admirers, most notably Theodor Adorno and Max Horkheimer, the leading lights of the newly established School of Social Research at the University of Frankfurt. The latter two thinkers were particularly influenced by Lukács' anti-doctrinal conception of Marxism, and developed an analytical method, 'Critical Theory', which was not afraid to be openly critical of the Marxist canon. Adorno in particular persevered with this adversarial attitude towards orthodox Marxism throughout his life, as his attack on traditional interpretations of the nature of the dialectic in *Negative Dialectics* reveals.[9] Lukács' emphasis on method in *History and Class Consciousness* is enthusiastically appropriated by the School in general, almost all of whom proved to be dissenting voices in one way or another within the Marxist tradition – to the point where they have been seen as precursors of post-Marxism.[10] The Frankfurt School influenced many others in their turn, becoming one of the main forces within the development of Western Marxism, thereby ensuring that the self-critical spirit of *History and Class Consciousness* became an integral part of that movement's ethos. Lukács himself, ironically enough, felt compelled by the initial response to *History and Class Consciousness* to present a less self-critical face to the world, drawing criticism from Adorno in the process.

Lukács and Realism

During the 1930s and 1940s Lukács produced several studies defending realism as a literary style. He developed his own canon of approved authors, with Scott, Balzac, Stendhal, Tolstoy and Gorki, for example, repeatedly being used to score points over such figures as Hugo, Flaubert and Zola. The major criterion for success as a realist, in Lukács' opinion, was the ability to reveal how socio-historical processes affected individual development. Scott was a particular favourite of Lukács in this respect, despite the reactionary nature of his political views. Scott's Scottish novels, with their clash between older ways of life – such as the semi-feudal clan system of the Highlands – and new ones emanating largely from England, depicted Scotland as a culture in transition. There was clearly a great deal of sympathy for the older ways in the author, not to mention a fair degree of romanticisation on his part of Highland life, but also a recognition that, regrettably or not, the world had moved on and the old ways were no longer viable. Modernity was extending its reach even into the more backward areas of Scottish culture.

Scott was one of the greatest exponents of the 'historical novel', and Lukács was particularly drawn to this genre as a site for Marxist literary analysis. As he explained in the preface to a later edition of *The Historical Novel* (1947), what the form provided for the Marxist critic was the basis for 'a theoretical examination of the interaction between the historical spirit and the great genres of literature which portray the totality of history'.[11] It was that interaction that Lukács found in the work of Scott, whose strong sense of historical necessity (the supersession of feudalism by modern bourgeois society) commended him to Lukács. The author's conservative politics could be set to one side by the Marxist critic, for whom the narratives themselves helped to reinforce the Marxist historical scheme of a progress through class struggle towards the 'dictatorship of the proletariat'.

Balzac, too, successfully communicates a sense of dialectical process in history, with Lukács regarding his novel sequence the *Comédie humaine* as an 'extension of the historical novel into an historical picture of the present'.[12] Once again Lukács manages to identify virtues in an ideological adversary, with Balzac being praised for showing us all that is contradictory in the development of nineteenth-century capitalism. *The Peasants* may set out to be a portrayal of the decline of the aristocratic estate in post-revolutionary France from Balzac's characteristically 'feudal, romantic viewpoint', but what it actually reveals is the collapse of the peasant smallholding in the face of the new capitalist order.[13] *Lost Illusions* demonstrates how the capitalist ethic came to dominate all aspects of French life, including the production of literature. Over the course of the *Comédie humaine* the right-wing Balzac turns into one of the most effective chroniclers of the rise of capitalism in France.

Tolstoy is another writer whose work transcends his class background to become an important source of evidence for Marxism's historical thesis. Whereas the more orthodox Marxist critics of the time were prone to judge authors on the basis of their known political commitments, Lukács demonstrated how Marxist aesthetics could escape the straitjacket of doctrinaire thought to appropriate the work of even apparent class enemies in its cause. It was not simply a case of bourgeois politics generating bourgeois literature of interest to the bourgeoisie only. As Lukács insisted in *Studies in European Realism* (1950): 'reactionary traits in the world-view of great realist writers do not prevent them from depicting social reality in a comprehensive, correct and objective way'.[14] It is a lesson that Western Marxist critics have taken to heart, reading against the grain of literary works to see what they can be made to reveal about the ideological forces at work in their society.

Realism is not a particularly precise concept in Lukács, although he does try to flesh it out somewhat in two essays of the 1930s reprinted in the collection *Writer and Critic* (1970), 'Narrate or Describe?' and 'The Intellectual Physiognomy in Characterisation'. The essays provide guidelines as to how to recognise realism in terms of narrative form and characterisation practice. Lukács contends that narrative can be organised either by 'active narration' or 'passive description'. The former method involves careful selection of detail in each scene such that everything included contributes meaningfully to the overall effect of the narrative; whereas the latter tends to provide an indiscriminate mass of details which do not necessarily further the progress of the narrative. Active narration makes us aware of historical process, and the importance of individual events within it; passive description tends to hide this from us by its overload of irrelevant information, which distracts the reader's attention away from what is taking place. When it comes to characterisation Lukács demands that authors observe 'typicality', giving us characters who are both representative of their culture but also in possession of individual traits (that is, not simply allegorical 'types' as in, say, *The Pilgrim's Progress*). Typical individuals similarly help to reveal the workings of historical process to us. This is the kind of narrative form and characterisation practice that Lukács finds in Scott, Balzac and Tolstoy, and fails to find in Flaubert or Zola. It is also the kind of narrative and characterisation that Lukács expects writers of his own day to provide, which brings him into collision with more modernist-minded Marxist aestheticians, most notably with the playwright Bertolt Brecht.

Brecht is scathing of Lukács' theory of realism, arguing that it would represent a backward step for writers of his generation if implemented. The gist of his criticism is that Lukács wants modern writers to be mere imitators of Lukács' approved canon from the nineteenth century, and that realism is not a fixed concept anyway: 'Were we to copy the style of these realists, we would no longer be realists.'[15] As far as Brecht is concerned Lukács is a reactionary thinker who has failed to notice how the world has changed, and he adheres to his own concept of epic theatre as a more effective way of making the audience think about the ideological problems of his own time. Modernism continued to be treated with suspicion by the Soviet authorities, however, and the Lukács–Brecht controversy revealed tensions within Marxist thought which to this day have never been resolved totally. What is at stake is not just artistic freedom, which the control-minded Soviet system could not countenance, but the relationship between the arts and mass culture. Both Lukács and his socialist-realist colleagues are opposed to anything that smacks of élitism, and since modernism rarely aspires to a mass audience it is always vulnerable to attack on this score. Adorno also clashed with Lukács on such issues, being a confirmed modernist in aesthetic matters and in favour of innovation in the arts.

Anti-modernism

The Meaning of Contemporary Realism (1958) is Lukács' most sustained attack on literary modernism, which eventually crystallises for him into a choice between the fiction of Franz Kafka and Thomas Mann. These two writers come to symbolise for Lukács all that is most distinctive in modernism and critical realism respectively. Kafka teaches us that alienation is humankind's natural condition, and that individuals exist in a state of isolation from their fellow human beings. Alienation is presented as an ahistorical condition, rather than, as a Marxist like Lukács would prefer to interpret it, a state brought on by the effects of capitalist ideology. Although there are elements of Kafka's work which Lukács admires, he condemns the overall despairing view of the human condition that he finds there. For Lukács, in works like *The Trial* and *The Castle*, 'the world is an allegory of transcendent Nothingness', where humanity seems powerless to effect any meaningful change.[16] While the anxiety felt by Kafka's protagonists is understandable, given the oppressiveness of capitalism as a social system, Lukács refuses to believe that it cannot be overcome by concerted political action. Anxiety is for Lukács a temporary rather than a permanent state of affairs, to which Marxism has an answer. Kafka is criticised for turning his own individual experience into a universal condition, and in consequence reinforcing the dominant ideology of capitalism. It is worth noting in passing, however, that in his early career Lukács was something of a cultural pessimist himself. Thus in *Soul and Form* we are to oberve him bemoaning the existence of an 'unbridgeable void between one human being and another'.[17] It is a sentiment worthy of Kafka, but Marxism was soon to excise the pessimistic strain from Lukács' thought.

Thomas Mann is the obverse to Kafka, a modern author whose work reveals the socio-economic pressures that lie behind the development of individual character. Instead of the limbo in which Kafka's characters discover themselves trapped, in Mann's fiction, 'place, time and detail are rooted firmly in a particular social and historical situation', enabling us as readers to see what problems the characters are confronted by in their social existence.[18] For Lukács, Mann's own political beliefs are as irrelevant to his thesis as those of Scott or Balzac are. What counts is that Mann's work does not fall into the modernist trap of treating alienation as humanity's natural lot, but that he makes us aware, instead, of alienation's social roots. Mann's novels show historical process at work, and that is enough to qualify for critical realist status. The choice that faces the writer of fiction nowadays, therefore, is a choice between the approach taken by Kafka and that taken by Mann, with the former representing a choice in favour of capitalist ideology. Other modernist authors such as Beckett, Musil, Faulkner and Joyce are treated as equally suspect in terms of their world-views.

Lukács' Legacy

Lukács' legacy continues to inform Western Marxist thought, right through to its current dialogue with postmodern thought. Jameson commends Lukács' critical project as 'a continuous lifelong meditation on narrative, on its basic structures, its relationship to the reality it expresses, and its epistemological value when compared with other, more abstract and philosophical modes of understanding'.[19] It is the grasp of historical process in Lukács' writings on literature in particular that attracts Jameson, even if he does detect weaknesses in the *The Theory of the Novel*'s historical thesis. There is, for example, a tendency to romanticise classical culture in the work, as well as what is for Jameson an excessively metaphysical conception of human existence that betrays Lukács' Hegelian roots. Where *The Theory of the Novel* is to be applauded, however, is for showing how the development of capitalism has reduced the epic dimension to individuals' lives. Jameson is in full agreement with Lukács on the symbiotic relationship between literature and socio-historical process, and in his own criticism has carried forward such ideas into an exploration of the postmodern aesthetic. Postmodernism has revived debates about the ideological character of modernism, and, although for very different reasons than motivated Lukács, has encouraged a return to realist styles of writing – if only in the form of pastiche, one of the most characteristic of postmodern literary practices. Lukács' critique of modernism takes on a new relevance in this context, although postmodernism's generalised suspicion of authority, Marxism included, would have jarred with a thinker so concerned to exercise control over the social totality.

Something of Lukács' spirit of creative interpretation of Marxist theory also survives in post-Marxism, as well as his dislike of determinist models of historical process. The work of the writing team Ernesto Laclau and Chantal Mouffe can be cited as representative of the ethic.[20] One crucial difference, however, is that post-Marxism has all but given up on the communist party as the facilitator of revolution on behalf of the masses. What is favoured instead is much looser forms of political organisation and a far less regimented approach to political action. Even Jameson, who has resisted the drift towards post-Marxism on the left in recent decades, admits that the character of the class struggle has changed, and he awaits the emergence of a 'new international proletariat' to contest the dominance of late capitalism.[21] *History and Class Consciousness* still has relevance to debates on the left, therefore, although it is invariably the early Lukács that speaks to that constituency nowadays. The Lukács who came to an accommodation, however pragmatic, with the

Soviet establishment's line on Marxist philosophy has little appeal in the aftermath of the Soviet empire's collapse. Adorno's verdict on him as 'a man who is desperately tugging at his chains', sums up Lukács' predicament in this respect.[22]

Those chains are probably less apparent in the critical writings, which are still highly regarded by the critical community. Western Marxism has in general taken a more relaxed attitude towards modernism than Lukács ever did, but his insistence on the close relationship between literary form and historical process continues to be a guiding principle of Marxist aesthetics. Yet at the very least, we can say that the issues which Lukács engaged with in critical matters are still current, and that his views transcend their Marxist context. Marxism is now very much out of fashion, but Lukács remains a significant voice in critical theory and a key point of reference for some of the field's major debates. Certainly, anyone analysing the relationship between literary form and historical process – as, for example, both new historicists and discourse theorists continue to do in their own particular way – will have to orient themselves against Lukács, whose own researches have done so much to establish the parameters of enquiry.

Notes

1. See Fredric Jameson, *Postmodernism, or, the Cultural Logic of Late Capitalism* (London and New York: Verso, 1991).
2. Lukács, *Lenin*, p. 12.
3. Lukács, *Theory of the Novel*, p. 56.
4. See, for example, such influential studies as Ian Watt, *The Rise of the Novel: Studies in Defoe, Richardson, and Fielding* (Harmondsworth: Pelican, 1972), and Michael McKeon, *The Origins of the English Novel 1600–1740* (London: Radius, 1988).
5. Lucien Goldmann, *The Hidden God: A Study of Tragic Vision in the 'Pensées' of Pascal and the Tragedies of Racine*, trans. Philip Thody (London: Routledge and Kegan Paul, 1964), p. 315.
6. Lukács, *History and Class Consciousness*, p. 1.
7. Ibid., p. 42.
8. Ibid., p. 330.
9. Theodor Adorno, *Negative Dialectics*, trans. E. B. Ashton (London: Routledge and Kegan Paul, 1973 [1966]).
10. See, for example, the argument in Chapter 5 of my *Post-Marxism: An Intellectual History* (London and New York: Routledge, 2000).
11. Lukács, *Historical Novel*, pp. 9–10.

12. Ibid., p. 96.
13. Lukács, *European Realism*, p. 78.
14. Ibid., p. 139.
15. Bertolt Brecht, 'Against Lukács', trans. Stuart Hood, *New Left Review*, 84, 1974, pp. 33–53 (p. 51).
16. Lukács, *Contemporary Realism*, p. 53.
17. Lukács, *Soul and Form*, p. 107.
18. Lukács, *Contemporary Realism*, p. 78.
19. Fredric Jameson, *Marxism and Form: Twentieth-Century Dialectical Theories of Literature* (Princeton, NJ: Princeton University Press, 1971), p. 163.
20. See their *Hegemony and Socialist Strategy: Towards a Radical Democratic Politics* (London: Verso, 1985).
21. Jameson, *Postmodernism*, p. 417.
22. Theodor W. Adorno, 'Reconciliation Under Duress', trans. Rodney Livingstone, in Ernst Bloch et al., *Aesthetics and Politics* (London: NLB, 1977), pp. 151–76 (p. 175).

Major Works by Lukács

Essays on Realism, trans. David Fernbach, ed. Rodney Livingstone (London: Lawrence and Wishart, 1980 [1948]).

The Historical Novel, trans. Hannah and Stanley Mitchell (Harmondsworth: Penguin, 1969 [1947]).

History and Class Consciousness: Studies in Marxist Dialectics, trans. Rodney Livingstone (London: Merlin Press, 1971 [1923]).

Lenin: A Study on the Unity of his Thought, trans. Nicholas Jacobs (London: NLB, 1970 [1924]).

The Meaning of Contemporary Realism, trans. John and Necke Mander (London: Merlin Press, 1963 [1958]).

Political Writings 1919–1929: The Question of Parliamentarianism and Other Essays, trans. Michael McColgan, ed. Rodney Livingstone (London: NLB, 1972).

Soul and Form, trans. Anna Bostock (London: Merlin Press, 1974 [1911]).

Studies in European Realism: A Sociological Survey of the Writings of Balzac, Stendhal, Zola, Tolstoy, Gorki and Others, trans. Edith Bone (London: Merlin Press, 1972 [1950]).

The Theory of the Novel: A Historico-Political Essay on the Forms of Great Epic Literature, trans. Anna Bostock (London: Merlin Press, 1971 [1916]).

Writer and Critic and Other Essays, trans. and ed. Arthur Kahn (London: Merlin Press, 1970).

The Young Hegel: Studies in the Relations between Dialectics and Economics, trans. Rodney Livingstone (London: Merlin Press, 1975 [1948]).

Suggestions for Further Reading

Arato, Andrew, and Brienes, Paul, *The Young Lukács and the Origins of Western Marxism* (New York: Seabury Press, 1979). Useful study of Lukács' impact on the development of Western Marxism, by authors sympathetic to the latter phenomenon.

Bernstein, J. M., *The Philosophy of the Novel: Lukács, Marxism, and the Dialectics of Form* (Minneapolis: University of Minnesota Press, 1984). An investigation of Lukács' theories of the novel, emphasising the continuity between his pre-Marxist and Marxist writings.

Feenberg, Andrew, *Lukács, Marx and the Sources of Critical Theory* (Oxford: Martin Robertson, 1981). Useful account of Lukács' impact on Adorno and his circle.

Gluck, Mary, *Georg Lukács and his Generation, 1900–18* (Cambridge, MA: Harvard University Press, 1985). Contextualises Lukács' thought within trends in Central European intellectual life in the early twentieth century.

Heller, Agnes (ed.), *Lukács Revalued* (Oxford: Basil Blackwell, 1983). Includes an analysis of Lukács' main ideas by several of his former students.

Kadarkay, Arpád, *Georg Lukács: Life, Thought and Politics* (Oxford and Cambridge, MA: Basil Blackwell, 1991). The most comprehensive recent study of Lukács' career.

Lichtheim, George, *Lukács* (London: Fontana/Collins, 1970). A somewhat hostile survey, which is particularly critical of Lukács' later work.

Lowy, Michael, *Georg Lukács – From Romanticism to Bolshevism*, trans. Patrick Camiller (London: NLB, 1979). A perceptive account of Lukács' development as a political thinker in his early career.

Sim, Stuart, *Modern Cultural Theorists: Georg Lukács* (Hemel Hempstead: Harvester Wheatsheaf, 1994). A reassessment of Lukács' work from the perspective of post-Marxism and postmodernism, with a detailed account of his theories of realism.

9

Theodor W. Adorno (1903–69) and Max Horkheimer (1895–1973)

Matt F. Connell

Adorno and Horkheimer in the Critical Tradition

Adorno and Horkheimer can be located with little difficulty in the critical tradition because of the obvious influences on them of Kant, Hegel, Marx, Nietzsche, Freud and Weber. The work of these two thinkers and the Frankfurt School generally can be characterised as a philosophically informed, psychologically interested and culturally oriented version of Marxism. Kant's moral philosophy provides them with the ethical standards of treating humans as subjects rather than objects, but Adorno and Horkheimer do not share Kant's Enlightened faith that rational understanding and control of the natural world of objects will be matched by the autonomous, morally rational conduct of human affairs when subjects attain maturity. For them, Enlightenment is a dialectical process, such that the antinomies identified by Kant, particularly the one between contradictory perspectives of humans as both free subjects and controlled objects, are symptoms of the real social contradictions at work in modern society.

Adorno and Horkheimer's understanding of Enlightenment through the dialectic reveals their indebtedness to Hegel and his attempts to understand social contradictions as a totality. However, they preferred to remain with the symptoms of Kant's antinomies rather than what they took to be Hegel's false reconciliation. Adorno rejected the totalitarian implication of Hegel's 'identity' thinking, according to which a fully self-conscious collective human subject becomes identical with the world by recognising that the world is the product of human activity. In Adorno's view, 'identity' thinking is a way of subsuming difference and otherness under a self-absorbed subjective identity. It is the philosophical expression of the dominant, bourgeois subjectivity of modernity to which both capitalism and administration force every other form of subjectivity to submit.

Adorno and Horkheimer found expression but not explanation of the dark side of the dialectic of Enlightenment in Nietzsche. The nihilism described by Nietzsche was understood by the Frankfurt theorists as a symptom at the level of personality and culture of the social contradictions of mass capitalist society. Nietzsche also offered them a genealogy of the rise of scientism, according to which science is allocated the role of religion but has already undermined the possibility of faith. Weber's reformulation of Nietzsche's genealogy of modernity also influenced Adorno and Horkheimer. His account of the disenchantment of the world through modernisation as specialisation explains how science could both be credited with and fail to live up to the holistic world-pictures that religions had provided. Moreover, Weber's distinction between instrumental reason and substantive reason, which picked up on Kant's delineation of the faculties of theoretical understanding and moral reason, was the basis for Adorno and Horkheimer's critique of the domination of instrumental reason. Weber's analysis of the rise of the state and rationalisation of politics and law as bureaucratisation was also central to their picture of the totally administered society. Moreover, his fundamental ambiguity about modernity fitted their assessment of the dialectic of Enlightenment. In that respect their position is distinct from Heidegger's negative view of modernity and regressive yearning for pre-modernity, a yearning which led him into political affiliation with the Nazi regime, which he hoped would revivify German life. Adorno and Horkheimer were not only diametrically opposed to Nazism politically and personally, but remained committed, in spite of their cultural pessimism, to the hope that modernity could be realigned with emancipation.

Adorno and Horkheimer's commitment to human emancipation is a feature of their Marxist legacy. They were not comfortable with the orthodox Marxism of their time, which is why they were struck by Lukács' break with the doctrine of economic determinism. They, as did he, attached much importance to the political and cultural forms of capitalism and its opposition. Their focus on the commodity form of mass culture drew heavily on Lukács' concept of reification, while in general his literary criticism provided them with a model for understanding the interaction between mode of production and cultural forms as part of a social totality. Adorno and Horkheimer also extended the range of Marxist analysis by drawing on Freud to examine the interaction between individual personality and social structure. The theoretical richness of the work of Adorno and Horkheimer owes much to their critical appropriations and original juxtapositions of concepts drawn from a wide range of predecessors.

Introduction

Born in Stuttgart in 1895, Horkheimer was the son of wealthy and conservative Jewish parents. He established a new dimension to the work of the Institute of Social Research at Frankfurt (founded in 1923). Under Carl Grünberg the Institute had amassed an archive on the workers' movement and produced a traditionally Marxist analysis of it. Horkheimer officially succeeded the ailing Grünberg as director of the Institute in 1930, but had already been influencing its direction. Horkheimer had strong philosophical and literary leanings and widened the scope of the Institute's academic work by recruiting an interdisciplinary group of scholars, who eventually formed the philosophically sophisticated Freudo-Marxism which Horkheimer called 'Critical Theory', and which people tend to mean when they use the retrospective term 'Frankfurt School'.

Horkheimer's circle was part of the Western Marxist milieu also represented by Kracauer, Bloch, Benjamin and Lukács. This milieu had its roots in the work of Kant, Hegel, Marx, Weber, Nietzsche and Freud, and widened Marxism from political and economic matters to include psychology and cultural analysis. Adorno and Horkheimer try to critically refigure the discredited image of the 'man of letters', arguing that in an age of specialists without spirit (Weber), an essayistic combination of interdisciplinary social-scientific research, speculative philosophy and cultural critique provides a corrective to the academic terrorism that polices the boundaries between ossifying disciplines: 'The departmentalization of mind is a means of abolishing mind.'[1] As Paul Connerton explains, 'Critical Theory' is Horkheimer's name for a combination of theories capable of unmasking traditional power relationships and revealing the ideologies that cloak them:

> Critique is here grounded in a specific experience, which is set down in Freud's psychoanalysis, in Hegel's *Phenomenology of Mind*, and in Marx's critique of ideology: the experience of an emancipation by means of critical insight into relationships of power, the strength of which derives, at least in part, from the fact that these relationships have not been seen through.[2]

Horkheimer established an association between the Institute and one of his student friends, a precocious young music critic called Theodor Wiesengrund-Adorno (born in Frankfurt in 1903). Adorno's hot-house education as a musician and philosopher culminated in his involvement during the 1920s with the cutting edges of modern music and social theory represented by, respectively, Schönberg's New Viennese Music and the Horkheimer circle in Frankfurt. Adorno's influence on the Frankfurt School was to prove crucial to its direction, as Horkheimer's relations with Adorno developed over more than forty years from academic superior, examiner, mentor and employer, to intellectual companion, lifelong friend and co-director of the Institute. It was a slow process, however, as Adorno did not become a full member of the Institute until 1938, while in exile in America.

At first Horkheimer was rather sceptical of Adorno's philosophy, which he saw as a philosophy of interpretation overly involved with Benjamin's theology, but was nonetheless gradually influenced by it, just as he encouraged Adorno's at first reluctant engagements with the methods of empirical social science. Adorno makes several dedications to Horkheimer which portray their thought as one entity, masking their differences, but accurately reflecting their developing tendency to work intensely together. Their cooperation reached its zenith during their wartime exile in America in the 1940s. Adorno had by this time succeeded, by a series of rather Machiavellian manoeuvres behind the scenes at the Institute, in becoming Horkheimer's theoretical aide-de-camp. Feeling caught between fascism, Stalinism and consumer capitalism on the West Coast of America, they worked together on a series of studies on prejudice. They also met regularly for extensive philosophical discussions that formed the kernel of their most famous work, a dark critique of modernity published in a limited mimeograph edition in 1944 as *Philosophical Fragments* and released in an expanded form as *Dialectic of Enlightenment* in 1947.

A few years after the war, Horkheimer and Adorno returned to Germany to re-establish the Institute. Horkheimer was appointed rector of Frankfurt University. Building on their American research into proto-fascistic personalities, Adorno and Horkheimer organised large studies into the political awareness of the West German population, disappointingly finding a good degree of nostalgia for the recent Nazi past. Adorno suggested that the persistence of fascism within democracy was now more important than anti-democratic fascism.

Pressurised by the anti-semitic resentment which still persisted within Frankfurt University, preoccupied with the rectorship from which he was soon to retire and involved in the reform of German higher education, Horkheimer rather faded into the background at the Institute, and Adorno became co-director from 1955 onwards. During these years, Adorno published a plethora of works on music and literature. Adorno, often caricatured as a withdrawn intellectual, also took on a public role as an educator and critic dedicated to the de-Nazification of German society and the prevention of another Auschwitz. He made over 160 radio broadcasts, on everything from art to education.

In the 1950s and 1960s, the teachings of Adorno and Horkheimer inspired and frustrated the generation of young radicals who exploded on to the streets in the late 1960s. Adorno was cautiously sympathetic but could not endorse the students' violent methods. In the end he too became a target, with disruptive occupations and protests at the Institute culminating in his calling in the police, an action for which Herbert Marcuse (who remained in America as a darling of the New Left) berated him.[3] Adorno was convinced that his own best political contribution was to complete his late masterworks, *Negative Dialectics* (1966) and *Aesthetic Theory* (1970). In this he was probably right. For Adorno, in their very alienation from practical politics, experimental forms of philosophy and art make an important political intervention by preserving forms of freedom which have vanished from actual political life. As it turned out, Adorno only just had time to complete these projects. He died in 1969 and Horkheimer followed him in 1973.

Some Elements of Adorno and Horkheimer's Critical Theory

Secular Theology[4]

The mostly Jewish members of the Institute for Social Research often engaged in debate and discussion with the scholars and theologians at Frankfurt's famous Free Jewish School (at which Fromm and Löwenthal had been important teachers prior to their full involvement at Horkheimer's Institute). Horkheimer and Adorno had different views on theology, but a theological moment persists in both their work, and the rise of German anti-semitism forced them to grapple with their Jewish identities. The political-messianic element of the Frankfurt reading of Judaeo-Christian thought appropriates the scriptural promise of the redemption of historical suffering in heaven, and turns it into a secularised hope for an earthly revolution in social conditions. Horkheimer was concerned to rescue the critical potential of religious and metaphysical thought from positivism, but suggested theology should be sublated by political philosophy: 'criticism of the status quo which found expression in earlier times as a belief in a heavenly judge today takes the form of a struggle for more rational forms of societal life'.[5]

Influenced by Bloch and Benjamin, as well as his mother's Catholicism, Adorno's more dialectical mediation of religious themes of redemption and reconciliation through materialism deepened the engagement with theology, yet was still thoroughly atheist: 'A restoration of theology, or better yet, a radicalization of the dialectic into the glowing centre of theology, would at the same time have to mean the utmost intensification of the social-dialectical, indeed economic, motifs.'[6] Horkheimer was not convinced that any sort of rescue of religion was advisable (though he became more interested in it towards the end of his life), but certainly always understood that the core of revolutionary political economy shares features with Judaism. As Adorno explains, Marx resisted 'positive blue-prints of socialism'.[7] Such blueprints usually reduce utopia to current ideas of pleasure, ideas stained by current economic pressures. Marx's resistance to blueprints is a secular equivalent of the Jewish ban on naming or depicting God: 'Materialism brought that ban into secular form by not permitting Utopia to be positively pictured.'[8]

Remaining true both to Benjamin's desire to wed theology and materialism, and Horkheimer's resistance to the theological sublimation of suffering, Adorno uses a social dialectic which conserves a messianic promise through a strict attention to the social repression of the body: 'At its most materialistic, materialism comes to agree with theology. Its great desire would be the resurrection of the flesh.'[9] This desire for the end of suffering and repression is not only Judaeo-Christian and Marxian, but also Romantic and Freudian too. It is the hope for a life that really lives, a new type of subjectivity, born from the satisfaction of libidinal and material needs.

Freudo-Marxism

Horkheimer's move towards psychoanalysis was an early symbol of his drive to 'leave the traditional Marxist straightjacket behind' when he took over the Institute.[10] Horkheimer wanted to engage with psychology in order to delineate recognisable connections between the economy, class, ideology and psychic structure.

Although he left the Institute in 1939, Fromm's distinctive early version of the Freud–Marx synthesis had a lasting impact on the social-psychological dimension of Horkheimer and Adorno's work. Fromm refused the orthodox Marxist rejection of Freud's 'bourgeois psychology', by pointing out some intriguing commonalities:

> [Freud's] drive theory was compatible with Marxism, Fromm argued, since the 'drive-constitution' only manifests itself in a dialectical interaction with the socio-historically specific 'life experiences'. Marx, in his early writings, had referred to man's 'drives' or 'instincts' (*Triebe*), and in *Capital* he accepted the primary nature of certain drives, referring to 'human nature in general' and 'human nature as modified in each historical epoch'.[11]

Because human drives are more malleable than the economic forces of capitalism and the pressured form of family relations they foster, they can be trained to desire the conditions that deform them, acting as social cement rather than becoming revolutionary dynamite. Psychoanalysis and Marxism show how the crumbling structure of the family, besieged by the capitalist organisation of the working day and economic instability, fosters developmentally crippling patterns of child-rearing, training children for the authoritarian hierarchies of adult life.[12]

Spurred on by the need to explain the success with which fascism had mobilised the anti-semitic forces which forced the Frankfurt School into exile in the 1930s, Horkheimer and Adorno worked throughout the 1940s and 1950s on projects funded by the American Jewish Committee investigating the links between social, familial and psychological processes in the formation of prejudiced and conformist personality types. The most famous of these is *The Authoritarian Personality* (1950). Authoritarians, broken and rendered weak by the power relations of their family, prop themselves up with fantasies of strength and the acceptance of hierarchy. They adopt a surface conformity to authority figures beneath which seethes a dark ambivalence, which in later life may seek displaced discharge through the projective hatred of social outgroups, especially if this course is legitimised and manipulated by powerful ruling authorities.

Although Adorno contributed to these projects by drawing on Fromm and Horkheimer's perspectives on Freud, his major methodological contribution to Frankfurt School theory meant that at a philosophical level no simple Freudo-Marxist synthesis was possible. Adorno championed a theoretical approach in which no dimension is privileged and in which the contradictions between different levels of analysis become the tenuous home of truth through their determination not by lack of theoretical clarity, but by real social contradiction and conflict. The 'shotgun marriage'[13] of Marxism and psychoanalysis could not be theoretically consummated in a fully coherent system. For Adorno, the recalcitrant incompatibility of psychological and social analysis is a product of the modern estrangement of individual and society, and of the child from the adult he or she will become. As we grow into the social world, we also become alienated from ourselves. Freud and Marx cannot be unified because self and society are not unified. A social psychology which subsumes the individual level under the social ends up unconsciously mimicking the situation it ought to be criticising.

Philosophical Constellations and the Critique of Totality

As the dialectic of sociology and psychology shows, every theoretical element of Adorno's interdisciplinary critical theory contributes something essential to his 'anti-system',[14] which eschews all foundational concepts in favour of a non-hierarchical 'constellation' of ideas. This concept owes something to Nietzsche's 'perspectivism', and a lot to Benjamin. A theoretical constellation is a conceptual rearrangement of traditional notions, aimed at releasing their critical potential. Imagine a star to be a theoretical perspective, and consider the figures our minds flesh out around stars in the night sky. The British look at the northern sky and see a plough, but others see a big dipper, or an animal. When tradition regards itself, it sees only the shapes it is accustomed to. The critical reorganisation of the customary constellation into a new force field attempts to draw the fragments into an illuminating formation showing how the original image involved a coercive relationship, yet was also a distorted echo of a potential togetherness through diversity, which is Adorno's utopia. It is possible to trace histories in the night sky of our conceptual inheritance other than those identified by tradition.

But this cannot proceed as a purely utopian rearrangement of recalcitrant material. The new constellation can actually do little more than clearly expose the distorting influence holding the pattern in its traditional format. The aim of Adorno's dialectical approach to competing realms of validity, for example the social and the psychological, is therefore to mediate each extreme through the other, avoiding a theoretical reduction of either, unless particular historically and materially specific conditions force theory to reflect honestly the real dominance of certain patterns.

As Nietzsche demonstrated, theory must not seek to completely tidy up the chaotic state of affairs that confronts it, because the result is inevitably the proliferation of huge systems, like Hegel's, whose only harmony is ultimately provided by the wish for a positive unity and the denial of an existing bad totality. This bad totality is Adorno's Weberian image of the totally administered society. The predominance of the social in Horkheimer and Adorno's work is to be understood as an imposition, the result of a certain historical situation which acts as a stumbling block for the theory that yearns to abolish hierarchy. Totalising systems of thought and the closed societies which produce them terrorise anything other to, 'non-identical' to, their own forms. What is different is envied, hated and feared, and forced to conform to the dominant order, by either conceptual or actual violence. But this alienated otherness is as vital to closed philosophical and social systems as is the Jew to the Nazi: without a projection board for screening their discontents, those systems would collapse under their own tensions.

The Critique of Enlightenment

While busy studying the particular psychoanalytic aetiologies of fascistic personalities, Adorno and Horkheimer were also working on a critique of the general pathologies of modernity which determined them. The Western Enlightenment emphasised the progressive side of reason, but in *Dialectic of Enlightenment* Adorno and Horkheimer pay attention to its darker side in an age of social catastrophe. According to its champions, such as Kant, Enlightened reason would free immature humanity from the apron-strings of natural immediacy and religious mythology, allowing the mature organisation of life through the rational scientific and technical control of natural forces ordered in a society of free individuals. The trouble is, without the guarantees of theology, the mainstream writers of the Enlightenment could not satisfactorily demonstrate that reason requires morality. For Adorno and Horkheimer, the Enlightenment unleashes an instrumental reason dedicated to a form of self-preservation that becomes exploitative.

This is revealed by those dark writers (such as de Sade and Nietzsche) who did not shrink from the unpleasant consequences of the Enlightenment's shedding of the dead-weight of religious moral authority:

> Unlike its apologists, the black writers of the bourgeoisie have not tried to ward off the consequences of the Enlightenment by harmonizing theories. They have not postulated that formalistic reason is more closely allied to morality than immorality. Whereas the optimistic writers merely disavowed and denied in order to protect the indissoluble union of reason and crime, civil society and domination, the dark chroniclers mercilessly declared the shocking truth.[15]

Enlightened reason seeks to externalise its darker side, attacking alleged irrationalists such as de Sade and Nietzsche, without comprehending the internal link between their cultural productions and reason itself. *Dialectic of Enlightenment* maintains that de Sade's critique of the Enlightenment works in its service by being an instantiation of its worst elements. He reveals the psychosexual apogee of unreflectively Enlightened reason, a distorted erotic relation between people who are reduced to instrumentalised objects of collective pleasure. Instrumental reason is the immanent truth of both de Sade's sexual-gymnastic torture pyramids and modernity alike. The pursuit of pleasure has lost its substantive link with the social development of the good life, and has become a mechanised pursuit of personal gratification. This logic of sexual domination also characterises the loss of a capacity for the sensuous enjoyment of nature. The methodical exploitation of the Sadean victim is a ghastly presentiment of what the factory does to the worker's chance of sensuous interaction with objects.

In order to uncover the roots of this problematic, Adorno and Horkheimer disrupt Enlightenment's self-confident opposition to mythology, by showing that the two are in fact entwined. Mythology always already involved an attempt to influence natural forces through magical means. Mature Enlightenment becomes a form of modern mythology in which we kneel not to the gods, but to science, while losing the mythological respect for nature. We still sacrifice animals, but in the laboratory no apology equivalent to the mythological appeasement of nature is made for this.

Furthermore, the development of technical and instrumental reason has outstripped the development of social reason, which is frozen and caught up within insane forms of political organisation. The rapid collapse of democratic Germany into the technocratic horrors of fascism starkly revealed the complicity of technical progress with social regression, and *Dialectic of Enlightenment* treats the repressive side of the Enlightened reason of modernity as a form of self-deception complicit with the things it condemns. Yet Adorno and Horkheimer are not irrationalist opponents of Enlightenment: they champion a self-reflective form of Enlightened Enlightenment, capable of emancipation not just from natural ties, but from Enlightenment's own social limitations. These limitations are rooted in historical splits between mental and manual labour, between spirit and matter and between humanity and nature, splits that a real Enlightenment would have to overcome. The *Dialectic* is a tragic funeral oration for Western reason, not so much in opposition to it as in mourning for it. The hope in the chance of a resurrection, a reconnection of reason with the bodily good life through a reconciliation of reason and nature, may operate at a level hidden by the tone of despair, but it is there nonetheless.

The problem with scientific Enlightenment is that from the beginning of human history, the control of nature has been achieved not through social freedom, but through domination. The control of nature relies on the repression of not only external nature but also of humanity's own inner nature. Adorno and Horkheimer present the primal history of the development of human subjectivity as a separation of the ego from the bosom of natural immediacy. This separation of subjectivity from nature involves a hardening of the self, celebrated by the ego as its identity, laboriously pulled away from nature but reproducing the violence of nature in its ruthless sacrifice of its own natural sympathies and in its domination of otherness.

The emancipatory side of the control of nature is secured for some social classes to the detriment of others, for those at the bottom of the social hierarchy do the dirty work that frees their masters. Here, Hegel's dialectic of lord and bondsman is crucial for Horkheimer and Adorno. They use it to provide a reading of Homer's *Odyssey* which portrays Odysseus as the prototype of the Enlightened bourgeois individual who achieves mastery over natural forces and the gods, primitives and women who, he believes, are still ruled by their natural impulses.[16] Primitive yearnings to give up the effort of separation from mother earth threaten humanity's new-found freedom from natural ties. These tabooed desires constantly seek expression. Odysseus, having controlled himself, has to control the regressive tendencies of his unruly crew in order to ensure their continued capacity to labour for him. In a series of similar episodes in the *Odyssey*, the oarsmen seek uncivilised bliss on the island of the lotus-eaters, become swine, and finally die as a result of their inability to spare the sacred cattle of the sun god. In these acts, the crew fail in the basic task of civilisation, that of deferring gratification and instead freely submit to their desire to return to a state of nature.

Today, the yoke of civilisation represented by Odysseus has been carried longer and fits better. But, like the oarsmen, the modern individual still yearns to throw it off, as is made clear in the constant worries, voiced by the industrial and political élite and those psychologically identified with them, about the lazy, immoral and primitive tendencies of the masses, who endanger their capacity for labour in the unrestrained pursuit of gratification. Those who express these worries most loudly are often the potential supporters of fascism. Their worry is a negative trace of their own desire to join in the transgression of civilised norms.

Culture and Art

Dialectic of Enlightenment also examines the socially approved channels for the discharge of these discontents of modernity. An ideology critique of the 'culture industry' uncovers a hideous side to cultural products usually seen as a bit of harmless fun. For Adorno and Horkheimer, the technologically advanced entertainment industry is a form of Enlightenment as mass deception, which stabilises capitalist economies by promulgating the ideologies of the status quo. They generally use the term 'culture industry' in preference to 'mass culture' or 'popular culture', because these latter terms imply a form of culture of the masses, whereas the former suggests something dished out to the masses from above.

The content, form and mode of consumption of entertainment all suppress insight into capitalism's domination of the masses. The content is generally conformist. Just as in economic life, we know in advance who the winners and losers of a story will be, but an ideological tinge is added in which somehow this seems meritocratic, with good and bad characters getting their just desserts. In formal terms, these products present narratives in which the status quo is disturbed and then restored with a mechanical predictability which mirrors the repetitive operations of the factory system. The consumption of these products seems to take place in our free time, but this free time is not genuine leisure, for it is coupled to the working day as a form of recuperation to get us back on our feet ready for the next day's labour. The infantile content and unchallenging form of everything from the hit record to the popular film is dictated by this mode of consumption. Exhausted workers need soothing pre-digested pap, not the unpalatable and sometimes disturbing products of autonomous art.

This well-known excoriation of the culture industry has been dogged by either exaggerated endorsement by modernist mandarins or indignant rejection by cultural populists. With some justification, the accusation is made that the critique of the culture industry adopts a lofty transcendental perspective, never engaging with popular culture as sensitively as Adorno and Horkheimer approach traditional art objects. A more subtle dialectical reception is possible, which follows Adorno's notion that high and low forms of art are not diametrically opposed but are the torn halves of a freedom which cannot at present be reunited. The culture industry forces the two together, for instance when adapting classical music for film scores, losing the critical component of both. The administered products of the culture industry are not to be confused with genuine popular or low forms of culture, such as the circus or festival, whose disruptive element is levelled by rationalisation and censorship when absorbed by the industry. The best products of that industry retain some of the critical energy of low culture in the form of absurd comedy: Adorno and Horkheimer are quite sympathetic towards Ed the Talking Horse, the Marx Brothers and Charlie Chaplin. Nor are the products of the culture industry to be opposed by a simple élitist or conservative endorsement of traditional high art, whose ideological content Adorno and Horkheimer attack with the same venom they pour over the culture industry.

Adorno's assessments of artworks are as stringent as his critiques of the culture industry, but his surrender to the immanent concerns of artworks more sympathetically links the contradictions and failures of those aesthetic concerns with the contradictions and failures of society. This sympathy gives a voice to traces of utopian negativity embedded in the lines, flaws and fractures which have been inscribed on the yearning face of the autonomous artwork by the social totality upon which it mutely gazes. It is the critic's role to facilitate this communication through the critical completion of the work: a notion with Romantic origins. At its best, criticism allows the artwork to speak and also follows Nietzsche's maxim 'You may lie with your mouth, but with the mouth you make as you do so you none the less tell the truth.'[17] Accordingly, even ideological culture can communicate a negative imprint of the truth, but Adorno's favoured forms of art come close to carrying through this critical process on their own account, adopting a self-reflexive stance which brings their contradictions and limitations to the fore rather than drawing an ideological veil over them.

Adorno defends experimental aesthetic freedom as a plenipotentiary of a better way of being, against the conservatives who loathe it for just that reason. Adorno's commitment to modern art is clear in his devotion to the avant-garde music of Schönberg, who overturned the classical system of musical tonality at the end of the nineteenth century with his atonal compositional techniques. Adorno became a minor composer in this style. Whereas the great works of Bach and Beethoven duplicate Hegel's idealism in a strained harmonic closure which mimics the confidence of the bourgeoisie and the control of nature on which it is based, the dissonant and fractured new music takes the strain past breaking point, snapping that confidence in an authentic reflection of the crisis of culture in the barbaric twentieth century. Similarly, Adorno privileges the painting of Klee and Picasso and the literature of Kafka, Beckett and Joyce. For Adorno, challenging art is one of the last refuges of critical thought in a society capable of absorbing most forms of political resistance. Some see this as a pessimistic abandonment of practical politics, but others portray it as a beacon of optimism in a dark world, as evidence that the totally administered society has not yet fully expunged the critical consciousness.

Contemporary Receptions of Adorno and Horkheimer

Since the deaths of Adorno and Horkheimer, a whole generation of academics have worked on their legacy. A group of their ex-students are sometimes referred to as the 'second-generation Frankfurt School'. The most well known of these is Jürgen Habermas, who was Adorno's assistant during the 1960s. He has produced an important critique of Horkheimer and Adorno,[18] suggesting that their analysis of Enlightened reason is too pessimistic and overly conditioned by their bleak historical situation, as is Adorno's retreat from politics to aesthetics. He develops the moments of their critique which see Enlightenment as an unfinished project, devoting himself to uncovering its positive potential in a theory which finds a normative utopia in the notion of unconstrained communication and consensus. In this, Habermas places himself on the middle ground between those Marxist critics of Adorno and Horkheimer who see them as too liberal, and those liberal critics who see them as too Marxist. Frankfurt School Marxism has survived the collapse of communism quite well, because of its heterodox critique of Stalinism and its scepticism about the chance of the proletariat becoming the revolutionary agent of historical change – a scepticism which never becomes an endorsement of capitalist society.

Although there are signs of a renewal of interest in Horkheimer, his theoretical star has been eclipsed somewhat by Adorno's. The relationship between the Frankfurt School and contemporary philosophies of postmodernism and deconstruction has focused on Adorno's critique of closed systems, and his occasionally ambiguous commitment to a Marxist paradigm also attracts varying types of attention from these quarters. Peter Uwe Hohendahl identifies four main positions: 'a strategy of (political) distancing, the poststructuralist rereading, the postmodernist critique, and a return to the "authentic" Adorno'.[19] These form a constellation of opposed tendencies, and some strange alliances. For example, modernist Adorno purists may defend Adorno by using critiques of Habermas seemingly similar to those of resolute postmodernists. Postmodern and poststructuralist takes on Adorno vary enormously, ranging across the positive and negative poles. Some celebrate Adorno's alleged abandonment of Hegelian Marxism; others berate or applaud him for keeping hold of it. Poststructuralist uses of Adorno endorse the alleged rejection of Enlightened reason that Habermas condemns, whereas those who seek a purified return to Adorno insist that his critique of reason is a defence of it. The range of these positions, and the fertile conflicts between them, suggests that the legacy of Adorno and Horkheimer will continue to provoke productive critical debates for the foreseeable future.

Notes

1. Adorno, *Minima Moralia*, p. 21.
2. P. Connerton, *The Tragedy of Enlightenment: An Essay on the Frankfurt School* (Cambridge: Cambridge University Press, 1980), p. 25.
3. Lessons for our times can be gleaned from these events. The debate between Adorno, Marcuse and the students on how best to protest in a non-revolutionary social situation is being unconsciously repeated on the streets by anti-capitalists today, usually at a lower level of reflection.
4. This section on theology is largely condensed, by permission of

Palgrave Publishers, from my 'Through the Eyes of an Artificial Angel: Secular Theology in Theodor W. Adorno's Freudo-Marxist Reading of Franz Kafka and Walter Benjamin', in P. Leonard (ed.), *Trajectories of Mysticism in Theory and Literature* (Basingstoke: Macmillan, 2000), pp. 198–218.

5. Horkheimer, 'Thoughts on Religion', in *Critical Theory*, pp. 129–31, p. 129.
6. Adorno, 'Letters to Walter Benjamin', trans. H. Zohn, in T. W. Adorno et al., *Aesthetics and Politics*, ed. and trans. R. Taylor (London: Verso, 1980), p. 114. Adorno was commenting on a draft by Benjamin.
7. Adorno, *Minima Moralia*, p. 156.
8. Adorno, *Negative Dialectics*, p. 207.
9. Ibid.
10. Jay, *The Dialectical Imagination*, p. 87.
11. P. Slater, *Origin and Significance of the Frankfurt School: A Marxist Perspective* (London: Routledge and Kegan Paul, 1977), p. 96.
12. Horkheimer, 'Authority and the Family', in *Critical Theory*, pp. 47–129.
13. M. Jay, *Adorno* (London: Fontana, 1984), p. 85.
14. Adorno, *Negative Dialectics*, p. xx.
15. Adorno and Horkheimer, *Dialectic of Enlightenment*, pp. 117–18.
16. The following account of the *Odyssey* is extracted from my 'Body, Mimesis and Childhood in Adorno, Kafka and Freud', in *Body and Society*, 4 (4), 1998, pp. 67–90.
17. F. Nietzsche, *Beyond Good and Evil*, trans. R. J. Hollingdale (London: Penguin, 1990), IV, § 166.
18. J. Habermas, *The Philosophical Discourse of Modernity*, trans. F. Lawrence (Cambridge: Polity, 1987).
19. P. U. Hohendahl, *Prismatic Thought: Theodor W. Adorno* (Lincoln and London: University of Nebraska Press, 1995), p. 4. This discussion of Hohendahl is compressed from my consideration of a range of recent Adorno criticism in 'Imagining Adorno: Critical Theory under Review', in *Theory, Culture and Society*, 17 (2), 2000, pp. 133–47.

Major Works by Adorno

Philosophy of Modern Music, trans. A. G. Mitchell and W. V. Bloomster (London: Sheed and Ward, 1973 [1949]).

The Authoritarian Personality (with others) (New York: Harper, 1950).

Minima Moralia: Reflections from Damaged Life, trans. E. F. N. Jephcott (London and New York: Verso, 1994 [1951]).

Negative Dialectics, trans. E. B. Ashton (London: Routledge, 1990 [1966]).

Aesthetic Theory, trans. R. Hullot-Kentor (London: Athlone, 1997 [1970]).

Major Works by Horkheimer

Critique of Instrumental Reason: Lectures and Essays since the End of World War II, trans. M. J. O'Connell et al. (New York: Seabury, 1974). Includes Horkheimer's *Eclipse of Reason* [1947].

Critical Theory: Selected Essays, trans. M. J. O'Connell et al. (New York: Continuum, 1982).

Between Philosophy and Social Science: Selected Early Writings, trans. G. F. Hunter et al. (Cambridge, MA: MIT Press, 1993).

Major Co-authored Work

Dialectic of Enlightenment, trans. J. Cumming (London: Verso, 1986 [1947]).

Suggestions for Further Reading

Benhabib, S., et al. (eds), *On Max Horkheimer: New Perspectives* (Cambridge, MA: MIT Press, 1993). Range of essays demonstrating a renaissance of interest in Horkheimer.

Held, D., *Introduction to Critical Theory: Horkheimer to Habermas* (Cambridge: Polity, 1990). Accessible introduction.

Jarvis, S., *Adorno: A Critical Introduction* (Cambridge: Polity, 1998). In-depth guide, with a philosophical emphasis.

Jay, M., *The Dialectical Imagination: A History of the Frankfurt School and the Institute of Social Research 1923–1950* (Berkeley: University of California Press, 1996). Scholarly account from the 1970s, now with a new introduction.

Wellmer, A., *The Persistence of Modernity* (Cambridge, MA: MIT Press, 1991).

Wiggershaus, R., *The Frankfurt School*, trans. M. Robertson (Cambridge: Polity, 1994). Huge tome, with excellent balance of history, biography and theory. Currently the standard comprehensive guide.

Zuidervaart, L., *Adorno's Aesthetic Theory: The Redemption of Illusion* (Cambridge, MA: MIT Press, 1991). Helpful explanation of a difficult aspect of Adorno's theory.

10

Edmund Husserl (1859–1938)

William Hutson

Husserl in the Critical Tradition

Husserl marks a return to the tradition of German critical philosophy established by Kant and reformulated by Hegel, but which by Husserl's time had lost influence. Positivist views, according to which philosophical investigation should be modelled on the success of the natural sciences, had come to predominate since the 1850s. From Husserl's perspective, such scientific philosophy operated on one side of Cartesian dualism of mind and matter, in that it was capable of a determination of objects but not in their relation to subjectivity. He thus returned to the Kantian concern for reconciling the objective achievements of science with subjective life, which he did by focusing on subjectivity as the grounds for objectivity. But although Husserl developed a transcendental phenomenology, he diverted from both Kant and Hegel. For Husserl as for Kant, transcendental refers to conditions of possibility for experience, an aspect of which is active engagement of consciousness in the world. But Husserl drops Kant's distinction between phenomenal and noumenal realms. For Husserl, theoretical understanding of the phenomenal realm could produce only a theoretical abstraction, whereas phenomenological philosophy could provide an account of meaningful experience gained through the interaction of consciousness and world. However, as the chapter explains in detail, Husserl's phenomenology is quite different from Hegel's.

Husserl's philosophical influence on those who followed him was immense, particularly on his students Heidegger and Gadamer, but also on those such as Merleau-Ponty and Sartre, who continued the phenomenological-existential tradition which he is credited with founding. Heidegger took Husserl's examination of the reciprocal relation between subject and world in a new direction, both continuing and critically dismantling Husserl's methodology. For Heidegger, Husserl's analyses of intentional acts of consciousness did not go far enough, because they overlooked Heidegger's crucial question of being. Husserl's reliance on absolute consciousness for his model of intentionality left him within the Western metaphysics which was the main target of Heidegger's critique. Moreover, neither Heidegger nor Gadamer followed Husserl's extended theory of meaning, which covered all intentional acts of meaningful expression in a way that made language dependent on a pre-linguistic intuitive sphere of consciousness. Gadamer's reception of Husserl was mediated through Heidegger, who was also less concerned than Husserl was in developing a phenomenological basis for epistemological objectivity. Gadamer developed Husserl's theory in a hermeneutic direction by drawing on the latter's notion of intersubjectivity, according to which humans experience each other as co-subjects in similar bodies. Gadamer was particularly drawn to Husserl's concept of horizons as the pre-given context in which humans find themselves, and which must be fused according to Gadamer if dialogical understanding is to occur.

Introduction

The name of Edmund Husserl is as inseparable from the term 'phenomenology' as Sigmund Freud's is from the term 'psychoanalysis'. This chapter gives a broad definition of phenomenology and discusses major themes in Husserl's work, which is treated as a coherent and on-going response to particular philosophical problems. This will contrast with the view that Husserl's philosophical career can be seen as a series of stages. Husserl was born in 1859 in Proßnitz in Mähren, then part of the Habsburg Empire, and now part of the Czech Republic. He died in Freiburg in south-west Germany in 1938. His early studies were in physics, astronomy and mathematics. It was after hearing lectures by Wilhelm Wundt and Franz Brentano that Husserl devoted himself to the study of philosophy. At various points in his career he taught at the universities of Halle, Göttingen and Freiburg. At Freiburg, even though he had officially retired, Husserl was banned from teaching and publishing activities by the Nazi regime because of his Jewish background. However, this did not prevent him from delivering important lectures in Vienna and Prague towards the end of his life. After his death, Husserl's manuscripts were smuggled out of Germany and hidden in diplomatic bags in Belgium until the end of the war. Husserl left some 40,000 pages of unpublished manuscripts, many of which are written in idiosyncratic shorthand, so his collected works are still being published.

There can be no question as to Husserl's importance in the development of philosophy since Kant. As the founder of modern phenomenology, Husserl's influence on thinkers and intellectual movements within the continental philosophical tradition is as significant as that of Marx, Nietzsche, Freud and Heidegger. Some examples of this can be shown from a cursory glance at thinkers whose own work stands in relation to Husserl's: Martin Heidegger, as a former student of Husserl's, radicalised and carried phenomenology into new areas of questioning; Theodor Adorno's early text *Against Epistemology* is a critique of what he saw as foundationalist tendencies in Husserl's thought; and, in sociology, the work of Alfred Schütz is marked by an engagement with phenomenological themes.

Towards a Definition of Phenomenology

What, then, is phenomenology? The term was probably first used by the eighteenth-century philosopher J. H. Lambert, from whom Kant borrowed it, followed by Hegel and the American pragmatists Peirce and James. However, Hegel's usage of the term is quite different from Husserl's. Dialectical method is alien to Husserl's thought, while Hegelians object to many features of the later thinker's work. On a basic level, phenomenology means the science of phenomena, that is, a study of appearances. An appearance in phenomenological terms is not simply disorganised sense-data or an undetermined object of experience. For phenomenology, any object which appears is already in a relationship to consciousness; there is no gap to be 'filled up' between them. The appearance of an object, or of objectivity as such, has no meaning outside of this relationship. Thus, one can characterise an appearance as anything that shows itself *for* consciousness. While this was not a new problem for philosophy, Husserl's novelty was to consider consciousness as being fundamentally different from reality; that is to say, he did not view consciousness as being one entity in the world that is merely relative to any other. In the philosophical milieu in which Husserl spent his formative years, it was generally accepted that consciousness was but one empirical object among many.

In the modern era, this question of subjective knowledge and its relation to the world has its origin in the thought of Descartes. In his *Meditations on First Philosophy*, Descartes divides reality into two substances: *res cogitans* (the mind) and *res extensa* (extended bodily substance) in order to reach a secure foundation for knowledge. Through such a division of reality, one of the key themes of modern philosophy is established: how is it possible for the mind to have knowledge of the external world? Although Husserl's thought shares many of the motivations of Descartes', such as the question of what can be known and what can be doubted, it should not be seen simply as a continuation of Cartesian method. Husserl himself has this to say of the conclusions that Descartes reached: '... be very sceptical, or rather critical'.[1] Contemporary Husserl scholars such as Anthony Steinbock and Donn Welton have shown, using recently published and unpublished works, that Husserl's thought cannot be reduced to a version of Cartesianism or foundationalism. Welton, for example, convincingly shows that Adorno's view of Husserl's thought as a foundational epistemology is ultimately unworkable, and that Derrida's critique rests on a misunderstanding of the philosophical relationship between Husserl and Heidegger.[2]

The initial motivations for Husserl's work can be understood against the background of late nineteenth-century German academic philosophy. From the 1850s on, German philosophical life had been marked by a general dissatisfaction with the idealism of Kant, Schelling, Hegel and Fichte. In general (Schopenhauer, Dilthey and Nietzsche being exceptions), German philosophy had become increasingly determined by the methodology of the natural sciences and saw empirical psychology as its proper field of enquiry. In contrast, it is one of the fundamental claims of phenomenology that consciousness cannot be treated as an object within nature, and that there are phenomena that cannot be explained by the methodology of natural science.

Throughout his career Husserl strove for a philosophy free from presuppositions concerning the nature of reality. The aim of phenomenology is to suspend empirical notions regarding reality and to focus on the manner in which they are given to consciousness. The task of phenomenology is not to say what objects are empirically, but to describe how they are presented to us. Thus, phenomenology does not consider consciousness to be in a causal relation to the world and its objects, but rather it considers the world as a *correlate* of consciousness; one is impossible without the other.

From this point of view, Husserl's fundamental discovery consists in showing that no subjective act is without an object; we are always in a relation to an object or field of objects. I may be mistaken in thinking that my own shadow is someone else moving towards me, but for the act of seeing it is an object nevertheless. Of the ineluctability of always being in relation to objects, even when in error, Husserl states:

> I now see things, these things here, they themselves; I do not see images of them, nor mere signs. Obviously I can also be deceived. But on what basis does it prove to be deception? On the basis of a reliable seeing, tested time and time again, that is a seeing of real things themselves.[3]

Following this, one can see that the relation to objectivity, even if incomplete or mistaken, is built into the very structure of subjectivity. Of this structure, Levinas remarks: '... *access to the object is part of the object's being*'.[4]

From this, a number of consequences follow. First, phenomenology shifts the emphasis of philosophical enquiry from the 'correctness' of empirical facts to the meaning that appearances have for consciousness. Second, for Husserl, there can be no 'true' world hidden behind the world of appearances. Third, phenomenology undermines the subject–object dichotomy that has troubled philosophy at least since Descartes. For phenomenology, neither the solitary subject nor the extant object is the prime concern, but rather the relation that obtains between them. In his late work *The Crisis of the European Sciences*, Husserl writes that: '... the point is not to secure objectivity but to understand it'.[5] Understood phenomenologically, thinking can never be 'neutral'; for Husserl, thought is always directed towards something. This directedness is the very structure of thinking. It is the task of phenomenology to describe this structure.

To understand exactly what is at stake here, one needs to understand a key term in Husserl's thought, that of *constitution*, which is the act whereby an object becomes meaningful. The presence of objects becomes meaningful only through the flow and structure of consciousness. In phenomenology, the world can have no meaning apart from consciousness, just as consciousness can have no meaning apart from the world. Things appear only in the manner in which consciousness experiences them, but they are experienced only insofar as they are present for consciousness. The unfolding of this reciprocity, in which objectivity is achieved, is the phenomenological meaning of constitution. This reciprocity is important because we never simply perceive objects; our experience is considerably more complex. As well as 'direct' perception, any experience can potentially involve different modes such as expectation, memory or imagination. This is to say that from the phenomenological point of view the description of experience is concerned as much with absence as it is with presence.

Phenomenology can also be understood as a move from particular thoughts to the fullness of thought as such. Rather than being an 'ossified' theory that merely arranges the desultory nature of sense-data, phenomenology seeks to uncover modes of experience in their continual flow. Husserl's thought draws attention to the ever-flowing 'stream of experience' as the basis for any conception of rationality. Reason, understood phenomenologically, is something that is lived; it is an openness towards the world. In phenomenological reflection we focus on the relation between ourselves and in the manner in which objects of the world are present to us. This points to a broader definition of phenomenology: it is the description of experience and objects of experience in their essential structure.

Intentionality and the Theory of Meaning

Husserl's first published work, *The Philosophy of Arithmetic* (1891), was concerned with foundational problems in mathematics. This work sought to clarify hitherto 'indefinable terms' such as number, multiplicity and unity, by means of psychology. The conclusion drawn is that mathematical functions are not 'pre-given' but have an empirically intuitive foundation. However, the logician Gottlob Frege accused Husserl of psychologism. This is the theory that logic is reducible to empirical psychology. According to Frege, it seriously undermined philosophy's ability to give any coherent account of meaning. Husserl took heed of the criticisms, although he moved in a different direction to the formalist semantics of Frege's theory of meaning, seeking rather to maintain the connection between subjectivity and objectivity. The divergence between the two thinkers is usually seen as the origin of the different paths that continental and analytic philosophy take in the twentieth century, although thinkers such as Michael Dummett have shown how the two traditions have their origins in similar problems.[6]

In 1901 Husserl published the two-volume work *Logical Investi-*

gations, where one can find the first fully explicated phenomenological analyses. If logic is broadly taken as the theory of formal rules of thought, the question is: on what ground does it stand? Husserl saw that logic could not be founded on empirical psychology because it would become hopelessly self-contradictory: psychology would have to employ logic in order to justify itself. If logic is to be objectively valid, it cannot come from particular empirical facts. Husserl sought to describe formal conditions for logic which would amount to a 'theory of theory' not reducible to psychologism. Furthermore, if there are objective conditions which account for the validity of objective laws, there must also be subjective conditions otherwise they could never be known. Yet, this sounds like a contradiction given Husserl's rejection of psychologism. Hence, Husserl's aim is to explain how logical laws can be subjective without being reduced to the empirical. Husserl comments that in contrast to empirical psychology:

> Phenomenology ... lays bare the 'sources' from which the basic concepts and ideal laws of *pure* logic 'flow', and back to which they must once more be traced, so as to give them all the 'clearness and distinction' needed for an understanding, and for an epistemological critique, of pure logic.[7]

This means that Husserl has to give an account of the subjective conditions for knowledge, without reducing them to empirical conditions within any particular subject. These must be *a priori* conditions which are grounded in the 'form of subjectivity in general'.[8] In *Logical Investigations*, Husserl referred to his method as the description of the way in which knowledge appears; it is an account of the relation between logical meaning and its sense in experience. He called for a 'return to the things themselves', a recursion to what originally shows itself to consciousness. Phenomenologically, the term 'origin' does not mean 'beginning' as it does for the natural sciences, but rather the structural relatedness of consciousness and what appears.

Intentionality

The key to grasping Husserl's thought is his concept of *intentionality*. The concept of *intentio* was used in medieval scholastic philosophy to indicate a yearning towards God. It re-emerged in the late nineteenth century in the work of Husserl's teacher Franz Brentano, whose work centred around the accessibility of psychic phenomena in experience. For Brentano, there is a radical difference between psychic acts (which have the capacity for representation), and physical objects. Every mental representation, claims Brentano, contains a special category of object causally connected to the external world. He referred to this as the 'intentional in-existence' of the object. For Husserl, however, intentional acts do not somehow contain represented objects, but are always tending towards objects. In this sense, intentionality is not so much a capacity of consciousness, but its very structure. In this view, consciousness is not an empty vessel bombarded and filled up by sense-data, but is essentially always directed towards something: the seen is something seen, the loved something loved, the judged something judged. Of this structure, Husserl comments:

> we do not experience the object and beside it the intentional experience directed upon it, there are not even two things present in the sense of a part and a whole which contains it: only one thing is present, the intentional experience ... I do not see colour-sensations but coloured things, I do not hear tone sensations but the singer's song.[9]

The intentional object is not a content, but rather something lived; intentionality is a lived experience, in contrast to desultory sensory experience. It is this character of intentionality that phenomenology seeks to describe. From this, phenomenology can be understood as the description of the lived experience of thinking in its various modes.

All experience, for Husserl, is intentional in that it is always directed towards something. Because of this intentional structure, the intentional object is not just an external reality (as it would be for natural science) but rather something meant, so that objects are brought to presence by intentional acts. Intentions can be 'empty' in the sense that the intended object may not actually be 'bodily present': I can imagine Nelson's Column even though it is not actually here; if I were to stand in Trafalgar Square, this intention would become filled. This does not mean that the filled intentional is now complete; it is part of the depth-structure of experience to find ever new determinations of the object. Likewise, flights of fancy and fiction belong in the intentional sphere: even though a blue cow with fourteen legs may not actually exist, or Stephen Daedalus may be a character in a novel, they are nevertheless intentional objects. Objectivity is not an impression as empiricism would have it, but a meaning that is an achievement of consciousness. For phenomenology, empirical experience is relative and desultory; it is intentionality that gives on-going unity to experience, which Husserl called 'sense' (*Sinn*).[10]

Meaning and Language

Meaning, for Husserl, is the possibility of the same being articulated in different acts. His theory of meaning distinguishes an intentional act and an intended meaning. As was shown above, the question for phenomenology is to account for the relationship between the two, and to explicate how an intention is 'filled' by meaning, which is understood as a correlate of an intentional act. In *Logical Investigations,* Husserl refers to the 'ideality of meaning', according to which any meaning can potentially be communicated again and again. However, according to Husserl, meaning is not primarily linguistic, but rather intentional.

This understanding of meaning allows Husserl to hold that language (whether written or spoken) is not the original bearer of meaning; it is only through intentional acts that meaning can be explicated. For the Husserl of the *Logical Investigations,* language belongs to the category of signs, of which there are two types: indication and expression. Indications are signs that have no significatory function; they merely point out a state of affairs that pertains between objects: 'the Martian canals are signs of the existence of intelligent beings on Mars, that fossil vertebrae are the signs of the existence of prediluvian animals etc.'.[11] In indication there is no necessary connection between the states of affairs, only one that is empirically contingent. As indications, signs (whether written or verbal) can only be understood as empirical objects.

Expressions, on the other hand, are meaningful signs that relate back to an intentional act. In communication, expressions function as indications, that is, they intimate an expression. Expressions refer to objects and to sense-fulfilling acts of intentionality. In this manner, Husserl considered that he had widened the concept of meaning (*Bedeutung*) beyond that of the linguistic sphere to include all intentional acts. Husserl's theory of meaning and language has been sharply criticised by a wide range of subsequent thinkers. This theory of meaning has become controversial because it claims that language refers back to a pre-linguistic intuitive sphere. It is for this reason that philosophers such as Heidegger, Gadamer, Merleau-

Ponty, Ricœur and Derrida give critiques of Husserl's view of language. Husserl did, however, deepen his own understanding of language, through his later analyses of intersubjectivity and the lifeworld.

Transcendental Phenomenology

Husserl became dissatisfied with the analyses undertaken in *Logical Investigations*; he came to see that the account that he had hitherto given did not go far enough in explaining the relationship between consciousness and the world. Descriptive analysis could only be but one attempt to clarify how we come to have knowledge of the world. Husserl would come to call descriptive analysis 'static phenomenology'. What was needed was what he later called 'genetic phenomenology', which would be an account of the movement of consciousness in the world. In his 1911 article entitled 'Philosophy as a Rigorous Science' he programmatically set out the further aims of phenomenology, claiming that philosophy is structured differently to the natural and human sciences, both of which cover up experiential life with theory.[12] It would be self-contradictory for philosophy to attempt to explain the natural and human sciences if it resorts to their methodologies. If philosophy is to be the ground of both the natural and human sciences it must turn to phenomenology. For this to be accomplished, a radical new method was needed. Husserl's thought underwent a 'transcendental turn'. In a similar fashion to Kant, Husserl's use of the term 'transcendental' refers to possible conditions of possibility for experience. However, unlike Kant, Husserl does not differentiate between the phenomenal and noumenal realms. Furthermore, unlike Kant, Husserl does not consider the world to be a mathematical totality which is primarily ordered according to Newtonian physics. For Husserl, this would be an abstraction from experience. The term 'transcendental' is used by Husserl to indicate the realm of consciousness that cannot be affected by reduction, a notion to which I will turn below.

In his work of 1913, *Ideas I*, Husserl gives a comprehensive account of his transcendental philosophy. Here he distinguishes between what he calls the natural attitude and the phenomenological attitude. The natural attitude is the naive acceptance of reality as a domain of facts independent of consciousness. The natural attitude is also the realm of data which are collected and analysed in the natural and human sciences. In this attitude, everything is naturalised, including consciousness, which becomes understood as a causal process or a biological occurrence. The natural attitude cannot give an account of itself or of the manner in which the world becomes meaningful. For Husserl, we need to modify the natural attitude and turn to the phenomenological attitude.

The phenomenological attitude is a return to the source of the world's meaning. A clue to this can be found in Husserl's account of perception. I look at a table: it is rectangular; I can walk around it and view it from a different angle; if the light changes the table takes on a different hue; I can crouch under it and see it from yet another angle. In perception, the table is never fully given. It has what Husserl called shadowy profiles (*Abschattungen*) throughout which something remains constant: the table's givenness to consciousness. What this shows is twofold: first, there is a difference between the table as a real object and its profiles; and, second, that this difference can only be accounted for in the unity of the acts in which the profiles appear. This manner of appearance is the clue to the phenomenological attitude.

The aspect of the appearance of an object that remains invariant throughout the perception of profiles is called by Husserl its *essence*. Phenomenologically, an essence is a new type of object which must become the subject of phenomenological reflection. For Husserl, an essence is that which holds throughout all possible perceptions of an object. Husserl's notion of essences should not be understood as a version of Platonic ideas, but rather as correlates of facts. Essences are brought to light by an act which Husserl calls eidetic intuition, which involves subjecting an imagined or perceived object to possible variations. With the aid of memory, changes in perception and imagination, one investigates what changes can be made in the object without it ceasing to exist. In this process of variation an invariant moment arises that can be intuitively grasped. Intuition is not 'added on' to consciousness, but is rather the originary presentation of objects to consciousness. Intuition of essences is the *a priori* activity of consciousness that accounts for the structure of the empirical world. The analysis of intuition shows how objects are present for consciousness *as* essences. This implies that we are free to become disengaged from the real world of facts. Husserl called this the phenomenological *epoché*, in which any judgements concerning the factual existence of the real world are suspended or 'bracketed'. This is not a return to scepticism or Cartesian doubt: it is a methodological device to question the presuppositions upon which the natural attitude rests. Through the *epoché* a step-by-step method emerges that Husserl calls the phenomenological reduction, after which a residuum remains. This residuum is the realm of transcendental consciousness, which is the region proper to phenomenological research.

The phenomenological reduction does not, however, destroy the world; it shows how it is possible for us to have belief in the world and how we are originally involved in the world prior to any theoretical positing. The objective world is shown, through the reduction, to derive its meaning from this transcendental realm. The phenomenological reduction is the turning of consciousness towards its own movement, a movement in which causality gives way to meaning. Transcendental phenomenology is the attempt to comprehend the origin of how the world becomes meaningful for consciousness. It is in this sense that phenomenology discloses the world as the correlate of transcendental subjectivity.

Intersubjectivity and the Lifeworld

The transcendental move described above led to accusations that Husserl's thought inevitably leads to solipsism, that is, it is concerned purely with the self. Husserl was not unaware of these objections and sought to address them. In *Cartesian Meditations*, published in 1928, he discussed the problematic of *intersubjectivity*, a theme he had been developing in lectures and manuscripts for some time. The phenomenological reduction would seem to show that others are simply objects for a solitary subject. If this were so, then the world could not be a possible world for everybody. However, there is something given in experience that shows that the other is also a subject and that the world is shared among a community of subjects. If phenomenology raises the question of how an objective world is possible, then the question of others sharing this world must also be raised. For this question to be coherent, Husserl must show how the constituting activities of the subject correspond to those of others. In *Cartesian Meditations*, Husserl writes: 'The existence-sense of the world includes ... thereness-for-everyone.'[13] If it were not so, the unity of the world would collapse.

Husserl's theory of intersubjectivity is based on empathy (*Einfühlung*), which is not understood psychologically, but rather as an intentional act that allows the other to be experienced as a co-subject. Within the reduction, the body is shown to be the immediate way in which the subject encounters the world. Within this context, the subject encounters other bodies, which while similar to mine cannot be experienced directly. The other is encountered through *appresentation*, an act through which something is made present through something else. Empathy is based on the similarity between bodies. This similarity motivates a transfer, through which the other is encountered as having perceptions and experiences analogous to one's own subjectivity. My body and the other's body are given in a continuous context of reciprocity. The other appears as an alter-ego, but one that is in communion with my own. If this co-constitution is clarified then it necessarily includes an open plurality of human beings as subjects of possible communication. It is within this framework that Husserl came to see transcendental subjectivity as including an analysis of transcendental intersubjectivity.

Related to Husserl's analysis of intersubjectivity is the explication of the lifeworld (*Lebenswelt*). His theory of perception shows how objects are originally given in ever-changing profiles. In his later work, he refers to the notion of horizons. The perceived object has internal horizons: the perceived object appears in its manifold of profiles. Added to this is the idea that a given object also has external horizons: the table has a book resting on it; it is in a room; the room is in a house; the house is in a city and so on. Horizons are not appearances as such, but rather the pre-given context in which we find ourselves. Horizons are connected to other horizons, which yield to yet further horizons. The 'horizon of horizons' is the world. The horizon of the lifeworld is co-given with each object. This is not the theoretically ordered world of Newtonian physics, but rather the experiential world with which we are involved. This pre-theoretical world, the background to all theoretical and cultural achievements, is the lifeworld. Indeed, the difference between lifeworld and theory only makes sense within the phenomenological disclosure of the lifeworld itself. Husserl writes:

> every practical world, every science, presupposes the lifeworld; as purposeful structures, they are *contrasted* with the lifeworld, which was always and continues to be 'of its own accord.' Yet, on the other hand, everything developing and developed by mankind (individually and in community) is itself a piece of the lifeworld.[14]

In other words, there is an experiential background prior to the world being wrapped in theoretical data, and it is from the lifeworld that the theoretical world arises.

However, the lifeworld is not normally theoretical evident. For it to become so, we need a special type of reduction called dismantling (*Abbau*). For Husserl, the history of theoretical achievements has thrown a 'garb of ideas' over the experiential world. These sedimented idealisations must be subject to a 'destruction' which will disclose both the lifeworld and the subjectivity to which it is indubitably linked. Of this, Husserl comments: 'The retrogression to the world of experience is a *retrogression to the "lifeworld"*, i.e., to the world in which we are always already living and which furnishes the ground for all cognitive performance and all scientific determination.'[15] The Husserlian notion of dismantling has resonance to both Heidegger's *Destruktion* of the history of philosophy, and Derrida's *déconstruction*. However, there are important differences: for Heidegger, Husserl's transcendental analyses always relate back to intentional acts without examining the *being* of such acts; and for Derrida, subjectivity cannot be the final move in any deconstruction. Yet, Husserl's late work does move in this direction. In *Ideas II*, one finds Husserl asking: 'Does the "infinity" of the world, instead of referring to a transfinite endlessness ... not rather mean an "openness"? What can be meant by this?'[16]

Husserl's Legacy

The influence of Husserl's work has been pervasive throughout twentieth century thought, particularly in France and Germany. In France, Emmanuel Levinas, a student of Husserl's, introduced phenomenology to Jean-Paul Sartre and found the initial impetus for his own thought in phenomenology. Through Sartre, Husserl's thought became crucial for thinkers such as Maurice Merleau-Ponty and Jean Hyppolite. Likewise, Jacques Derrida's early work is devoted to a critique of phenomenological problems and Jean-François Lyotard's first publication was an introduction to phenomenology. The continuing influence and importance of Husserl's thought can be seen in the work of contemporary French thinkers such as Françoise Dastur. In Germany the influence of Husserl has been no less important. As a student and assistant of Husserl's, the young Martin Heidegger found one of the ways into his own path of thinking through phenomenology. The hermeneutics of Hans-Georg Gadamer is also marked by an encounter with Husserl's thought. In the critical theory of Theodor Adorno one finds a critique of Husserl, and more recently Jürgen Habermas has appropriated Husserl's concept of the lifeworld into his theory of communicative action.

In this chapter I have tried to show two main features of Husserl's thought: first, that phenomenological analyses are in principle on-going, and that the whole of Husserl's work is in fact an instantiation of this; and, second, that Husserlian phenomenology has provided an indispensable impetus to subsequent thinking. Phenomenology is an on-going attempt to interpret the meaning of objectivity in relation to subjectivity. Phenomenology is also inherently self-critical. This is why Husserl often referred to himself as a beginner in philosophy. Heidegger, reflecting on his own philosophical debt to Husserl, wrote: '... phenomenology is not a school. It is the possibility of thinking, at times changing and only thus persisting, of corresponding to the claim of what is to be thought.'[17] It is this possibility that Husserl considered to be the ultimate self-responsibility of humanity.[18]

Notes

1. Husserl, *The Idea of Phenomenology*, p. 39.
2. See Welton, *The Other Husserl.*
3. Husserl, from unpublished manuscript 'Einleitung in die Philosophie', cited in Welton, *The Other Husserl*, p. 13.
4. Levinas, *Discovering Existence with Husserl*, p. 95.
5. Husserl, *The Crisis of the European Sciences*, p. 189.
6. See Dummett, *The Origins of Analytical Philosophy.*
7. Husserl, *Logical Investigations vol. I*, pp. 249–50.
8. Ibid., p.136.
9. Husserl, *Logical Investigations vol. II*, pp. 558–9.
10. In Husserl, *Sinn* is used in distinction to *Bedeutung* (reference or signification). Some translators use 'meaning' for *Bedeutung* and 'sense' for *Sinn.*
11. Husserl, *Logical Investigations vol. I*, p. 270.
12. Husserl, *Phenomenology and the Crisis of Philosophy*, pp. 71–147.
13. Husserl, *Cartesian Meditations*, p. 92.
14. Husserl, *The Crisis of the European Sciences*, pp. 382–3.
15. Husserl, *Experience and Judgment*, p. 41.
16. Husserl, *Ideas II*, p. 299.
17. Heidegger, 'My Way to Phenomenology', in *On Time and Being*, trans. Joan Stambaugh (New York: Harper and Row, 1972 [1969]), pp. 74–82.
18. Husserl, *The Crisis of the European Sciences*, p. 400.

Major Works by Husserl

Cartesian Meditations: An Introduction to Phenomenology, trans. Dorion Cairns (The Hague: Martinus Nijhoff, 1960 [1950]).

The Crisis of European Sciences and Transcendental Phenomenology: An Introduction to Phenomenological Philosophy, trans. David Carr (Evanston: Northwestern University Press, 1970 [1954]).

Experience and Judgment: Investigations in a Genealogy of Logic, trans. James Churchill and Karl Ameriks (Evanston: Northwestern University Press, 1970 [1948]).

The Idea of Phenomenology, trans. William Alston and George Nakhnikian (The Hague: Martinus Nijhoff, 1964 [1958]).

Ideas Pertaining to a Pure Phenomenology and to a Phenomenological Philosophy, First Book: General Introduction to a Pure Phenomenology, trans. F. Kirsten (Dordrecht: Kluwer Academic Publishers, 1983 [1913]).

Ideas Pertaining to a Pure Phenomenology and to a Phenomenological Philosophy, Second Book: Studies in the Phenomenology of Constitution, trans. Richard Rojcewicz and André Schuwer (Dordrecht: Kluwer Academic Publishers, 1989 [1952]).

Logical Investigations, Vols 1 and 2, trans. J. N. Findlay (London: Routlege and Kegan Paul, 1970 [1900–1]).

Suggestions for Further Reading

Adorno, Theodor W., *Against Epistemolgy: A Metacritique*, trans. Willis Domingo (Cambridge, MA: MIT Press, 1982 [1970]).

Derrida, Jacques, *Speech and Phenomena*, trans. David B. Allison (Evanston: Northwestern University Press, 1973 [1967]).

Dummett, Michael, *The Origins of Analytical Philosophy* (Cambridge, MA: Harvard University Press, 1994).

Kolakowski, Leszek, *Husserl and the Search for Certitude* (Chicago: Chicago University Press, 1987). A short but comprehensive account of the main themes of phenomenology.

Levinas, Emmanuel, *The Theory of Intuition in the Phenomenology of Husserl*, trans. André Orianne (Evanston: Northwestern University Press, 1973 [1930]). A key work for understanding the reception of Husserl's thought in France.

Levinas, Emmanuel, *Discovering Existence with Husserl*, trans. Richard A. Cohen and Michael B. Smith (Evanston: Northwestern University Press 1998 [1967]). A collection of Levinas' essays on Husserl from 1929 through to 1977.

Natansen, Maurice, *Husserl: Philosopher of Infinite Tasks* (Evanston: Northwestern University Press 1973). A broad-ranging account of Husserl's thought that focuses on the development of the notion of lifeworld.

Steinbock, Anthony J., *Home and Beyond: Generative Phenomenology after Husserl* (Evanston: Northwestern University Press, 1995).

Welton, Donn, *The Other Husserl: The Horizons of Transcendental Phenomenology* (Bloomington: Indiana University Press, 2000).

Zahavi, Dan, *Self-Awareness and Alterity: A Phenomenological Investigation* (Evanston: Northwestern University Press, 1999). This important work shows how phenomenology provides the basis for many contemporary debates surrounding the body, the self and other, and theories of society.

11

Martin Heidegger (1889–1976)

David Woods

Heidegger in the Critical Tradition

Heidegger's intellectual work is predicated on his view that the Western philosophical tradition since Plato, which he identifies as metaphysical, has lost its way by concealing and ignoring the question of being. It is easier to see him in opposition to his predecessors rather than as continuing their tradition. However, Heidegger did respond to a Kantian problem of the distinction between the world of appearances that can be understood through categorial conceptualisation and the world of things in themselves, or noumena. For Heidegger, the gulf between them was a symptom of the increasing philosophical oblivion of being. The Kantian appeal to noumena is only necessary because the distinction between the content of experience and the categories which give it its form misses how experience itself already carries a pre-understanding of being. Temporality, rather than being finally an inner mode of interrelating external experiences via the categories, indicates the essential intertwining of human being and its world which precedes any distinction between form and content. The finitude which this implies should be embraced, insisted Heidegger, whereas the German idealists who followed Kant, including Hegel, sought to escape finitude by identifying human destiny with grand concepts such as spirit. According to Heidegger's history of philosophy, the key to the forgetting of being is the increasing focus on subjectivity, so that Hegel's idea of reason becoming realised through the self-consciousness of the subject was particularly objectionable to him. On the face of it, Nietzsche's will to power is the culmination of the forgetting of being in that in modern times subjectivity is expressed as will. Yet Nietzsche is another ambivalent figure for Heidegger, as he is credited with bringing the problem of metaphysics to light – insofar as he shows the illusoriness of supposedly transcendent sources of value – but once again without grasping that the root of the problem was the forgetting of being.

Heidegger was heavily influenced by his teacher Husserl even though he came to reject some basic tenets of Husserl's phenomenology. Most significantly, Husserl's focus on subjectivity as the grounds of objective knowledge were alien to Heidegger's critique of the role of subjectivity in Western metaphysics and to his aletheic notion of truth as a single self-manifestation which did away with the problematic relation of subject and object with which Husserl was so concerned. However, Heidegger drew substantially on Husserl to develop his notions of everyday being-in-the world as a background to all forms of understanding. Husserl thought it possible for phenomenological analysis to bracket off the presuppositions of everyday existence and thereby reveal the operation of consciousness to itself. For Heidegger, however, phenomenology is a way of revealing the initially hidden unity between finite human beings and their world, and is thus indissolubly linked to issues of interpretation.

As a key founding figure in existential and hermeneutic phenomenology, Heidegger had a profound influence on his successors. Gadamer shared Heidegger's sense that human experience has more to do with being in a world which is already given to humans than with conscious reflection by subjects on a world of objects. He was particularly affected by Heidegger's later work on historicity, which identified the fundamental self-grounding philosophical knowledge of communities with different historical epochs. For Gadamer, it was less a question of there being a philosophical truth of historical communities and more an issue of understanding being possible against a shared background of tradition, which was itself the background in relation to which knowledge is possible. Although Arendt cannot easily be ascribed to the existential phenomenological tradition, she did adopt something of the conceptual form of Heidegger's philosophy and thinking about the world. However, she changes Heidegger's grand concepts to suit her purposes in social and political philosophy, such that for her authentic being and freedom are political action in concert.

Introduction

Martin Heidegger was born in 1889 in Meßkirch, Baden, in southwest Germany. His father was a cooper and sexton of the local Catholic church. Heidegger initially intended to spend his life in the priesthood, taking Theology and Scholastic Philosophy at Freiburg

University, but he turned away from this vocation and dedicated himself to philosophy, studying under Edmund Husserl. *Being and Time* (henceforth *BT*) was published in 1927, bringing him to international attention. Although he had shown little interest in politics to this point, in 1933 he associated himself with the National Socialist movement. He became Rector of Freiburg University, and in his now notorious Rectoral Address drew parallels between the direction of Germany under Hitler and what was proposed in *BT*. However, tensions mounted with the Party and his rectorship ended after one year. His writing subsequently became critical of modernity and technology, one incarnation of which was Nazism, seeing them as presenting a great danger to humanity. After the war he was banned from teaching, but from 1949 he gave lectures to small élite groups, and resumed lecturing in Freiburg in 1952. He was buried in Meßkirch in 1976.

Most of this chapter will examine *BT*, which lays out some key ideas that are indispensable for understanding Heidegger's work as a whole, including the notion of 'world', arguably one of Heidegger's most influential contributions to philosophy. Heidegger was, however, a thinker whose work underwent a significant change in direction, which is usually known as the 'turn'. The final section of the chapter will therefore consider why Heidegger thought the turn necessary, and examine briefly some of the key ideas that flowed from it.

Being and Time

BT is probably the most famous incomplete work in twentieth-century Western philosophy. As we are told on the first page of the text, its goal is to investigate the question of the meaning of being,[1] and to show that time is the ultimate framework within which any understanding of being must be situated. Why time should have this role is taken up below, but the more immediate issue is what Heidegger means by the meaning of being. What are we saying when we say that something is? The very question sounds strange and perhaps disorienting to us, as the answer seems so obvious. The reason for this, Heidegger maintains, is that ontology – the study of being – as it has emerged in Western philosophy has been precipitate in determining what its own task is. Traditionally, ontology has been a conceptual investigation of particular regions of being, specifying what it is that entities of a given sort have in common and how they differ from other types of entity. Ontology thus provides foundations for the sciences which, since they deal explicitly only with entities, are contrastingly labelled by Heidegger as 'ontic'. *BT*, however, starts from the premise that ontology thus understood has already moved too quickly. In its focus on particular areas of being, it fails precisely to ask about the meaning of being generally: what is being? The question has rather been dismissed in one of several ways: being has been held to be the most universal concept; or to be indefinable; or to be self-evident. According to Heidegger all of these answers have led the tradition from Plato onwards astray, so that now the question seems obscure to us. Nonetheless, ontology 'remains blind and perverted from its ownmost aim'[2] until the meaning of being is clarified. What is required, then, is a 'fundamental ontology' which will take up the question anew.

Although the minimal existing answers are deficient, Heidegger's new enquiry begins from a clue in the fact that being is self-evident. In the very taken-for-grantedness of our everyday engagement with entities we show that we somehow understand the being of the entities which we encounter (for example in hammering a nail, contemplating a landscape or taking scientific measurements), even if we find it difficult to express that understanding adequately. We thus 'already live in an understanding of being' although the meaning of being is 'still veiled in darkness' (p. 23).

The initial step towards determining the meaning of being will thus be a close analysis of human being, or Dasein. (Why Heidegger chooses this term, meaning literally there-being, will emerge as the discussion proceeds.) Since Dasein has an implicit understanding (a 'pre-understanding') of entities other than itself, the enquiry finds a concrete starting point in Dasein's everyday activity. But Heidegger has other reasons for holding that Dasein has a mode of being which can provide better access to the meaning of being than any other entity. Most importantly, as it engages in its everyday activity Dasein leads its life, presses forward into possibilities. The possibilities which a particular individual realises do not express some pre-formed human essence, however, but rather go to constitute it as the specific Dasein that it is. As Heidegger puts it, Dasein's essence is its existence; the categories of nature, which presuppose that an entity has some fixed identity, are not appropriate for it. Further, in pressing forth into its possibilities, Dasein necessarily takes a stand on its own existence; it has a pre-understanding of itself. For these reasons Dasein must be conceived as a new ontological category, and one which has a privileged relation to the question of being. *BT* therefore begins with an 'existential' analysis whose aim is to uncover the ontological structures of Dasein, and thereby to specify the meaning of Dasein's being. Such existential structures underlie and are to be contrasted with the particular circumstances of and decisions taken by an individual Dasein, which Heidegger refers to as 'existentiell' matters. Once this analysis has been completed, the meaning of being more generally can be addressed.

The published version of *BT* consists of two divisions. The overarching task of Division I is to uncover a complex structure – Dasein's being-in-the-world – which prior to *BT* was unknown to us. Heidegger declares that he will use a phenomenological approach in laying out Dasein's existential structures, or 'existentialia', and thence being-in-the-world. Careful examination of the phenomena given in experience will reveal aspects of that givenness which are usually hidden or, in Heidegger's terminology, covered up. Although the preliminary discussion of Dasein has highlighted how it presses forward into possibilities, it is important to emphasise straight away that a key move of *BT* is to characterise Dasein as, fundamentally, not a conscious subject but rather a set of comportments or ways of acting. Counter-intuitively, consciousness appears late on in the existential analytic, and is seen to be a consequence of Dasein's being-in-the-world. Division II recasts the ontological structure of Dasein in terms of temporality, in accordance with the programmatic statement which begins the treatise, and includes an account of why phenomena needed to be attended to so closely for them to be rescued from being covered up. In the course of elaborating the structure of being-in-the-world Heidegger identifies among Dasein's various existentialia three which are at once fundamental and interrelated, or 'equiprimordial': understanding, moods and falling. Though each of them is given extensive consideration in *BT*, the following will be led by a focus on understanding; the broader significance of this tripartite structure will be revisited below.

Division I

For Heidegger, understanding is based in Dasein's projective capacities. We have already seen how Dasein is always pressing forth into its possibilities, projecting itself in a course of action, and Heidegger sets about demonstrating that this is the most fundamental mode in which it understands both itself and other entities. This argument begins with an analysis of Dasein's relationship to tools, or the 'ready-to-hand'. Following Heidegger's famous example, the most basic way for Dasein to understand a hammer, then, is simply to use it. However, this understanding is holistic: it is a condition of understanding how to use a hammer that Dasein be able to use (understand) a whole range of other tools and materials; in this case nails, chisels, planks and so on. Dasein normally relates to tools in a specific way whereby they figure in its concern with furthering its own ends. There are two aspects to this: invisibility and publicness.[3]

First, as it goes about its business Dasein takes the tool *as* something, but in a peculiar manner whereby the tool itself has a certain sort of invisibility. We do not pay particular attention to the hammer; rather it becomes a seamless component of our on-going activity. Heidegger refers to this sort of 'seeing', in which we have an un-self-reflexive awareness of what lies before us, as 'circumspection'. When someone enters a room they normally do not pay particular attention to the door; whether it is open or closed, they act appropriately, circumspectly, without giving it explicit attention. In circumspection Dasein, against an already-constituted practical understanding, uses a tool and thus implicitly identifies or 'assigns' this particular tool as being a certain entity, which in turn is part of a wider web of assignment relations which Heidegger calls 'the world'. Importantly, because of the holistic, open-ended character of understanding, the phenomenal content of these assignment relations cannot be summarised as a list of rules.

Second, this emphasis on Dasein's primarily practical character entails an irreducible reference to public usage. The production of a suit, for instance, involves 'an essential assignment or reference to possible wearers' (p. 153). Just as any tool must be understood as an element within a whole, so too must Dasein's ends be conceived of holistically. This points to one of the key ontological characteristics of Dasein: its being is a being-with others. Dasein encounters other Daseins primarily as the bearers of social roles; if for example someone provides material upon which we work, we find the supplier to be a good or bad one depending upon the quality and appropriateness of what they have delivered. Such an encounter is different from how Dasein encounters other entities, and Heidegger labels it 'solicitude' in contrast to 'concern'. Clearly, however, the other's role could in principle be taken on by me and vice versa, and this very interchangeability indicates the priority of the social role over the individual who happens to occupy it.

The major consequence of the argument so far is that Dasein is essentially constituted 'from the outside'. The individual projections of a Dasein do not first arise 'from within' such that they can then come to constitute a public realm by some process of comparison or negotiation with other Daseins. Rather it is only by taking over elements of a pre-constituted public realm of shared practices that Dasein can appear at all, and it does so most fundamentally in projecting itself by means of assignment relations; Dasein and world thus form a mutually supporting complex.

Heidegger's general term for the range of roles and institutional arrangements that precede and condition Dasein is *das Man*. This is usually translated as 'the they', although this arguably obscures the function of social roles, which indicate in a normative way what must be done if the role I am undertaking is to be fulfilled. In the discussion of the they Heidegger sets out to distinguish a third aspect of Dasein's being: being-oneself. For Heidegger, the self that emerges in the account of everyday Dasein is the 'they-self'. The ontological structures Heidegger has brought to light so far suggest that what we ordinarily take as obvious or natural practices or values have no basis beyond the activities in which a community happens to engage. Dasein can avoid this unsettling insight, however, in that, as Heidegger portrays it, the shared practices which constitute the they initially offer Dasein false consolation, an easy conformism and endless new things in which it can become inauthentically absorbed such that it never has to face its basic condition. The distinction between authentic and inauthentic Dasein will only come to fruition in Division II, but it is important to be clear that, despite the invective heaped upon the they because it makes Dasein start from a position of inauthenticity, it nevertheless remains one of Dasein's basic ungrounded conditions. Authenticity will be a matter of how Dasein relates to or 'takes over' the they, not whether it does so or not.

Even from this minimal account of concern, solicitude and being-oneself we can get some initial sense of Heidegger's conception of Dasein's everyday being-in-the-world: the world, far from its ordinary sense of a natural or cultural space in which people live has the ontological meaning of a complex set of structures and practices which enable and constrain Dasein's being but which normally pass unnoticed. Clearly, however, Dasein does not spend all its time dealing with the ready to hand. Sometimes people just stare at things, discuss how to overcome a problem or formulate theories. In his account of such phenomena Heidegger turns to a third ontological category: the present-at-hand. Dasein first encounters the present-at-hand when some sort of failure occurs in its dealing with ready-to-hand entities, for instance if a hammer is unsuitable for the task at hand. What is involved here is interpretation, which Heidegger portrays as a series of stages whereby Dasein emerges from un-self-reflexive action into an increasingly acute consciousness of its world. Interpretation is in the first instance non-verbal; Dasein wordlessly tries to swap the hammer for another. Presence at hand is, however, an ontological category to which Dasein attains full access when it has recourse to a certain type of speech, namely assertions (statements of the type 'S is P'). When an assertion is made about some entity, such as 'this hammer is too light', specific aspects of its being are highlighted, and Dasein's understanding alters to become much more like our commonsense notion of understanding. 'Only now are we given any access to *properties* or the like' (p. 200). Heidegger finds a number of intermediate stages where speech becomes increasingly detached from an immediate context of activity, culminating in theoretical assertions. The crucial point for Heidegger is the order of dependence involved in this process: what he calls the 'apophantical "as"' of assertions, which pick out entities in terms which are abstract to a greater or lesser degree, derives from the 'existential-hermeneutical "as"' of engaged, circumspective understanding. The sort of change-over involved when Dasein starts relating to entities as present-at-hand does not involve a change in the entity itself; Dasein had already understood the entity as something, and in assertions this 'as' simply gets expressed for the first time.

Heidegger thus claims that human being has a more basic mode than any developed explicitly by the philosophical tradition, precisely because the tradition has to a greater or lesser degree passed over the phenomenon of world. Indeed, the meaning of being in general has been conceived by the tradition in terms of presence-at-hand (though Heidegger finds in Aristotle an implicit understanding of what has been missed). This is not a mere accident, however, but is rather a consequence of Dasein's structure; by definition Dasein's understanding of entities is first raised explicitly in assertion, and so presence-at-hand misleadingly presses itself upon us as having ontological priority. For Heidegger one of the most decisive ways in which this appears in modern philosophy is in Descartes' division of reality into *res cogitans* and *res extensa* (roughly, mind and matter). On the basis of this distinction, certainty (and hence first of all self-certainty) becomes the criterion for establishing what is a ground, and truth is staged as a relationship between two present-at-hand entities, the knower and the 'external world'. Clearly, however, this move attempts to make foundational what in Heidegger's phenomenological analysis comes last; Dasein must already inhabit a world before it can take a step back and ask what it can be certain of. Once we have noticed the phenomenon of the world, the dualist model of consciousness and the epistemologies which follow from it become untenable.

> When Dasein directs itself toward something and grasps it, it does not somehow first get out of an inner sphere in which it has been proximally encapsulated, but its primary kind of being is such that it is always 'outside' alongside entities which it encounters and which belong to a world already discovered. Nor is any inner sphere abandoned when Dasein dwells alongside the entity to be known, and determines its character ... And furthermore, the perceiving of what is known is not a process of returning with one's booty to the 'cabinet' of consciousness after one has gone out and grasped it; even in perceiving, retaining and preserving, the Dasein who knows *remains outside*, and it does so *as Dasein.* (p. 89)

Thus Dasein is always already in a world in which it is disclosing entities; Dasein is its 'there'.

Division II

The exposition of Dasein's being-in-the-world has been guided by what Heidegger has found to be key phenomenal elements of Dasein's everyday existence. But how are we to be sure that some crucial aspect of Dasein's structure has not been overlooked? Towards the end of the division Heidegger draws together his findings in the most fundamental structure of Dasein identified so far, which he calls 'care'. The term has, of course, an ontological meaning and is to be distinguished from ontical attitudes on the part of Dasein. Care is summarised thus: 'the being of Dasein means ahead-of-itself-being-already-in-(the-world) as being-alongside (entities encountered within-the-world)' (p. 237). This initially opaque formula can be analysed into three separate components which align with the three equiprimordial existentialia mentioned above – understanding, moods and falling. First, Dasein is ahead of itself or oriented to the future (and is thus 'existential'); this corresponds to Dasein's understanding. Dasein is also already in the world; it is 'thrown' into a world that it did not choose but in which it has to make binding choices (and is thus 'factical'). That it cannot help but be affected by the world is revealed in its moods. Finally, in the course of this situated projecting Dasein is there 'alongside' entities, absorbed in dealing with them; Heidegger calls this 'falling'. The accumulation of hyphens in Heidegger's definition, however, indicates, as ever in *BT*, that these components form a unity. In Division II the source of this unity is shown to lie in temporality: projection corresponds to the future, thrownness to the past, and falling to the present. The task of Division II is thus to revisit the phenomena outlined in Division I, but with temporality now made thematic so as to dispatch any suspicion that the analysis may be incomplete. Further, the account so far has only dealt with inauthentic Dasein, so the second task of Division II is to spell out what authentic self-understanding might be. Between them, these steps deepen the account of temporality as the source of Dasein's unity.

The development of the notion of authenticity occupies a good deal of Division II with what is in effect a secularisation of Kierkegaard, whom Heidegger references explicitly. A tightly interrelated series of arguments track how a number of phenomena such as death, anxiety, guilt and conscience, all of which are first encountered by Dasein as existentiell matters, can give Dasein existential insight into its own constitution. In the broadest outline, authentic Dasein comes to see its own 'nullity' – that it is a finite being whose own existence issues from the sheer contingency of the they. Delivered from the illusion that life has an ultimate meaning and that it can be completely self-determining, authentic Dasein becomes more open to its 'Situation'. This is not necessarily a matter of rejecting out of hand whatever life Dasein is embarked upon, but rather of becoming free to be more responsive to what its particular circumstances demand if it is to live to the full what Heidegger calls its ownmost potentiality for being.

The discussion of authenticity results in a set of distinctions between authentic and inauthentic ways in which Dasein temporalises. For example, the 'anticipation' of the future which is required for Dasein to become authentically open to its Situation is contrasted with an 'awaiting' which never radically questions the terms supplied by the they. Nevertheless, whether authentic or not, Dasein is always temporal. Clearly, temporality here cannot have the ordinary meaning of time as a series of nows, with distinct dimensions of past, present and future. Rather Dasein is temporal in that it is factical, falling and existential. Dasein's having been, the present, and the future are designated 'ecstaces' to indicate the mutual necessity of these three aspects of Dasein, and Heidegger calls this more basic sense of temporality 'primordial time' to distinguish it from our ordinary notion of time. Temporality forms the horizon which is the condition of possibility both of Dasein (as a discloser of entities) and of the world (as an open-ended set of assignment-relations).

The significance of this becomes clearer through a comparison with Husserl. For Husserl, intentionality is fundamentally cognitive. Horizons form a context or background within which an object appears through an intentional act. The imaginative variations to which phenomena are subjected in phenomenology result in the pure, presuppositionless, intuitive presentation of essences, and thus knowledge of these essences is produced. In all of this, however, the basic mode in which intentionality, whether 'empty' or not, is fulfilled is modelled on sight; the variations are precisely variations in how the object appears to us. If, however, we recall the priority of the ready-to-hand it follows directly that for Heidegger 'even the phenomenological "intuition of essences" is grounded in existential understanding' (p. 187). That is to say, the temporal horizon within which Dasein intends objects is practical; the intention is fulfilled inasmuch as the entity Dasein encounters shows itself to be appropriate to its projections. Cognition, including the operations of Husserlian phenomenology, presuppose Dasein's being-in-the-world. We are now in a position to appreciate the significance of Heidegger's appeal to the hermeneutic circle, which in the introduction had been identified as the appropriate method for phenomenological enquiry. Phenomenology cannot be, as Husserl wished, a presupposition-free science; it must rather begin on the basis that Dasein is always already engaged in the world, and that hence the primary way in which it takes entities as particular things is indeed a properly hermeneutic one. Thus for Heidegger a return to the things themselves, far from involving a stripping away of presuppositions, requires rather a renewed investigation of their character.

'The Turn' and After

Towards the end of *BT*, Heidegger is sober about the discipline imposed by the hermeneutic circle which, since it entails a fore-conception – some expectation of what the outcome of the enquiry will be – necessarily sets *BT* along a specific path. However, 'whether this is the *only* way or even the right one at all, can be decided only *after one has gone along it*' (p. 487). And Heidegger indeed came to see that the direction taken by *BT* was inappropriate as a way of engaging with the question of being. Division II ends with a reiteration of the issue with which the treatise had opened: 'Does *time* manifest itself as the horizon of *being*?' (p. 488). The third division was to tackle the meaning of being in general, working from the demonstration that Dasein's being is fundamentally temporal, and Part Two was to be a 'destruction of the history of ontology' which would reconstruct the specific ways in which previous ontologies had effectively missed the phenomenon of world, thereby gaining insight into how the question of being presses misleading answers upon us. Though a good deal of work addressing these issues (as well as much else besides) was in fact published subsequently, the attempt to include it within the programmatic unity of the sort envisaged in *BT* was abandoned. This is the change which is usually referred to as 'the turn', and for some scholars it indicates a shift between earlier and later Heidegger, while others find early, middle and late periods in Heidegger's writing. An initial sense of what it is that changes can be found in a work first published in 1959. Here Heidegger says that the notion in *BT* that hermeneutics must take the form of a circle was 'superficial', and he substitutes for it the notion of a hermeneutic relation. In the word 'hermeneutic' we can hear a reference to Hermes, messenger of the gods:

> He brings the message of destiny; *hermeneuein* is that exposition which brings tidings because it can listen to a message ... it was this original sense which prompted me to use it in defining the phenomenological thinking that opened the way to *Being and Time* for me. What mattered then, and still does, is to bring out the being of beings – though no longer in the manner of metaphysics, but such that being itself will shine out, being itself – that is to say: the presence of present beings ... Language defines the hermeneutic relation.[4]

This dense passage contains in miniature many of the themes of later Heidegger. Perhaps the most striking thing about it is its mixture of continuity and change. The issue for Heidegger is still being in general, but from this later perspective *BT* is seen as part of metaphysics, which now appears as a trap to be avoided. *BT* replaces an explanatory model of human being based on a mistaken assumption about the primacy of the present-at-hand with one based on Dasein as a 'worldly', open set of comportments. This was conceived as a step towards the wider goal of specifying the meaning of being in general but, despite the originality and far-reaching consequences for philosophy of the notion of world, Heidegger now sees this goal as anthropocentric. Division II shows that temporality is the meaning of Dasein's being, but the question with which the division ends indicates that temporality is also to be the meaning of being in general; *BT* thus entails a Dasein-centred view of being. Temporality forms the horizon of Dasein and of the world, but given the design of the treatise there can be no consideration of, so to speak, the 'other side' of the horizon, of how conditions not originating in Dasein and the world allow the horizon to form.

Later Heidegger's response is to turn away from a search for possible answers to the question of being, as such a search treats being as a ground, a principle in terms of which beings could be explained. Heidegger had originally thought of his task as the extension of metaphysics, with the demonstration that time is the transcendental horizon for the question of being, as the title of Part One of *BT* has it. However, the emphasis now shifts to an exploration of the nature of the horizon within which we understand being, in order to bring out the being of beings in a non-metaphysical way. The later Heidegger historicises Dasein's understanding of being as set out in *BT*. (In *BT* Dasein is characterised as historical in that it is thrown into a particular community, but the existentiell experiences, such as anxiety and guilt, that gave access to existential structures, are understood to hold good for all Daseins.) Heidegger comes to conceive of human history as a sequence of epochs; being opens up a particular understanding, a set of answers to the question 'what is being?' which characterises a community, determining what sort of entities can appear for it and what therefore counts as truth. Thus for example in the epoch of Christianity, being is identified with a divine transcendent ground, and the world is full of creatures, while in modernity humans becomes the source of intelligibility, and the world is populated with objects. (It is in the latter context that Dasein's understanding of being set out in *BT* is now seen to stand.) Since the different understandings of being do not originate in Dasein they cannot be accounted for in terms of Dasein;

from our perspective all there is is the sheer succession of epochs beyond accounting, which Heidegger sometimes calls 'sending' or 'destining'.

The second important aspect of the quotation is that language is said to define the hermeneutic relation. The priority that Heidegger attributes to language should perhaps not be surprising. In *BT* language gave expression to the disclosedness in which Dasein encounters entities, and if now such disclosing is conceived as requiring more than simply human doing then language holds out the possibility of a uniquely intimate sort of access to the articulations of a world which constitute an epoch's understanding of being. The task of hermeneutics accordingly becomes that of bringing tidings by means of an exposition, a recovering of the hidden significance of the messages which are destined to us in language; hence the marked stylistic changes between early and later Heidegger, as well as the increased importance ascribed to the creative etymology which had always figured in his writing.

Heidegger's treatment of art in particular brings out key implications of destining and the presence of present beings. Poetry, as we might expect, is the most privileged example of art, but great art more generally in later Heidegger comes to be attributed with the capacity to reveal in a peculiarly totalising way the articulations of an understanding of being shared by a community. Thus of the Greek temple Heidegger says that it 'first gives to things their look and to men their outlook on themselves'.[5] As we might suspect, what is involved here is not a matter of representation; rather, the temple embodies the 'as'-structures which are available to that people. The temple, which houses the god, pulls together into a whole the particular ways in which 'birth and death, disaster and blessing, victory and disgrace, endurance and decline'[6] are for those who built it. Using an influential couplet of terms, Heidegger tells us that in 'setting up a world and setting forth the earth, the work is the fighting of the battle in which the unconcealedness of beings as a whole, or truth, is won'.[7] The notion of a 'world' here still has a sense of a horizon, while 'the earth' marks the resistance to our projects which we encounter through our particular 'as'-structures. Thus unlike the tool, whose materiality 'disappears into usefulness',[8] the temple gives access to the otherwise closed earth in a way that is not captured by physical measurement. 'The lustre and gleam of the stone, though itself apparently glowing only by the grace of the sun, yet first brings to light the light of the day ... its own repose brings out the raging of the sea.'[9] It is tempting to think of this couplet in the familiar terms of form and matter, but this would be misleading insofar as, clearly, the schema emphasises the permanent distinctness of the earth from our projections upon it. Further, the form/matter binary is itself clearly the product of a world. To put the point another way, to conceive of the earth as unformed matter would be to rejoin metaphysics, to forget that a world is destined rather than grounded and that we cannot get behind the specifics of particular 'as'-structures to give an explanation of them. In summary, the presence of present beings involves a double withdrawal of being. First, from the discussion of the work of art Heidegger wants to show that the way the world is for a community, its truth, is *aletheia*, an unconcealment which picks out entities or illuminates them in particular ways against an impenetrable background. Second, the horizon of each epoch is determined by *Ereignis* or 'the event of Appropriation';[10] that is, an understanding of being is destined to us, but it appears as an ungrounded happening which cannot admit of explanation.

Famously, Heidegger thinks that our current, 'technological' epoch has the character of nihilism: our understanding of being is that there is nothing but beings. Since Descartes, the objectivity of the object has been grounded in the subjectivity of the subject; *BT* itself had demonstrated that the most thoroughgoing explanation of this grounding was that objects gain their objectivity in conforming to Dasein's projective behaviour. In the present epoch the notion of truth as *aletheia* is forgotten and art, bereft of its totalising capacity, retreats to the margins of society. As Heidegger puts it, rather than setting forth the earth technology challenges it forth; now beings are only insofar as they are available to be illuminated totally through calculation and manipulation. Both objects and subjects come to be disclosed as raw material, part of a 'standing reserve' in the unlimited exploitation and consumption of nature. Technology is thus the most extreme version of subjectivism: an unrestricted will-to-power, an ends-driven rationality running beyond any control.

Nevertheless Heidegger holds that we do not have to despair. The technological understanding of being is ambiguous, in that whilst it threatens to reduce entities to the uniformity of the standing reserve, Heidegger says that 'we look into the danger and see the growth of the saving power'.[11] Since being is now understood as nothing, the distinction between being and beings disappears. As there are no misleading answers to the question of being – the question itself has no sense for a technological understanding – for the first time since the inception of metaphysics the possibility is opened for a post-metaphysical relation to being which experiences it as *Ereignis* rather than conceives it as a ground. Thus technology enables the preservation of a newly profound relation to being at the same time that it threatens to obliterate it. This move gives later Heidegger's writing a sense of historical self-reflexiveness as well as its rationale. Certainly, since understandings of being are destined to us, there is nothing we can do to effect a change ourselves; we are obliged to wait for a new understanding to arrive, which is what Heidegger means when he says that only a god can save us. Nonetheless, the attentive listening to the messages of different epochs preserves the significance of particular cultural practices or objects, such as the Greek temple, against the depredations of technological understanding, and can make us more alert to what true change will involve.

Conclusion

As thought-provoking as many of these points from later Heidegger and the account of the 'turn' may be, they are clearly problematic. There is a pervasive quasi-theological rhetoric in which meaningful human intervention in the world seems reduced to a sort of quietism, as well as a wholesale dismissal of what others might see as beneficial aspects of modernity. As regards early Heidegger, the potentially progressive notion of being-with others, once juxtaposed with the demands of authenticity, becomes transformed into a picture of a people drawn together through a 'co-historising' in which it faces up heroically to a shared thrownness, and thence it is a short step, for some critics, to Heidegger's aligning himself with the Nazi party in 1933.

Nonetheless, Heidegger's work has been massively influential in a number of fields. Of course, the existentialist thrust of *BT* was taken up (badly, according to Heidegger) by a generation of post-war French thinkers. On a different front, and despite their antagonisms, Heidegger and Adorno, albeit in very different ways, both look to art as a refuge from an all-encompassing instrumental rationality. Similarly, there are parallels between Heidegger's notion of epochality and Foucault's notion of the episteme, as well as between entities as standing reserve and the latter's studies of disciplinary apparatuses which, beyond any conscious organising force, ensue in 'bio-power' and subjects who bend themselves to the needs of the technological system. The list could be extended greatly, but what many of those influenced by Heidegger have in common is that they accept the broad outlines of his thought – the early notion of world is especially relevant here – but dispute key elements of it. Thus Levinas takes Heidegger to task for the underdeveloped notion of the other in the existential analytic, while Irigaray among others interrogates the same text for its notable omission of any consideration of sexual difference. Not least, perhaps, Derrida's sustained engagement with Heidegger separates the metaphysics of presence from the notion of destining; deconstruction is thus freed to tease out the heterogeneous forces which constitute such presence (in a mode of analysis which nevertheless follows Heidegger's insistence upon the primacy of language), and in so doing restores a fuller sense of human agency which nevertheless does not fall short of Heidegger's insights. What these and other such responses reflect, arguably, is the continuing relevance for contemporary thought of the radicalised versions of hermeneutics and phenomenology developed in Heidegger's work.

Notes

1. I have avoided the convention of capitalising 'being' because of the connotations it brings of a transcendent entity, which Heidegger is keen to avoid.
2. Heidegger, *Being and Time*, p. 31. Remaining page numbers will be in the text, and emphases throughout will be original.
3. The use of this term here should be distinguished from Heidegger's notion of publicness in *BT*, where it describes a particular – negative – aspect of 'the they'.
4. Heidegger, 'A Dialogue on Language', in *On the Way to Language*, pp. 29–30.
5. Heidegger, 'The Origin of the Work of Art', in *Poetry, Language, Thought*, p. 43.
6. Ibid., p. 42.
7. Ibid., p. 55.
8. Ibid., p. 46.
9. Ibid., p. 42.
10. Heidegger, 'Time and Being', in *On Time and Being*, p. 19.
11. Heidegger, 'The Question Concerning Technology', in *The Question Concerning Technology and Other Essays*, p. 33.

Major Works by Heidegger

Being and Time, trans. John Macquarrie and Edward Robinson (Oxford: Blackwell, 1962 [1927]).

Contributions to Philosophy (From Enowning), trans. Parvis Emad and Kenneth Maly (Bloomington: Indiana University Press, 1999 [1989]).

Early Greek Thinking, trans. David Farrell Krell and Frank Capuzzi (New York: Harper and Row, 1975 [1950–4]).

Poetry, Language, Thought, trans. Albert Hofstadter (New York: Harper and Row, 1971 [1950–60]).

On Time and Being, trans. Joan Stambaugh (New York: Harper and Row, 1972 [1969]).

On the Way to Language, trans. Peter D. Hertz (New York: Harper and Row, 1970 [1959]).

Pathmarks, trans. William McNeill (Cambridge: Cambridge University Press, 1998 [1967]).

The Question Concerning Technology and Other Essays, trans. and ed. William Lovitt (New York: Harper and Row, 1977 [1950–4]).

Suggestions for Further Reading

Dreyfus, Hubert L., *Being-in-the-World* (Cambridge, MA: MIT Press, 1991). Focuses mainly on Division I, drawing parallels with later Wittgenstein. Very helpful on a range of topics.

Mulhall, Stephen, *Heidegger and Being and Time* (London: Routledge 1996). An accessible explication of *BT* with helpful references to analytic philosophy and an account of the structural significance of authenticity to the work as a whole.

Pattison, George, *The Later Heidegger* (London: Routledge, 2000). A lucid examination of the key themes in later Heidegger. Sympathetic but measured.

Zimmerman, Michael E., *Heidegger's Confrontation with Modernity* (Bloomington: Indiana University Press, 1990). Contextualises Heidegger's stance on technology in terms of the social, cultural and political issues of 1920s and 1930s Germany, as well as elucidating the role of art in his later work.

12

Hans-Georg Gadamer (1900–2002)

Nicholas H. Smith

Gadamer in the Critical Tradition

Gadamer was a student of Husserl and Heidegger, and both exerted a profound influence on him. Husserl's influence is most evident in Gadamer's use of the notion of a 'horizon', that is, a background pre-given to the thinker against which thinking always takes place. But while Gadamer appropriates this thought, he also tries to bring out the intersubjective, dialogical character of understanding more fully than Husserl's phenomenology was able to do by introducing a distinctive notion of the 'fusion of horizons'. In this respect at least Gadamer is close to Hegel. His debt to Heidegger is even more marked. Gadamer was impressed not only by Heidegger's highly original interpretations of classical philosophical texts, but also by Heidegger's discovery of the ontological significance of interpretation itself. The latter insight, that interpretation is essentially a matter of being rather than knowledge, is the point of departure for Gadamer's own philosophical hermeneutics.

Whereas for Heidegger all of Western metaphysics had obscured the question of being, Gadamer is concerned by the way in which the more specific Enlightenment ideals of reason and truth give a distorted representation of the conditions of self-understanding. According to Gadamer, these ideals stand behind 'subjectivist' notions of aesthetic consciousness inspired by Kant as well as 'objectivist' approaches to history found in modern historicism. Following the basic Heideggerian insight that philosophy should not be modelled on the relation between subject and object, Gadamer's hermeneutics aims at recovering the world-disclosing, self-transformative meaning of works of art and historical texts. In Gadamer's view, this is at once a question of dismantling the Enlightenment's specific form of alienation from the artwork and historical tradition.

Although Gadamer opposed the Enlightenment's rejection of prejudice and tradition, he was not attracted to Nietzsche's iconoclastic critique of philosophy and its attachment to truth. Gadamer's conviction that truth possesses an irreducible and indispensable ideality meant that he could not be content with the genealogical critique of scientific truth, instead doing his best to develop a hermeneutic notion of truth through a recovery of the experience of understanding. On the face of it, Gadamer's Hegelian commitment to the ideality of truth and meaning puts space between his and Wittgenstein's projects. Yet, both Wittgenstein and Gadamer regarded language as the shared practice in which understanding is possible, so that for the former 'forms of life' and for the latter 'tradition' are fundamentally linguistic modes of intersubjectivity.

Introduction

Hans-Georg Gadamer was raised in Breslau, Silesia, then on the prosperous eastern fringe of the German Empire. His father was an accomplished professor of pharmaceutical chemistry, and while Hans-Georg would also go on to lead the life of learning, from an early age his passion was for the 'human' rather than the 'natural' sciences. In 1919 Gadamer went to Marburg University to study philosophy and philology. After completing his doctorate on Plato's concept of desire, in 1923 he went to study under Edmund Husserl and Martin Heidegger at the University of Freiburg. Gadamer was spellbound by Heidegger and continued to work with him after Heidegger's move to Marburg later that year. When Heidegger returned to Freiburg in 1927, Gadamer was just completing his *Habilitationshrift*, a phenomenological reading of Plato eventually published as *Plato's Dialectical Ethics* (1931). Gadamer was caught off guard by Hitler's rise to power, but unlike his Jewish friends and colleagues, such as Karl Löwith, he was able to adapt to the new regime and would even prosper under it professionally. In January 1939 Gadamer was appointed Professor of Philosophy at the University of Leipzig, where he remained until his resignation in 1947, soon to be succeeded by the Marxist philosopher Ernst Bloch. After a brief stay in Frankfurt, in 1949 Gadamer took up the chair vacated by Karl Jaspers at Heidelberg, a position he would occupy until his retirement twenty years later. Although Gadamer wrote continuously throughout his career, it was not until 1960, with the publication of his magnum opus *Truth and Method*, that he made a decisive contribution to the broad tradition of critical theory. In this work, Gadamer outlined the essential features of what he called 'philosophical hermeneutics'. Gadamer has also written many essays (most of them transcriptions of lectures) in which he draws out the implications of his hermeneutics for philosophical ethics, the arts, literary criticism, religion and public affairs.

Philosophical Hermeneutics

Gadamer's central idea is indicated obliquely in the title of his major work. There is a standing tendency in modern thought, Gadamer believes, to construe truth in terms of objectivity, where objectivity is secured by adopting the correct scientific method. The success of modern physics, chemistry, biology and so forth suggests that these sciences have indeed hit upon the right method for ascertaining the truths of nature. As Gadamer observes, the modern natural sciences now enjoy an 'unassailable and anonymous authority'.[1] According to one outlook, often referred to as 'naturalism', the general method employed in modern natural science is capable of telling us all there is to know about reality. But according to another, the dominant one in Germany during the time of Gadamer's training, knowledge of the human world must take a different path. For Wilhelm Dilthey (1833–1911), whose formulation of this view was particularly influential, this is because the human sciences succeed by reaching an understanding of their object domain. Since the method of physics, chemistry and so forth is geared towards causal explanation rather than understanding, it is mistaken to hold that the natural sciences provide a model for all knowledge. Naturalism is mistaken not because the human sciences do not themselves properly aspire to objectivity. Dilthey's point is rather that understanding and interpretation is a science in its own right, a form of objective enquiry with its own legitimate rules and procedures.

The name given to the science of interpretation is hermeneutics. Gadamer agrees with Dilthey that the human sciences are essentially concerned with understanding, or the interpretation of meanings, on account of which they have a different structure to the natural sciences. However, in Gadamer's view Dilthey's critique of naturalism was insufficiently radical. This is because Dilthey, indeed the whole tradition of hermeneutic theory going back to Schleiermacher (1768–1834), still saw the problem of the truth of hermeneutics as equivalent to the problem of the objectivity of the hermeneutic method. The limitations of this epistemologically centred approach, Gadamer believes, were first brought out by Heidegger. Heidegger convinced Gadamer that hermeneutics is much more than a method of knowing; in its original structure, understanding is a feature of *Existenz* or 'being-in-the-world'. Being-in-the-world is essentially characterised by a pre-theoretical, pre-reflective form of engaged understanding, and it is this, rather than any reflexive 'interpretative method' or 'science' of interpretation, that provides the point of departure of Gadamer's philosophical or 'ontological' hermeneutics.

Philosophical hermeneutics is an important task for our times, Gadamer thinks, because the link between truth and method insisted upon by modern epistemology tends to bury, distort or truncate the experience of understanding. To the extent to which we are under the sway of this epistemology, we need to recover the experience through philosophical re-articulation. Gadamer identifies two cases where the need for such retrieval is most palpable: the encounter with art and the encounter with history.

Aesthetic Consciousness

How does modern epistemology give rise to a truncated model of the experience of art? Gadamer's answer to this question is long and complex, but his account hinges on the emergence of the idea of the 'aesthetic'. It is a commonplace, Gadamer observes, to encounter a work of art as if it were the locus of a distinct kind of value: namely, 'aesthetic' value. The aesthetic value of an artwork is the worth it possesses simply as an artwork, a worth that is distinct, say, from whatever practical utility or moral merit the work may have. Now Gadamer observes that this way of thinking about art is significantly motivated by developments in epistemology that can be traced back to Kant. In his critical philosophy, Kant sought to determine the basis of the validity of modern science and morality. This could only be achieved, in Kant's view, by carefully differentiating the realm of application of scientific concepts and principles from that of moral concepts and principles. And just as science and morality had to be kept distinct in order to secure their validity, so art had to be allocated its own sphere of value. The legitimacy of aesthetic judgements, according to Kant, was neither the kind of validity that scientific claims enjoyed, because works of art, unlike propositions and theories, were not conveyors of truth; nor was it like the legitimacy of a moral demand, which is unconditionally and universally binding. Rather, the validity of an aesthetic judgement had its basis in the capacity of beautiful objects to elicit a pleasurable but disinterested feeling, an 'aesthetic pleasure', in the subject of the judgement, which Kant attributed to the free interplay of the human mental faculties. Thus, whereas the basis of the validity of science and morality was objective, 'aesthetic' validity had a merely subjective source.

But in Gadamer's view, the 'subjectivisation' of art that results from considering works of art as the locus of a distinct aesthetic value is untrue to the phenomenology of art. Or better, it reflects an alienated and impoverished form in which works of art 'appear'. For it blinds us to a potential that is in fact inherent in all great works of art: their capacity to reveal. Instead of distancing ourselves from an artwork and assessing its 'aesthetic merit', we can open ourselves to the world the artwork discloses, and, in doing so, have our own experienceable world transformed. Gadamer uses the term '*Erfahrung*' to designate this kind of self-transformative experience, an experience he contrasts with the subjectivistically foreshortened '*Erlebnis*' experience of aesthetic consciousness. In Gadamer's view, we can only make sense of *Erfahrung* experience if we construe it as a form of understanding, and for this reason 'aesthetics has to be absorbed into hermeneutics'.[2]

In Gadamer's view, the absorption of aesthetics into hermeneutics forces us to rethink the very nature of the artwork. Under the influence of modern epistemology, we are accustomed to thinking of an artwork as a created object that confronts a subject, a subject whose experience of the object is contained in his or her consciousness. On this account, to the extent to which we are able to say that the work has a meaning, it must be something fixed by a 'state of mind'. For Gadamer, however, consciousness cannot be the locus of the meaning; be it that of the artist/author or the spectator/reader. For just as, when we are at play, we are in a sense taken over by the game (and so constituted by something that, so to speak, has a life of its own) so the work of art exceeds the contents of any particular consciousness: it has an existence or 'mode of being' that goes beyond the realm of mental representations. Furthermore, just as play is a natural, rudimentary form of self-presentation, so art essentially has the character of 'being addressed': an artwork exists inherently, if more or less directly, 'for' someone. The proximity between play and art suggests to Gadamer that the work of art has the ontology of an event: 'the event of being that occurs in presentation'.[3] In Gadamer's view, it is fundamentally mistaken to construe the temporal endurance of a work of art as anything like the permanence of a substantial object. Rather, art is play, as Gadamer calls it, 'transformed into structure'.[4] Transformation into structure ensures the artwork's ability to be made manifest in multiple ways. It also enables the artwork to make a claim on an addressee. But the validity of the claim is not independent of the involvement and concerns of the addressees themselves. It follows that while no artwork is ever fully complete, it always invites completion through its various modes of manifestation and reception.

Gadamer's philosophical hermeneutics questions the 'subjectivism' of aesthetic consciousness by alerting us to the fact that artworks have the power to disclose a world and therefore to express a claim on the recipient of the work. As an appropriate response to this claim, the *Erfahrung* experience of art is essentially a form of understanding. But crucially, the understanding that is embodied in the experience of art is not understanding in the sense recognised by modern epistemology. We do not overcome aesthetic consciousness with our original notion of understanding intact. On the contrary, the absorption of aesthetics into hermeneutics forces us to revise our idea of what it is to understand something as much as it challenges us to rethink our model of what it is to experience a work of art. If our notion of what it is to understand something is to include the experience of art (and anything less, in Gadamer's view, would be arbitrary and dogmatic) then it must be comprehensive enough to be able to articulate the fundamentally dialogical, context-related, and incomplete character of *Erfahrung* experience.

Meaning in History

The predicament of the historian also points to the need for a more expansive notion of human understanding. Gadamer distinguishes two ways in which historians can orient themselves in relation to their subject matter. On the one hand, they can regard it as containing a meaning that is already there, mummified so to speak, in the historical past, waiting to be found and resurrected. They can then gear their interpretative activity towards the reconstruction of the antecedently given meaning. Gadamer observes that the meaning of particular historical documents, as well as history as a whole, can be understood this way, and he tries to show that such an understanding helped shape the German hermeneutic tradition from Schleiermacher, through the 'historical' school of the nineteenth century, up to Dilthey. In Gadamer's view, Schleiermacher introduced the idea that the temporal distance that separates the interpreter from classical literary and theological texts makes the avoidance of misunderstanding imperative. And the avoidance of misunderstanding can be secured by way of a procedure that reproduces the meaning-creating act expressed in the text. According to this model, successful interpretations manage to divine, if not the intention of the author, then the idea that originally motivated the author's productive activity. The goal of interpretation is thus a kind of restoration of the original meaning. While the leading figures of the German historical school, the historians Ranke and Droyson, did not suppose that the meaning of texts or actions could be located in the psychology of the authors or agents, and while they also rejected the Hegelian notion that history had some *a priori* meaning, a *telos* directing history 'behind its back', so to speak, they too, according to Gadamer, were committed to a version of the restorative model. For although the historical school sought to replace *a priori* philosophical speculation about the meaning of history with piecemeal empirical historical research, it remained bound to the project of universal history, which in turn presupposed the point of view of an ideal historical spectator who impartially observes the historical truth. So long as historical research aims 'to reconstruct the great text of history from the fragments of tradition',[5] it remains essentially restorative.

Gadamer by no means simply rejects the hermeneutics of Schleiermacher, the historical school, and Dilthey (who, according to Gadamer, synthesised these two approaches). And he certainly does not deny the importance of impartial scholarship in the study of history. But he does think there is something questionable about the reconstructive, restorative model of historical understanding. As Gadamer insists, it is futile to try to capture the meaning of the past as it was in the past. And even if such restoration were possible, it would hardly matter unless it were in some way connected with a live concern in the present. Furthermore, the thought that the historian should find orientation and legitimation in relation to an impartial, 'God's eye view' on history is quite misconceived, for it confounds a fundamental structure of human understanding: its finitude. For Gadamer, the finitude of human understanding, and the non-recuperability of temporal distance, can be acknowledged if we can think of the historian's task not as the reconstruction of self-contained totalities of past meaning but as a kind of integration of the past and present. To think of the historian's relation to his or her subject matter in this way, to think of it, as Gadamer writes, as 'thoughtful mediation with contemporary life',[6] is to transform a merely external relation to the past into an internal relation of involvement and participation: we move from mere consciousness of something from the past to a historical experience (*Erfahrung*) of our emplacement in tradition. This is the crux of Gadamer's key notion of 'historically effected consciousness'.

In Gadamer's view, the integration of past and present signalled by the principle of historical effect describes the historian's actual predicament. After all, historians pursue their research with a particular set of problems, and a particular set of interests, that must already possess significance. In possessing significance, the historian's work points forwards as well as backwards in time. Historical research is always undertaken from a contemporary, context-specific standpoint, which must somehow be integrated with that of the texts or text-analogues under investigation. For this reason, 'the abstract antithesis between tradition and historical research, between history and the knowledge of it, must be discarded'.[7] Gadamer does not consider himself here to be prescribing a particular method for discovering truths about history. His ambition is rather to reclaim the historicity of historical truth itself.

Reason and Tradition

Gadamer grants that, in a certain sense, the historicity of human understanding had already been demonstrated by Heidegger. The 'hermeneutics of facticity' elaborated in *Being and Time* satisfied Gadamer that understanding is conditioned by existential structures of 'thrownness' and 'projection': it is by finding our way about a world that is historically given to us, and by anticipating its unfolding, that we first come to understand, and all theoretical modes of understanding are derived from this primordial engagement. Gadamer then draws on Heidegger's account to elucidate the situation of an interpreter in relation to a text. The process of reaching an understanding of the text, Gadamer submits, has its own 'background' conditions that are comparable to those identified by Heidegger in his hermeneutics of facticity. However, in Gadamer's view the Enlightenment ideals of reason and truth prevent us from seeing this background, for they discredit the very concepts that are needed to articulate it. The concepts in question are prejudice, authority and tradition, and one of the central chapters of *Truth and Method* is provocatively dedicated to their rehabilitation.

Gadamer's proposal is much less shocking than it might appear at first sight. In current usage, the term 'prejudice' means an unfounded judgement, one that expresses a false but dogmatically held pre-conception about something. Gadamer points out, however, that this negative connotation is an invention of the Enlightenment. Originally, the term was used in a legal context to designate a provisional judgement, that is, a verdict reached on the basis of the available evidence, pending a final verdict. A prejudice is literally something that precedes judgement: it is a 'pre-judgement' (in German, *Vor-Urteil*). If we think of a prejudice in accordance with the original usage, it does not carry a connotation of unfairness, irrationality and erroneousness. Naturally, it is prejudice in its original sense that Gadamer wants to rehabilitate. We need to rehabilitate it, Gadamer argues, because it articulates a crucial background condition of interpretation and understanding. Prior to formulating an interpretative judgement, the interpreter has to work with pre-judgements (prejudices) about what the text or text-analogue might mean. Far from being obstacles to understanding, such anticipations of meaning are indispensable for any understanding whatsoever: without some prejudice or other the interpreter would have no access to the subject matter of the text. Moreover, there is something universal about this feature of the hermeneutic situation: 'the historicity of our existence entails that prejudices, in the literal sense of the word, constitute the initial directedness of our whole ability to experience'.[8]

With the rehabilitation of prejudice, authority and tradition win back some of the dignity stripped from them by the Enlightenment. The Enlightenment presented authority and tradition, like prejudice, as hindrances to the individual's free pursuit of truth and self-understanding. But if Gadamer's account of prejudices is correct, this cannot be the right view. For the prejudices that give me access to a world are not simply mine. They exceed my particular consciousness and should therefore be considered as expressions of something larger than myself; namely, the tradition in which I stand. For this reason, tradition cannot but exercise some authority over the individual. Of course, this is not to say that the authority of tradition can never be rationally questioned or criticised. Gadamer's point is rather that the rigid opposition set up by the Enlightenment between reason and authority makes us misunderstand what goes on when rational reflection happens. The Enlightenment model suggests that in adopting a rational point of view we are transported from the space of historical tradition altogether, when in fact, Gadamer argues, reason refines, loosens, and extends that space. The hermeneutic acknowledgement that understanding is 'always already' historically situated only entails a subordination of reason to authority and tradition if we remain within the false Enlightenment paradigm.

Practical Philosophy

In Gadamer's view, a better paradigm is to be found in Aristotle's practical philosophy. In the *Nicomachian Ethics*, Aristotle argued that human existence is not just a matter of survival but of living well by rational standards: human beings have the capacity for 'good' life as well as 'mere' life. But how can we know what the good life consists of? Aristotle saw that it is easy to be misled by the form of this question. For it can lead us into thinking that we can have knowledge of the good in the same way in which, say, a geometrician has knowledge of space, or a craftsperson knows how to perform some skill. We can suppose, in other words, that acquiring knowledge of the good is like learning a theory or mastering a technique. But as Aristotle observed, this is to miss the distinctiveness of ethical knowledge. The person who excels in ethical knowledge, or as Aristotle put it, the person who possesses practical wisdom, attends in the right way to what a particular situation demands. The aim of practical deliberation is to determine the action that 'befits' the situation, that is, the 'proper' action or the 'right' thing to do in the circumstances. Unlike scientific problem-solving, such determination is not a matter of applying a general theory to a particular case. And unlike the skilled craftsperson, the person with practical wisdom does not have a pre-given conception of what the right outcome will be. On the Aristotelian model, as Gadamer influentially interprets it, knowledge of the good is not independent of the process of becoming good through one's education, choices and actions. In being socialised into the ethos of a culture, individuals acquire an ethical 'character' or 'comportment' that in the normal case makes them responsive to particular ethical demands. But to be so moulded is by no means to receive a blueprint of how to live. The rationally favoured response to a situation does not come pre-packaged, as if the right thing to do could be read off the situation by applying some general theory. Similarly, it is misguided to think that reason should be able to justify ethical demands independently of a socialised, and so historically situated, concerned point of view on them.

Gadamer thus turns to Aristotle's ethics to show how the universal and the particular are interdependent. It also provides Gadamer with a model for dealing with the basic problem of hermeneutics. With Aristotle as his guide, Gadamer maintains that the task of understanding a historical text is inseparable from the task of bringing out its contemporaneity. Just as in practical reason we do not first justify the general rule and then apply it to the particular case, so interpretation is not a two-stage process involving, first, an understanding of the text's objective or universal meaning, and, second, an application of this meaning to the interpreter's subjective position. Rather the universal and the particular, the meaning and the application, are brought together in the one act of understanding. As Gadamer puts it: 'application is neither a subsequent nor merely occasional part of the phenomenon of understanding, but codetermines it as a whole from the beginning'.[9] The truth of an interpretation therefore has the character of practical insight in Aristotle's sense rather than the character of an objective, scientific statement.

Language and Dialogue

For Gadamer, understanding brings about a mediation of the universal and the particular as well as the past and the present. But even more important, it mediates the self and the other. Gadamer emphasises that understanding is impossible without some initial apprehension of the alterity of the text to be understood. The process of reaching an understanding requires that the interpreter is open to the questions addressed by the text itself, and it proceeds by working with the text about the subject matter. In other words, understanding has an essentially dialogical structure, and the truth it aims at is nothing more or less than the outcome of a successful conversation. And just as it is absurd to suppose that human conversation has some pre-determined terminus, so understanding is an on-going, never completed task. This is an important point to grasp, in Gadamer's view, because, again under pressure from modern epistemology, we are inclined to think that successful understanding issues in some once and for all grasp of a self-contained meaning, the meaning objectively contained in the statements or propositions that make up the text. But such a monological model is not only misplaced as an ideal: it misdescribes the experience of arriving at an understanding, which at its best involves a self-transformative encounter with the alterity, not simply the externality, of the text. Gadamer uses the term 'fusion of horizons' to describe this structure: in the 'event' of understanding, the horizon of the self's experienceable world is transformed through contact with another. As we have seen, this occurs in a particularly vivid way in the experience of art.

For Gadamer, dialogue provides the model not just for textual interpretation but for language in general. Departing from mainstream modern theories of language, Gadamer denies that the basic unit of linguistic meaning is the word, statement or proposition. Rather, it is the conversation. It is in the course of conversational interaction, by expressing desires and purposes, forming social relations, and so forth, that humans become the linguistic beings they are. Even solitary reflection is a kind of dialogue of the soul with itself. And just as Aristotle provides a corrective to modern theory-centric notions of reason and truth, so, as Gadamer reads them, Plato's dialogues offer a compelling reminder of the importance of conversation for philosophy. For it was his engagement in the practice of philosophical conversation that enabled Socrates to reach the abiding insight of hermeneutics: since the other person may be right, and the conversation that we are is unending, human wisdom is 'a knowledge of our own ignorance'.[10]

Gadamer and Contemporary Critical Theory

Many of today's most influential critical theorists owe a debt to Gadamer's work. Jürgen Habermas quickly saw the relevance of Gadamer's hermeneutics for the Frankfurt School's critique of positivism and instrumental reason, and the 'communicative turn' in critical theory urged by Habermas was impelled by his reading of *Truth and Method*.[11] *Truth and Method* also helped to inspire the so-called 'post-analytic' philosophy of Richard Rorty, and more recently of John McDowell.[12] Of course not all contemporary philosophers and critical theorists read Gadamer so sympathetically: notably, Jacques Derrida has contested Gadamer's basic approach,[13] and Manfred Frank has sought to retrieve the heritage of 'Romantic' hermeneutics from what he takes to be Gadamer's Heideggerian misrepresentation of it.[14] Even Habermas, together with his successor at Frankfurt, Axel Honneth, has grave reservations about philosophical hermeneutics, both as a theory of language and as a resource for legitimating and sustaining social criticism. Since the contemporary reception of Gadamer's work is still very much shaped by Habermas' critique, let me begin my concluding remarks there.

Above all, Habermas is impressed by the dialogical, intersubjective model of reason that emerges from Gadamer's hermeneutics. Gadamer rightly saw that the Enlightenment's monological ideal of rationality, that is, roughly, reason as the mastery of an object by a sovereign, self-contained subject, was both false and oppressive. In Habermas' view, Gadamer took the right direction by seeking to replace it with a dialogical conception, one that took the process of reaching an understanding between subjects as paradigmatic for rationality. Nonetheless, Gadamer's hermeneutics is flawed, Habermas argues, because it fails to show how radical critical reflection is possible, that is to say, reflection with a critical power that exceeds all traditionally legitimated norms and social relations. In the 1960s, Habermas used the Marxist model of ideology critique, recast in communication-theoretic terms, to expose the limited scope of hermeneutic reflection. Later, and with more conviction, he would draw on the liberal ideal of universal justice. For Habermas, the justice of a norm is scrutible only from a point of view that abstracts from pre-given traditions. By failing to recognise this, Habermas argues, Gadamer's hermeneutics falls victim to a crippling moral relativism and it illicitly endorses a fundamentally conservative attitude towards tradition.

Whether or not there is any truth to the widely held view that philosophical hermeneutics is inherently conservative (I believe that careful consideration of the matter will show that there is probably very little)[15] there is no doubt that Gadamer does not see himself as a radical. Gadamer's philosophy, unlike the critical theories of Habermas and other members of the Frankfurt School, is not intended to provide a basis for the critique of 'false consciousness' or systematic injustice in the modern world. Gadamer's overriding concern is the fragmentation of tradition and the implications this has for historical experience. Unlike the so-called 'masters of suspicion', Marx, Nietzsche and Freud, Gadamer is not in the business of demystifying tradition: it is rather the retrieval of tradition, and the critique of alienated forms of historical consciousness, that guides him. Admittedly, Gadamer's preoccupation with the problem of historical experience puts him in close proximity to another thinker of the Frankfurt School, Walter Benjamin. But while Benjamin's diagnosis of the impoverishment of historicism bears striking resemblances to Gadamer's, he has no remedial use for the concept of tradition in Gadamer's sense.

There are also certain similarities between Gadamer's hermeneutics and Derrida's philosophy of deconstruction. Gadamer and Derrida both owe a lot to Heidegger's dismantling (*Destruktion*) of the Western philosophical tradition. However, Gadamer and Derrida have very different ideas of what that project amounted to and where it fell short. Roughly speaking, Derrida attempted to correct Heidegger by turning to structuralist semiotics, or the theory of signs, as well as Nietzschean perspectivism. Gadamer, by contrast, was never drawn to Nietzscheanism, and his approach to language side-steps the structuralist problematic. The resulting tension between deconstruction and hermeneutics is highlighted in a skirmish that took place between Derrida and Gadamer in 1981.[16] Derrida suggested that in having recourse to the will of the interpreter, Gadamer's hermeneutics remains ensnared in a pre-Heideggerian metaphysics of subjectivity. However convincing one finds Derrida's objection, to which Gadamer himself offered a careful and elaborate response, it does raise an issue about the role of meaning-generating structures that operate 'behind the back' of the interpreter. Arguably, Gadamer's overriding concern with the experience of understanding leaves him ill-equipped to deal with the anonymous structures of signification that bring so much grist to the mill for deconstructive theory. It could also be maintained that Gadamer's worries about modern subjectivism lead him to overcorrect it by placing too much weight on the norm of truth. But if, from a deconstructive point of view, philosophical hermeneutics is therefore normalising and insufficiently distanced from logocentrism, for Gadamer the Nietzschean abandonment of the ideality of truth, and the structuralist reduction of meaning to content-independent structures of signification, reflects a formalism that has its roots in the very form of thinking deconstruction seeks to attack.

Rorty's take on *Truth and Method* is different again. Rorty embraces Gadamer's hermeneutics because it helps liberate philosophy from the shackles of foundationalism. Instead of viewing philosophy as a kind of master discourse that lays down the foundations of knowledge and arbitrates between the claims of different disciplines and cultures, Gadamer shows how philosophy can get by with a more modest self-image, one that is content to serve reminders of the open-endedness and diversity of human enquiry. If we follow Gadamer's lead and view human enquiry as nothing more or less than an on-going conversation, Rorty argues, we are less likely to be bewitched by the metaphysical thoughts that there is one true theory of things and one true goal of human life. Gadamer's hermeneutics thus provides a kind of model for what philosophy would be like in a liberal utopia. However, while such a minimalist spirit of openness does define what Gadamer calls the 'soul of hermeneutics', it is questionable that *Truth and Method* is most profitably read as a manifesto for philosophical relativism. For to read it that way is to risk losing from view the core phenomenological problem that motivates Gadamer's work: recovery of the experience of understanding.

Notes

1. Gadamer, *Philosophical Hermeneutics*, p. 3.
2. Gadamer, *Truth and Method*, p. 164.
3. Ibid., p. 116.
4. Ibid., p. 110.
5. Ibid., p. 218.
6. Ibid., p. 169.
7. Ibid., p. 282.
8. Gadamer, *Philosophical Hermeneutics*, p. 9.
9. Gadamer, *Truth and Method*, p. 324.
10. Gadamer, *Philosophical Apprenticeships*, p. 185.
11. See Habermas, 'A Review of Gadamer's *Truth and Method*', in Fred Dallmayr and Thomas McCarthy (eds), *Understanding and Social Inquiry* (Notre Dame: Notre Dame University Press, 1977), and 'The Hermeneutic Claim to Universality', in Joseph Bleicher (ed.), *Contemporary Hermeneutics* (London: Routledge, 1980).
12. See Richard Rorty, *Philosophy and the Mirror of Nature* (Princeton: Princeton University Press, 1979); John McDowell, *Mind and World* (Cambridge, MA: Harvard University Press, 1994).
13. See Derrida, 'Three Questions to Hans-Georg Gadamer', in Diane P. Michelfelder and Richard E. Palmer (eds), *Dialogue and Deconstruction* (Albany: SUNY Press, 1989), pp. 52–4.
14. See Manfred Frank and Andrew Bowie (eds), *The Subject and the Text* (Cambridge: Cambridge University Press, 1998).

15. See Nicholas H. Smith, *Strong Hermeneutics* (London: Routledge, 1997).
16. See the texts collected in *Dialogue and Deconstruction.*

Major Works by Gadamer

Truth and Method, 2nd edn, trans. Joel Weinsheimer and Donald G. Marshall (London: Sheed and Ward, 1989 [1960]).

Philosophical Hermeneutics, trans. and ed. David E. Linge (Berkeley, CA: University of California Press, 1976). Contains lucid recapitulations of *Truth and Method.*

Philosophical Apprenticeships, trans. Robert R. Sullivan (Cambridge, MA: MIT Press, 1985 [1977]). A highly readable intellectual autobiography.

Hermeneutics, Religion and Ethics, trans. Joel Weinsheimer (New Haven and London: Yale University Press, 1999). Contains the important essay 'On the Possibility of a Philosophical Ethics'.

Suggestions for Further Reading

Grondin, Jean, *Introduction to Philosophical Hermeneutics*, trans. Joel Weinsheimer (New Haven and London: Yale University Press, 1994 [1991]). An accessible brief history of the hermeneutic tradition sympathetic to Gadamer.

Michelfelder, Diane P., and Palmer, Richard E. (eds), *Dialogue and Deconstruction: The Gadamer-Derrida Encounter* (Albany, NY: SUNY Press, 1989). Texts by Gadamer and Derrida with extensive commentary. Advanced.

Smith, Nicholas H., *Strong Hermeneutics: Contingency and Moral Identity* (London and New York: Routledge, 1997). Situates hermeneutics in contemporary debates about ethics.

Warnke, Georgia, *Gadamer: Hermeneutics, Tradition and Reason* (Cambridge: Polity Press, 1987). A clear exposition of *Truth and Method*, good on Habermas' and Rorty's responses to it.

13

Ludwig Wittgenstein (1889–1951)

Simon Tormey

Wittgenstein in the Critical Tradition

It is difficult to locate Wittgenstein in the critical tradition that constitutes the background to contemporary critical theory, not least because he was a maverick figure in relation to that tradition, of which he remained deeply sceptical. His philosophical debts would appear to be mainly to Russell and Frege in the early stage of his work, from whom he took an emphasis on the logical structure of meaningful language, and to Moore's commonsense philosophy for his later work on ordinary language philosophy. Schopenhauer, whose key idea is that the fundamental reality is will, was the philosopher with whom the younger Wittgenstein was most taken, and from whom he seems to have developed an interest in the mystical aspects of life that evade human understanding. Perhaps he also absorbed the sense that what Nietzsche (who was also initially attracted to Schopenhauer) calls the philosophical will to truth cannot be sated.

At the same time, Wittgenstein's work was always a response to what he generally took to be the errors of philosophy, including his own. In that sense, he shares certain affinities with Nietzsche's critical genealogy of philosophy, in that both undermine the view that philosophy represents an assured route to truth. For example, the later Wittgenstein denounced the view that mathematics or logic are a paradigmatic language for describing the world, rather than being a particular language game, just as Nietzsche had claimed that physics is a way of interpreting the world. Nietzsche also regarded the philosophical notion of the subject as a fiction which rested on human faith that the world resembles the grammar of language. For Wittgenstein too, philosophy was led astray by the metaphysics of the subject, into the presupposition that the subject separated from the world of objects represented the latter to itself through language. In Wittgenstein's view, the subjects using language, the world represented through language and language itself are all aspects of the same world. In terms of the critical tradition covered in this volume, all efforts from Kant onwards to overcome Cartesian dualism by reconciling subject and object, or mind and matter, were attempts to solve a puzzle that philosophy had made for itself.

Additional philosophical affinities between Wittgenstein and others come to light given his implicit critique of the metaphysics of the subject and his stress on language and other practices. Wittgenstein held that philosophical puzzles could be solved best by returning concepts to their everyday context of use, in language games bounded by forms of life. Wittgenstein's forms of life bear some resemblance to Husserl's notion of *Lebenswelt*, just as Husserl's stress on the intersubjective character of meaning and language is paralleled by Wittgenstein's argument that language cannot be private. Wittgenstein's comparability with phenomenological hermeneutics is more pronounced in relation to Gadamer, for whom objective understanding is prior to knowledge. Just as Wittgenstein held that there are certain shared presuppositions that cannot be doubted from within forms of life if any statements are to be meaningful, Gadamer argued that historical traditions of intersubjective understanding are preconditions for judgements about what is to be regarded as true or false. On another level, Wittgenstein's perception of his philosophical approach as therapeutic was informed by the manner rather than content of Freud's work. Philosophical investigation could uncover the deviation of concepts from their everyday use, thereby allowing philosophers to see how they had become captivated by a picture.

Introduction

Wittgenstein is undoubtedly one of the most important and controversial thinkers of the twentieth century and one whose work has had an enormous impact on debates in critical theory. An iconic figure who published only one major piece of work during his lifetime, the *Tractatus Logico-Philosophicus* (*TLP*), he is nonetheless one of the key figures behind the so-called 'linguistic turn' which transformed critical theory in the latter half of the twentieth century.

Wittgenstein was born to one of the wealthiest families of the Austro-Hungarian Empire in 1881 and trained in Austria and Manchester as an engineer before turning to the philosophy of mathematics. It was this latter interest that led him to the door of Bertrand Russell with whom he studied in Cambridge until, with the onset of the Great War, he signed up for service in the Austro-Hungarian army. It was while serving as a soldier that Wittgenstein completed the *TLP*, a work that convinced him that he had solved the fundamental problems of philosophy. For the next ten years Wittgenstein pursued a variety of careers including spells as a gardener, school teacher and an architect for his sister's house in Vienna. It was not until the late 1920s that he was coaxed back into philosophy as the presuppositions of his earlier work seemed progressively less convincing both to his followers and to himself. It was these doubts that slowly convinced him to reject the findings of *TLP* and to develop a radically different account of the relationship between language and the world over the 1930s and 1940s. Although none of the work of his later years was published during his lifetime, the most important statement of his later philosophy, *Philosophical Investigations*, was published shortly after his death in 1951. Thereafter a stream of other work was published under the auspices of former students and colleagues, including, most notably, *The Blue and Brown Books*, which mark the transition between the early and later work, *Philosophical Grammar*, *On Certainty*, and *Remarks on the Foundations of Mathematics.*

Language, World, Form

Whilst the subject matter of the *TLP* is easily rendered, its contents are anything but. Despite being helpfully short, the *TLP* is virtually impenetrable to those without a training in logic and symbolic notation. Even the sections which are not rendered in such terms are likely to strike the non-specialist as at best opaque and at worst unintelligible. To describe the work in such terms is not, it should be noted, to offend against the memory of its author, for one of the paradoxes to be unravelled in discussing the *TLP* is that Wittgenstein himself describes the work as 'nonsense'. This is not, on the other hand, to say that it lacks rigour or interest. Far from it: the *TLP* is clearly one of the most extraordinary pieces of literature of the twentieth century. It may be, as his commentators admit, 'sibylline' and 'marmoreal', but even to those who understand little of its content it is clearly a work of genius.[1]

For the purposes of explication *TLP* contains two doctrines of importance for understanding the later philosophy and beyond that the 'linguistic turn'. The first is that of 'logical form' and the second the 'picture theory of language'. Following the lead of Russell and Gottlob Frege, Wittgenstein wanted to describe the relationship between language and the world in a fashion that would make clear the limits of what could meaningfully be said. Finding the limits of what could be said would in turn help delineate the function of critical enquiry generally and philosophy in particular, the hypothesis being that philosophy arises where there is a confusion concerning what is 'out there' (§1.1). The starting point for this enquiry is the notion of the world as the totality of 'facts', not of 'things'. To describe the world is to represent a given state of affairs using a combination of elemental atoms or words. These words are combined in 'logical form', which is to say that they conform to the nature of logical propositions which assert something 'to be the case'. If something is indeed the case, then by extension it is a fact about the world: it describes something that may or may not be true. In turn whether a fact is true depends on whether it can be said to picture the world accurately. As Wittgenstein remarks at §4.021, 'A proposition is a picture of reality: for if I understand a proposition, I know that the situation that it represents. And I understand the proposition without having had its sense explained to me.' The sentence 'Simon is typing these words' clearly possesses logical form because it gives us a proposition about a given state of affairs; it is also a fact in that it describes something true about the world. The sentence accurately pictures the world. If it did not, then it would strike us as nonsense or in some other way deficient. The point is that words can stand in many different combinations, but only some of those combinations will make sense, will constitute 'facts'. The function of language as Wittgenstein sees it is to provide the building blocks for describing the world, to describe the totality of 'facts', and part of the purpose of the *TLP* is to demonstrate that, to be meaningful, language can have no other function. This in turn implies that uses of language that do not have as their function the 'picturing' of the world must be nonsense.

It is in this description of the role of language that the central paradox of the *TLP* lies, for in describing language as picturing the world, it is implicit that any attempt to describe language itself must be metaphysical or nonsense. How, in other words, could statements about statements be true when they themselves fail to 'picture' anything? Consistent to the end Wittgenstein declares in conclusion that his own work is nonsense and should thus be thrown off like a ladder 'to see the world aright' (§6.54). Similarly, all forms of metaphysics, that is all attempts to talk about the nature of the world generally or about the nature of human relationships to it, are nonsense. The concerns of religion, ethics and philosophy can only be 'shown' in some non-linguistic sense. What a non-linguistic sense could amount to is never broached. The inference, however, is that the 'truths' of, say, religious teaching are not made apparent through the picturing of a state of affairs, but through the sense religion has for us as individuals. As Wittgenstein intones in the final ringing sentence of the *TLP*: 'Whereof we cannot speak thereof we shall remain silent' (§7).

The significance of the *TLP* is more immediate and striking for philosophy than for critical theory, for it pushed to the very limits a particular conception of language and thus a particular conception of the function of philosophy. Philosophers in the analytic tradition had long attempted to draw a parallel between logic and language with a view to developing an ideal or pure language that would accurately picture the world as it really is, as opposed to how it has long been described by metaphysicians, philosophers and the like. It was this hubristic project that Wittgenstein 'realised' in the *TLP*, albeit through the call for language to be purged of its sulphurous particularities and idiosyncrasies. It also suggested that philosophy itself had no function or subject matter of its own and thus that all it could aspire to being is a 'therapeutic' form of practice or immanent critique of philosophy itself. Some philosophers would helpfully remind other philosophers of the limitations of doing 'philosophy' as that term had traditionally been understood. In short, the *TLP* initiated a radically iconoclastic discourse not only on the aims and objectives of philosophical discourse, but on the very future of philosophy as a discipline and mode of reflection. Like all iconoclastic doctrines there were those who enthusiastically supported its prescriptions, not least the so-called Vienna Circle (Carnap, Schlick, Waissman and so on) whose own doctrine, 'logical positivism', bore similarities to that announced in the *TLP*. The *TLP* was, more generally, in tune with the tenor of the times, for in its high modernism, its arrogant sweeping away of old certainties and doctrines, it played the role philosophically that new movements such as constructivism and futurism played culturally. It was a manifesto for those alienated by the excesses of ornamentation, decadence and mystification associated with the philosophical *ancien régime*. The *TLP* was in its own way revolutionary; but it in turn legitimated a set of assumptions and beliefs which proved just as objectionable as those so recently displaced.

The End of the Beginning: Language as Practice

As became evident to Wittgenstein in the course of discussions with a succession of friends and colleagues who sought him out in his self-imposed 'exile', the *TLP*'s greatest strength, its startlingly lucid account of the limits of language, was also its greatest weakness. What became increasingly apparent to Wittgenstein was that the role he had assigned to language, namely picturing the world, described only one of its functions. The more he looked at the matter, however, the more it seemed that language performed a range of functions, only one of which could be described in such fashion. It was also clear that rather than possessing 'logical form', the rules and procedures of language were determined by those functions rather than the reverse. The various transitionary works of the 1930s and 1940s such as *The Blue and Brown Books* and *Philosophical Grammar* show this dawning realisation graphically as a monocausal explanation of the function of language is transformed into a progressively richer account of language's possibilities and potentialities. It was this anomaly that was to become the basis for Wittgenstein's account of 'language games', which in turn is one of the most important and influential findings of his later philosophy. The culmination of this challenging of the descriptive, picturing function of language is reached in *Investigations,* where Wittgenstein unceremoniously demolishes the one-dimensionality of his former account by reference to the myriad forms in which language is used. Language, as he now insists, should be looked at as a set of tools for performing a range of different functions. At §23 he asks:

> But how many kinds of sentence are there? Say assertion, question and command? There are countless kinds: countless different kinds of use of what we call 'symbols', 'words', 'sentences'. And this multiplicity is not something fixed, given once and for all; but new types of language, new language games, as we may say, come into existence, and others become obsolete and get forgotten ... Here the term 'language game' is meant to bring into prominence the fact that the speaking of language is part of an activity, or of a form of life.

In a radical inversion of the account given in the *TLP,* the principal claim of the later philosophy is thus that it is a mistake to see meaning as in some sense determined by the world. Rather meaning is now seen as determined by 'use'.

So what then is 'use'? Where does use come from? What became increasingly apparent to Wittgenstein was that to invoke the use of a term, the meaning of a word, was to invoke the extant practices and customs of a *Lebenswelt*, or 'form of life', hence it is to these practices and customs that we must look to find the meaning of any given word. The meaning of the term 'white' should not, in other words, be regarded as being determined by some inherent 'whiteness' lying in the world, but rather by the manner in which the term is used within a form of life. By extension knowing what 'white' is is not a question of understanding the essence of colour, but of learning how the word is used through examples, questions and so on. What Wittgenstein was keen to avoid, however, was giving the impression that ultimately all language is in some sense equivalent to all others, so that we could still (*pace TLP*) imagine the generation of a universal language able to traverse the totality of different ways of living. Wittgenstein wants, rather, to stress the diversity and plurality of possible forms of life and hence the plurality and diversity of language and meaning, making such an enterprise ultimately futile if not nonsensical. It is for this reason that a feature of Wittgenstein's later work is his constant reference to possible or imagined communities that are radically different to our own. This is particularly important to arguments he makes in relation, for example, to the boundedness of mathematics which philosophers such as Russell, Frege and of course Wittgenstein himself considered the paradigmatic language for describing the world 'as it is'. In the work of the later Wittgenstein even mathematics is, somewhat shockingly, regarded as the product of a particular form of life, just another language game with its own rules and procedures. The point he makes is that what we call maths is still our maths, the maths of our culture, and as such it is only one possible mathematics. Other cultures may have other needs and other conceptions of quantity and quality, and in these cases they would inevitably have developed a different mathematics. What is determinant therefore is not 'the world', but rather our needs, which in the context of mathematics means the uses that calculation and computation may serve for us.

The above discussion is in turn important in highlighting what might otherwise remain puzzling in Wittgenstein's analysis, which is the question of the boundary between 'forms of life'. The emphasis on language in Wittgenstein's work is such that it is tempting to equate the term 'form of life' with linguistic communities, so that the French would be regarded as one form of life and the Germans or the Russians quite another. As the discussion above makes clear, this is not what Wittgenstein has in mind. His point is rather that a form of life is built on a particular *Weltanschauung* which may or may not be shared across a linguistic divide. The Germans and French may on this view have a similar *Weltanschauung* in the sense that what French and German people do, how they conceive of the world, is in broad terms similar. Both, for example, compute and calculate in the same way and so both deploy the same maths. It is for this reason that French can be satisfactorily translated into the German (give or take problems of nuance). The same could not be said of French and, say, Azandi. Here the differences in *Weltanschauung* may make translation of certain terms much more difficult because of the lack of, as it were, equivalence between the two forms of life. Some practices in one culture simply do not have an equivalence in the other, and where practices depart radically so too does the prospect of mutual understanding. As Wittgenstein idiosyncratically puts it, 'If a lion could talk, we could not understand him' (s. II ix).

The description of Wittgenstein as a 'cultural relativist' is therefore accurate, but not perhaps in the way in which that term is ordinarily employed. It is not, for example, important to Wittgenstein's argument that the differences between communities are more significant than the similarities, or even that human diversity and plurality is somehow intrinsic to the human condition. His argument is not concerned with demonstrating the plural and diverse nature of the world as such, but rather that what is 'in the world' is a product of culture and not the other way around. If it could somehow be shown that 'culture' is in the process of 'universalisation' (as post-Hegelians have long argued), then we could imagine the development of a universal language. Yet the point would still be that even this development would not invalidate what Wittgenstein has to say about the relationship between language and world and, by extension, about the availability of 'different' worlds and realities. Even were everyone to speak the same language, this would not in itself change the nature of the relationship between language and world, which is to say that 'the world' remains the world as it appears to us, rather than as it is in some extra-cultural sense.

'Letting the Fly out of the Bottle'

This view of the relation between language and world has crucial ramifications for considering the role of philosophy. Intriguingly, Wittgenstein's view of what philosophy is able to achieve remains similar if not, indeed, the same as that articulated in *TLP*. On this later view philosophical problems are still regarded as essentially metaphysical in character, though in *Investigations* Wittgenstein characterises such problems not as 'nonsense' per se, but more picturesquely as instances of language 'going on holiday' or 'idling' (§38, 132). Philosophy, he argues, arises through the 'bewitchment' of language (§109). This is to say that it is the product of our dwelling on the essence of terms such as 'being', 'existence' and 'thought', instead of looking at how they are used within everyday language. The similarity with the view expressed in *TLP* rests with the conviction that philosophy is bereft of a subject matter of its own. There are no specifically philosophical issues or questions and thus the role of the philosopher consists merely in 'assembling reminders' for those who would insist that the nature of the world remains hidden from view, difficult to access or otherwise obscured. As Wittgenstein bluntly puts in *Investigations*: 'Philosophy simply puts everything before us, and neither explains nor deduces anything. – Since everything lies open to view there is nothing to be explained. For what is hidden, for example, is of no interest to us' (§126).

As in *TLP* so in the later work, philosophy appears as a therapeutic practice, essentially a method for resolving the perplexities caused by too much straining after the 'real' meaning of the world, as if such a meaning could be found independently of the uses to which it is ordinarily put. Philosophy is thus the intellectual equivalent of the fly buzzing around in a bottle. The fly makes a great deal of noise, but ultimately to no great effect or use. Philosophy should be dedicated to letting the fly out of the bottle: it should illustrate the way in which words are used so that the 'buzzing' ceases (§309). Philosophy should be a method for curing the imprecise, the incomprehensible and the incoherent. It should bring us back to what we always-already know as members of a linguistic community. In this sense, 'philosophy leaves everything as it is'. The difference between the *TLP* and *Investigations* thus concerns that outcome rather than the form of philosophical practice. Whilst both regard philosophy as in essence a method for curing puzzlement, they differ as to what it is that is privileged as the source of transparency. In *TLP* it is the idea of a perfect language, of language as a 'pane of glass' (to invoke Orwell) through which the world can be seen. In *Investigations* it is the always-already extant grammar of the diverse language games of our way of life that provides the basis for clarity.

The 'Linguistic Turn' and Critique

The importance of the view of language and the role of philosophy associated with Wittgenstein's later thought are difficult to underestimate. First, the notion that reality is determined by language challenges several cherished notions of Western philosophy. The first is the notion that the world exists independently of the subject and thus has to be interpreted by him or her, such interpretations being more or less accurate depending on the degree of knowledge or self-consciousness possessed by the subject. Such a conception of the subject appears in various guises from Descartes' positing of subjective experience as prior to knowledge of the world through Kant's notion of 'Das Ding-an-Sich' ('the thing-in-itself'), Hegel's concept of the subject coming to Absolute Knowledge and Marx's concept of 'false consciousness'. Wittgenstein's work clearly anticipates the findings of structuralist and poststructuralist theory in positing subjectivisation as a process of insertion into a pre-existing sociality. On a Wittgensteinian view there is no beyond or outside of the world into which we are inserted, and thus the prospects of generating subjects who are in a sense in control of their own 'world' is rejected. The post-Renaissance view of humanity as author of the world is reversed, placing in question the entire edifice of expectations that compose what modernists and postmodernists alike refer to as the 'Enlightenment Project'.

Second, the notion of philosophy as a privileged domain giving access to universal truths or insights into the condition of existence is similarly rejected not merely as élitist, but as wholly misguided. The point of Wittgenstein's repeated admonition to regard the world as 'open to view' is to stress that philosophy itself contributes nothing in terms of clarifying or demystifying the world. Far from it: on Wittgenstein's reading philosophers have succeeded merely in producing bewilderment and bafflement as the link between language and activity becomes obscured to the point where words become unhinged from the context and usage in which they make sense. The notion of philosophy as a therapeutic corrective to the wilfully obscure manipulations of the 'philosophers' is a recurring motif in critical theory, and his position echoes the scepticism regarding the claims of philosophy found in earlier thinkers. Marx, for example, famously juxtaposed philosophy and *praxis* in the eleventh thesis on Feuerbach ('the philosophers have only *interpreted* the world ...'), and in *The German Ideology* he characterises the relationship between philosophy and 'the study of the real world' as analogous to that between 'masturbation' and 'sexual love', which gives some indication of Marx's hostility to academic philosophy.[2]

The notion of philosophy as a therapeutic method which has as its object the critique of metaphysics also links in obvious ways to Nietzsche and post-Nietzschean philosophy. Nietzsche had a similarly dim view of the 'achievements' of philosophy and the metaphysical assumptions that underpinned it. His exasperation with the self-evidently ideological function that philosophy plays in justifying and legitimating various forms of domination builds from similar premises about foundational discourse generally. Nietzsche is no doubt more significant as a direct inspiration for the development of deconstruction, yet the connections and overlaps are readily apparent. Despite their very different intellectual and philosophical backgrounds, Derrida and Wittgenstein share the vision of philosophical critique as method (as Henry Staten shows), but a method directed against the self-image of philosophy itself.[3] In both, philosophy is transformed into an immanent critique *of* philosophy, one whose result is not, however, negation as reconfirming the status quo (as implied in the statement 'philosophy leaves everything as it is'); but negation as the necessary prelude to thought, reflection and action freed from the dead hand of 'philosophy'.

Wittgenstein's significance in relation to critical theory nonetheless extends considerably further than the notion of philosophical method underpinning both the early and the later philosophy, but also to the substantive claims he makes about the relationship between language and the world. If the world is constituted through language then of course this privileges the distinctiveness of linguistically discrete communities and at the same time undermines the post-Enlightenment goal of 'universalism'. In this sense Wittgenstein can be seen as anticipating the thrust of postcolonial theory in wanting to reject the tendency within critical theory to privilege the experience of occidental culture (*qua* universal culture), in favour of a series of subordinate or 'subaltern' cultures. This is certainly a reading which Wittgenstein's thought lends itself to, as the thrust of the later work is to emphasise that differences between cultures and communities cannot be translated in terms of the relative position of those cultures vis-à-vis some extra-cultural norm. The strong impression Wittgenstein's work gives is that of a thinker deeply appreciative and protective of 'difference' in all its manifestations, not least in terms of cultural difference. Of course this defence of difference is read by some as a sign of Wittgenstein's innate conservatism, for what it also seems to imply is that we should defend any and all forms of social practice no matter how objectionable to the occidental gaze. As I suggested in a previous section, Wittgenstein's defence of difference is not in fact a defence of cultural difference per se, of 'tradition', or of the immutability of social practices. It is a defence of the idea of the availability of different forms of cultural, linguistic and symbolic orders and hence of the arbitrariness of social life itself. This is to say that social life or ways of living resist reduction to something outside of themselves, to something like 'tradition' on the one hand or, say, 'production' on the other. There is no outside of sociality, no code by which we can read the 'real' or underlying meaning of social existence. As Wittgenstein himself puts it: 'What has to be accepted, the given, is – so one could say – *forms of life*' (s. II xi).

A final point in relation to the above is that Wittgenstein's later thought is evidently a key resource for the development of anti-essentialist forms of critique. Wittgenstein, as we have noted, was himself preoccupied with the critique of 'essentialism' in the human sciences, which he took to be the theoretical equivalent of metaphysics in philosophy. The thrust of his observations on social life in the later work is the futility of attempting to explain social practices in terms that go beyond the account given by participants in those practices themselves. All action, he seems to be claiming, is situated in a given context and can only be made sense of within that context. In this sense the role of the social researcher is not 'explanation', or revealing the 'cause' of particular social 'effects', but rather an appreciation of social action from the stance of empathy and understanding of the particular way of life under investigation. In this sense Wittgenstein's work links to concerns of the hermeneutic tradition and in particular to that of Hans-Georg Gadamer, whose ideas concerning the centrality of *Verstehen* to social investigation is similar to that of Wittgenstein. Both stress the limited function that explanation may play in a context where it is people, cultures and societies that are the object of study. It also links to the poststructuralist stress on revealing the discursive structures that underpin social life to evade the trap of an essentialist discourse that insists on pan-cultural points of 'first origin' to ground explanation. Foucault's proposed schema for the human sciences, namely the pursuit of critique that is 'archaeological in its method' and 'genealogical in its design', is one that mirrors Wittgenstein's concern to contain the imperialism of metanarratives.[4]

Wittgenstein and Critical Theory

Wittgenstein cannot be meaningfully described as a 'critical theorist' in most of the senses in which that term is used. But what should by now be apparent is how his work cross-cuts and intersects with the concerns of those who are more readily identified in such terms. What is also undeniable is that his work has been a direct influence on many of the latter over the course of the second half of the twentieth century. Of these one of the most significant receptions of Wittgenstein's work has been that of Jürgen Habermas in defence of his project to develop a theory of communicative action. Of course a number of thinkers and schools influenced Habermas' move to develop an intersubjective basis for critical theory, not least Weber and the American pragmatists, but the debt to Wittgenstein is clear. What impressed Habermas was evidently Wittgenstein's insistence on the always-already constructed domain of the social and in turn on the irreducibility of social life to something outside of itself. This appeared to undercut the Marxian insistence on the availability of an 'origin' in production and thus on the idea of emancipation as the recovery of a lost 'Man' rooted in the collective recovery of the productive process. Instead Habermas argued that emancipatory theory should be orientated to the revitalisation of the realm of communication, of discourse and argumentation and thus of the symbolic order itself. It has to concentrate on the properties of sociality and in particular of speech which under alienated conditions is 'distorted' by hidden interests or manipulation. In this way Wittgenstein's work was invoked to reshape the basis of emancipatory theory.

Side by side with the attempts of 'traditional' or emancipatory critical theory to deploy Wittgenstein for progressive causes has been the utilisation of his work in the service of postmodern theory. The work of Jean-François Lyotard is particularly marked by his reading of Wittgenstein and indeed pays explicit homage to

Wittgenstein (*Just Gaming*). For Lyotard, Wittgenstein's thought speaks to the irreducibility of difference in human life. 'Sameness' is a discursive construct serving political purposes rather than a property of objects or people. Wittgenstein is a philosopher who, in his own words, 'teaches differences', and thus who destabilises the constructs of thought, who resists closure of all kind and thus who accentuates the contingent, open nature of existence. In this sense he is, to Lyotard and others, an ally of the postmodern, which revels in the play of differences, the play of signs and the openness of social forms. What in particular Lyotard takes from Wittgenstein is the concept of language games and by extension the notion of language as 'decentred', non-linear, fragmented. Such a characterisation of language and social life again undercut the Marxian metanarrative of 'progress', which Lyotard was keen to attack. We can note, however, that Lyotard is not uncritical in this borrowing. Indeed in later work he dispenses with the idea of games, which imply a knowingness and intentionality on the part of actors, with the idea of regimes of 'phrases'. Nonetheless, Lyotard's debt, and the debt of much postmodern theory, to Wittgenstein is clear.

Wittgenstein's influence is also clear in the work of Richard Rorty, an Anglo-American philosopher happy to engage with 'continental' theorists and themes. Wittgenstein's importance for Rorty lies, first, in his augmenting of the pragmatist account on the nature of the relationship between language and the world and thus in giving fresh ammunition to those critical of the universalist tendencies of post-Enlightenment philosophy. Rorty endorses Wittgenstein's view of philosophy as essentially an on-going discourse concerned with the clarification of concepts and ideas, rather than a discipline with its own subject matter. It should not in other words attempt to provide a final account of the Truth or the fundamental questions of life, but rather to partake in the eternal conversation about how we should live, about what the limits of knowledge are, about what ideals and values it is worth upholding or rejecting. As for Lyotard, so for Rorty, the importance of Wittgenstein's work is in the manner in which it resists closure and totalisation through the constant reassertion of an anti-essentialist, anti-foundationalist stance. Where they may be said to differ is in regard to the normative project that such a stance sustains. Whereas Lyotard is keen to maintain a critical stance vis-à-vis liberal-capitalist institutions and practices, for Rorty the latter represent the best guarantee against the form of theoretical and political closure that Wittgenstein was so keen to undermine. In short, for Rorty Wittgenstein is the archetype of an ironical 'bourgeois' liberal content with the flux and uncertainty of liberal culture. Whichever account seems persuasive, what is evident is that Wittgenstein's work has been and remains a crucial resource for the development of post-foundational forms of critique and beyond that, post-foundational forms of normative discourse.

Notes

1. P. M. S. Hacker, entry for 'Wittgenstein' in T. Honderich (ed.), *The Oxford Companion to Philosophy* (Oxford: Oxford University Press, 1995), p. 913.
2. Karl Marx and Friedrich Engels, *The German Ideology*, ed. C. J. Arthur (London: Laurence and Wishart, 1974 [1846]), p. 103.
3. Henry Staten, *Wittgenstein and Derrida* (Lincoln, NE: University of Nebraska Press, 1986).
4. Michel Foucault, 'What is Enlightenment?' in Paul Rabinow (ed.), *The Foucault Reader* (New York: Pantheon Books, 1984), p. 46.

Major Works by Wittgenstein

The Blue and Brown Books, ed. R. Rhees (Oxford: Blackwell, 1975 [1958]).

Culture and Value, ed. G. H. von Wright, trans. P. Winch (Oxford: Blackwell, 1980).

Lectures and Conversations on Aesthetics, Psychology and Religious Belief, ed. C Barrett (Oxford: Blackwell, 1966).

On Certainty, ed. G. E. M. Anscombe and G. H. von Wright (Oxford: Blackwell, 1969).

Philosophical Grammar, ed. R. Rhees, trans. A. Kenny (Oxford: Blackwell, 1969).

Philosophical Investigations, ed. G. E. M. Anscombe and R. Rhees, trans. G. E. M. Anscombe (Oxford: Blackwell, 1953).

Remarks on the Foundations of Mathematics, ed. G. H. von Wright, R. Rhees and G. E. M. Anscombe, trans. G. E. M. Anscombe (Oxford: Blackwell, 1978 [1958]).

Remarks on the Philosophy of Psychology, vol. 1, ed. G. E. M. Anscombe and G. H. von Wright, trans. G. E. M. Anscombe (revised edition) (Oxford: Blackwell, 1978 [1956]).

Tractatus Logico-Philosophicus, trans. D. Pears and B. McGuinness (London: Routledge, 1961 [1922]).

Zettel, ed. G. E. M. Anscombe and G. H. von Wright, trans. G. E. M. Anscombe (Oxford: Blackwell, 1981 [1967]).

Suggestions for Further Reading

Brill, Susan, *Wittgenstein and Critical Theory* (Athens, OH: University of Ohio Press, 1995). An interesting attempt to utilise Wittgenstein's work in the service of literary theory and critique.

Cavell, Stanley, *The Claim of Reason: Wittgenstein, Skepticism, Morality and Tragedy* (Oxford: Oxford University Press, 1979). A highly influential work of interpretation showing the significance of Wittgenstein's work for contemporary philosophy.

Glendinning, Simon, *On Being with Others: Heidegger, Wittgenstein, Derrida* (London: Routledge, 1998). A useful analysis of the overlaps and continuities between Wittgenstein and continental theory.

Grayling, A. C., *Wittgenstein* (Oxford: Oxford University Press, 1988). One of the better short introductions to Wittgenstein's thought.

Habermas, Jürgen, *The Theory of Communicative Action,* 2 vols (Cambridge: Polity, 1995/1998). Massive, multi-layered attempt to redevelop the basis of social theory through the integration of pragmatic and linguistic philosophy.

Heaston, Susan, *Humanist Marxism and Wittgensteinian Social Philosophy* (Manchester: Manchester University Press, 1983). Shows the affinity of Wittgenstein's iconoclastic and critical philosophy to left radical theory.

Lyotard, Jean-François, *The Differend: Phrases in Dispute* (Manchester: Manchester University Press, 1988 [1983]). Influential rereading of Wittgenstein's work in the service of postmodern theory.

Monk, Ray, *Ludwig Wittgenstein: The Duty of Genius* (London: Jonathan Cape, 1990). Standard biography which shows the extent to which the life is the 'text'.

Pitkin, Hannah, *Wittgenstein and Justice* (Berkeley, CA: University of California Press, 1972). Imaginative and original attempt to develop a Wittgensteinian basis for normative theorising.

Rorty, Richard, *Contingency, Irony, and Solidarity* (Cambridge: Cambridge University Press, 1989). Wittgenstein in the service of liberal culture and practice.

Staten, Henry, *Wittgenstein and Derrida* (Lincoln, NE: University of Nebraska Press, 1986). Still the standard point of reference for discussions about the degree of overlap between Wittgenstein's work and deconstruction.

14

Hannah Arendt (1906–1975)

Richard H. King

Arendt in the Critical Tradition

Arendt's relation to the critical tradition that constitutes the background to contemporary critical theory is not easily defined, but there are several interesting points of contact, the diversity of which indicates the unique blend of her thought. From Kant she borrowed the notion of aesthetic judgement, which she treated as the model for political judgement. Just as for Kant aesthetic judgements could not be authorised by theoretical understanding or reason, yet were expected to enjoy the assent of an aesthetic community, so for Arendt did political judgements depend on the assent of a political community rather than empirical proofs or moral principles. She pictured people operating in the public sphere in response to events rather like art critics responding to works of art and trying to convince others of their point of view. The vitality of Arendt's public sphere in which political actors engage with each other agonistically bears a resemblance to Nietzsche's sense of struggle as agonism, but Arendt's version is firmly located in the context of participatory democracy. Like Kant, Arendt was interested in how freedom could be instituted politically for all.

Arendt's unfailing advocacy of human freedom also shapes her other philosophical affiliations and aversions. She regarded Hegel's teleological historiography as a determinist account that denied freedom, and hence also objected to Marxist versions of the grand narrative of history. For Arendt, the political is foremost of human activities, whereas Marx subordinates it to production. Yet, she was not entirely unsympathetic to Marx and Marxist politics insofar as it embraced a notion of political action as praxis, rather than the implementation of theoretical ideas. She regarded both the workers' movement and the political revolutions they led to, some of which she witnessed in her youth, as significant episodes of freedom. Yet, at its core Marxism had an attenuated idea of human activity as productive labour rather than political action. Moreover, Marx's prioritisation of the social problem of poverty and material necessity in general led to a politics oriented not towards the maintenance of freedom but to state control of society and ultimately to totalitarianism.

Arendt disagreed with most of her fellow contemporary German-Jewish intellectuals, many of whom were associated with the Frankfurt School, partly because of their underlying Marxism, though she did have an interest in Benjamin. The key to freedom for her was collective political action rather than the utopian promise of avant-garde art that resisted commodification. She also had little time for the Freudian influences on their work as she held that Freud offered causal explanations of human behaviour that denied the possibility of freedom of action. Arendt shared this disagreement with Freud with other thinkers in the tradition of phenomenological existentialism, to which she was related through her mentor Heidegger. Arendt adopted something of Heidegger's manner of thinking through large ideas, but she changed his key ideas to suit her purposes in social philosophy. Arendt thus preferred being in the world with others (*Mit Sein*) to *Dasein,* perhaps reflecting a Husserlian interest in intersubjectivity. The primary existential fact of human existence in her view was not finitude and death, but natality, which is the coming in to the world of a new being, or Dasein, which could achieve its freedom only by acting in concert with others. For Arendt, only political action (which Heidegger disregarded) is authentic being, meaning the appropriate response to being thrown into the world. In contrast, both philosophising and mass existence geared to satisfying material needs are forms of egoism that isolate humans from each other and from the world.

Introduction

A product, as she once insisted, of 'the German tradition of philosophy',[1] Hannah Arendt was born of secular Jewish parents in Königsberg in 1906. A student of Martin Heidegger and Karl Jaspers in the Weimar years, she escaped the Nazis in 1933, spent the rest of the decade in Paris, and then reached the United States in 1941. Most of the detainees in Gurs, the camp where she was held in southern France, ended up in Auschwitz. Once in America, Arendt rapidly established herself as an intellectual force among the newly emerging, and predominantly Jewish, New York intellectuals. After the war, she worked for Jewish organisations and Schocken Books, while also reviewing books for *Partisan Review* and *Commentary* and later for *The New Yorker* and *The New York Review of Books*. Over the years, she returned to the university as a visiting and part-time teacher in several American universities, eventually taking a full-time position at the New School for Social Research in New York. She and her husband were strongly opposed to McCarthyism in the 1940s and 1950s, but never seriously considered returning to Europe, unlike her friend Bertolt Brecht, who fled after being questioned by the House Un-American Activities Committee, or her enemy, Theodor Adorno, who returned to Frankfurt to help revive the Frankfurt School there in the early 1950s.

By her death in 1975, Arendt was among the most prominent and controversial American intellectuals. In particular, she was severely attacked for the unconventional opinions she expressed in *Eichmann in Jerusalem* (1963). Later, as her papers were made available after her death, she was criticised about her relationship with Heidegger, her mentor and one-time lover. She was accused of being gullible about his involvement with the Nazis and for allegedly taking charge of the rehabilitation of his personal and philosophical reputation in the 1960s.

Arendt's intellectual reputation has gone through several distinct phases. With the publication of *The Origins of Totalitarianism* in 1951 until roughly the mid-1960s, she was seen primarily as an analyst of the historical-political crisis of modernity, which had produced totalitarianism not only in Germany but the Soviet Union. From the early 1970s and to the 1990s, she was considered mainly as a political thinker, whose central theme was the revival of politics and the public realm. For this, she repaired to the Greek polis as the great political moment in the history of the West. This divided focus between the ancient and modern worlds reflected an ambivalence in her own thought, making her in the words of Seyla Benhabib a 'reluctant modernist'.[2] More recently, students of Arendt's thought have been busy primarily with two matters. The first is the reconstruction of her personal life and intellectual *Bildung*, especially the philosophical influences on her work. Second, her mature work has been analysed in terms of its philosophical underpinnings, with emphasis falling upon the ideas she developed in response to Heidegger's thought, 'natality', 'world' and 'plurality', and the faculty of 'judgement' deriving from Kant.

Through it all, her style of thinking, which she once referred to as 'thinking without banisters', has attracted considerable attention.

Her combination of philosophically informed historical ruminations and historically charged political speculation has seemed foreign to political scientists and historians on both sides of the Atlantic, particularly in Britain. On the other hand, her reputation in the United States and in Germany has remained generally high and attention to her work has grown apace even in poststructuralist circles. Though no friend of feminism in her lifetime, her work has recently been taken up by feminist academics and some have grouped her with Simone Weil and Rosa Luxemburg as among the most important public intellectual figures among women in the twentieth century.

In what follows, I want to examine Arendt's thinking in two areas: totalitarianism and politics. My thesis is that Arendt had two distinct notions of each concept, both of which need understanding before her thought can be accurately assessed. I will then finish by relating the style and concerns of her thought to contemporary theory, especially political thought.

Totalitarianism and the Problem of Evil

In two respects, *The Origins of Totalitarianism* was mis-titled. First, Arendt herself preferred the first British title, *The Burden of Our Time*; and, second, the term 'origins' misrepresented her intentions for the book. Begun just at the end of World War Two, as she and her husband, Heinrich Blücher, were reeling from the discovery of the enormity of what had happened to European Jewry, *Origins* was originally intended to be about Nazi Germany, with 'racial imperialism' as its focus. However, in the late 1940s, Arendt added the Soviet Union as an example of a regime where 'terror and ideology' had established their sway. It was important to Arendt that both regimes be seen as 'totalitarian', despite the obvious differences in their origins and development, of which she was well aware. Totalitarianism, she insisted, was not a peculiarly German phenomenon. It was rather a trans-European manifestation of the modern assumption that 'everything is possible'. As a corollary, she also claimed that totalitarianism, particularly the racial form it assumed in Germany, could not be explained by the history of ideas going back to Plato and the Greeks. It was unprecedented and represented a radical break with the intellectual, spiritual and political traditions of the West.

Also puzzling was Arendt's organisation of the book. The first section was entitled 'Anti-semitism' and represented a fascinating, if idiosyncratic, essay on the history of post-Emancipation Jewry in Europe; the second large section was called 'Imperialism', while the third was named 'Totalitarianism'. Arendt did not intend to construct a neat explanatory narrative of the emergence of totalitarianism but to present, even juxtapose, the components out of which totalitarianism 'crystallised'. Above all else, she did not want to imply that totalitarianism had been inevitable. To do so would be to deny the possibility of freedom in human history and would imply that totalitarianism was somehow justified. Here, she was arguing against the Hegelian thought that: 'World history is the judge of the world'; and against the conception of right-wing Hegelians that 'whatever is, is right'. Thus, Arendt's organisation of the text was not quite so idiosyncratic as it first seemed.

In a book of startling claims, one of the most original was that modern anti-semitism differed from traditional anti-semitism in three respects. First, it was not religious but scientific: anti-semitism had become racialised. Second, by the late nineteenth century, it had become ideologised, by which Arendt meant that anti-semitism increasingly stood at the centre of an entire world-view rather than being one belief among others. And, third, it became politicised, the core belief of several political parties in Germany and the Austro-Hungarian Empire. Thus she insisted that modern, European anti-semitism was something new.

Two large claims were made in regards to imperialism. The first was, and still is, daring and speculative. According to Arendt, the significance of European imperial expansion in the late nineteenth century had been threefold. It deepened white racism against people of colour, particularly in Africa. It strengthened the political techniques of subversion, domination and rule by decree not law against duly constituted governments abroad. And, finally, it encouraged the ceaselessly expansionist tendencies of European capital. What was learned and developed in the colonies came back, boomerang-like, to Europe and helped feed the burgeoning fascisms there. At the same time, on a separate 'track', the nation-state was destabilising, along the fault line which divided the 'people' and 'the citizen-body', the *ethnos* and the *polis*, communal exclusivity and universal natural rights. Where the promise of the French Revolution had been the republic of equal citizens, by World War One the impulse was to privilege nation over state and cultural-racial over political loyalties.

All of this was waiting to be crystallised by the massive destruction of European institutions wrought by the Great War. National and stateless minorities and refugees reflected the destabilisation of European polities and societies. The condition of literal homelessness was matched by political statelessness and social superfluousness. The result was what Arendt referred to, drawing upon her mentor Heidegger, as a deeply experienced 'worldlessness' on a massive scale. Whether this condition fed the desire for totalitarian movements in Germany or was created by totalitarian regimes such as Stalin's, the interwar years saw the coming to fruition of the preconditions for the triumph of totalitarianism.

Finally, in her 'Totalitarianism' section Arendt offered a kind of phenomenological analysis of the logic of totalitarianism in practice. Her central thesis was that totalitarianism was not just authoritarianism grown nasty or a modern form of tyranny. For her, totalitarian regimes depended centrally upon 'ideology and terror'. The term ideology referred to more than just a general world-view or political position; rather, ideology articulated the logic of the idea of race or class as it was implemented in historical reality. The upshot was that ideology did not mirror common reality but replaced it with a construct, all but immune to empirical or logical refutation. But it was terror, as embodied in the camp-system of both totalitarian systems, that Arendt saw as constituting the historical uniqueness of totalitarianism.

Again, Arendt's point was both innovative and deeply disturbing. The camps were not just badly run institutions of economic exploitation, examples of modern slavery, as it were; nor were they dependent on sadists and criminal perverts for their functioning. The truth was that that they served no useful economic or military purpose that justified the enormous expenditure needed to stock, staff and maintain them. This was even true, she claimed, of the Soviet slave labour camps. Their purpose, she claimed most radically, was to be places of experimentation in transforming human nature. Indeed, this was a process that not only the inmates but also the guards and staff who operated the camps were to undergo.

The dehumanisation of the inmates, she argued, involved a three-stage process. First, the legal-juridical status of the inmate was denied. Punishment was meted out for everything and nothing, while the term of incarceration was open-ended. Second, the inmate was stripped of any moral stature. Impossible moral dilemmas were posed for mothers who had to choose which of their children should live or die, while inmate resistance was met with such disproportionate response that moral heroism brought down untold suffering on fellow inmates. Finally, Arendt insisted that the camps existed to destroy the very individuality of the individual. Their goal was to create a massive population of human beings 'without qualities' and thus superfluous, interchangeable and lacking both the individuality or the sense of collective solidarity which were the characteristics of what she later referred to as 'worldliness'. To be human was to transcend natural needs and, in the deepest sense, to have a culture. Above all, the camps sought to stamp out all 'spontaneity', all capacity to initiate thought or to act with other people. This was, for her, hell on earth, an embodiment of 'radical evil', which we 'can neither punish nor forgive'.[3]

Ten years after the publication of *Origins*, Hannah Arendt covered the Jerusalem trial of Adolf Eichmann for *The New Yorker*, where her five-part coverage was first published and then republished as *Eichmann in Jerusalem: A Report on the Banality of Evil* in 1963. Not only was the book enormously controversial, it also represented a rethinking of several aspects of *Origins*. There, Arendt had used the term 'radical evil', though without defining it very extensively; but in her *Eichmann* book, she used, actually only once in the text itself, the phrase 'banality of evil'. As she was later to observe, she realised that, contra *Origins*, there need not have been any deep ideological motivation behind the implementation of the Final Solution. Though Arendt was not now claiming that all Nazis from Hitler and Himmler on down were merely time-servers, her point was that the system did not need fanatic anti-semites to function effectively. Nothing about Eichmann suggested an evil genius or will to evil. The effect was to stress the routinisation of evil under Nazi domination as contrasted with the dramatic and even darkly glamorous, highly intelligent figures of evil such as Milton's Satan or Melville's Ahab that populated the Western literary imagination.

Most disturbing about an Eichmann was the enormous disparity between his sense of his own motivations, on the one hand, and the horrific results of his action as a central figure in the extermination of millions of people, on the other hand. His failure was a failure to 'think from the standpoint of somebody else', 'thinking' here referring more to a failure of moral imagination than of rationality in the conventional sense of the term. Indeed, Arendt's Eichmann study might best be read as an exploration of 'the case of the conscience of Eichmann'. What that revealed was that 'Evil in the Third Reich had lost the quality by which most people recognise it, the quality of temptation'.[4] As Arendt later wrote: 'my opinion now is that evil is never "radical", that it is only extreme and that it possesses neither depth nor any demonic dimension'.[5] Arendt later returned to the relationship between thinking and moral capacity, as suggested by Eichmann's failure to 'think what he was doing', in her all-too-brief consideration of Heidegger's thought in 1971 and then more fully in *The Life of the Mind* (1978). Arendt's expanded view was that thinking was the capacity to unsettle one's own settled views, to call one's typical ways of being in the world into question. Too much thinking took one out of the 'world' entirely and created political stupidity, as was the case of Heidegger, while too little thought on fundamental matters led to the utter moral conventionality of an Eichmann.

Politics and Freedom

But how was it that Arendt's thought shifted from a preoccupation with totalitarianism and the nature of evil to the nature of politics and participatory freedom? After *Origins* Arendt realised that she needed to better acquaint herself with Marx's thought and the tradition of political philosophy generally, if she wanted to identify what it was in the tradition that had made it so ineffectual in countering the reality of totalitarianism, and what it was in Marxism, if anything, that had facilitated the development of totalitarianism in the Soviet Union. She concluded that, for a variety of reasons, the Western political tradition had always been profoundly suspicious of politics and that there were aspects of Marxist thought which reenforced this hostility to politics, as Arendt understood the term.

Arendt was also heartened by a contemporary historical event – the Hungarian Revolution of the autumn of 1956. The revolt there against the Soviet puppet government revealed to her that politics, in the form of a spontaneous emergence of the council-system form of government, was still possible from within the heart of totalitarianism. Thus history supplied the provocation to think about what authentic politics might be. Besides Hungary, the examples Arendt came up with were the Greek polis, in the first instance, and the tradition running from the political upheavals of the late eighteenth century in America and France through the Paris Commune, down to the emergence of the council (Soviet) system in Russia during the Revolution and the post-World War One councils (*Räte*) in Germany, in the second instance. While most analysts of the post-war political condition, much less of totalitarianism, feared mass and/or participatory politics, Arendt thought otherwise. As the Cold War began to thaw, she emerged as more democratic in her political thinking. Indeed, her thought anticipated, and in some case influenced, New Left thinking as it emerged in the 1960s.

What then did she mean by politics? Though an enormous topic, a few basic things can be said. First, *Origins* already contained the building blocks of the Arendtian view of politics, specifically the concepts of 'world', 'plurality', and 'natality', along with the moral-political standard she proposed near the end of *Origins*, namely, 'the right to have rights'. Arendt largely abandoned the language of rights after *Origins*. *The Human Condition* (1958) took as its central concerns, first, the political space that would guarantee the right to have rights. Second, it moved beyond the defensive implications of that criterion by proposing that in such a space individuals could appear and determine together the common affairs of the polity through speech and action. This speech and action in public not only furthered the cause of freedom: it was the way political freedom appeared in the world. In terms of her two models of politics, the Greek polis of *The Human Condition* marked the originary instance of this conception of politics, while the tradition laid out in *On Revolution* (1963) traced the re-emergence of the politics of freedom in the modern world. It was her alternative to the Jacobin–Bolshevik revolutionary tradition. Moreover, where *The Human Condition* focused on the disappearance of the Greek model of politics and the rise of what she called 'the social', thus implying a narrative of decline in Western politics, the re-emergence of the politics of freedom in the American Revolution and elsewhere suggested that it was wrong to see the history of Western politics in such negative terms.

Underlying her idea of a public, political space was the assumption that to be human was to have a 'world', a general field or network of human meaning and signification, where individuality and difference are preserved. Only insofar as we are distinct from others, only where there is an 'in-between', can we speak and act with others. Individuality is not an obstacle to, but a prerequisite for, collective deliberation and action. In turn, 'natality', literally the way novelty comes into the world and also a trope for new beginnings, prefigures the possibility of free action. Overall, the central point of politics was to preserve and strengthen the world, while worldliness was what made politics possible.

This being-defining vision of politics was meant to remedy the flaws in the tradition of political thought in the West. First, both the classical and the Christian traditions of thought were suspicious of 'the world' and of politics in general. In the modern world, the Renaissance notion of 'the state as a work of art', the Marxist revolutionary plans for a classless society and utopian socialist models were all hostile to genuine plurality. From another point of view, the Greek tradition of thought contrasted political rhetoric, whose purpose was persuasion, with rational speech, which aimed at truth. Thus, the politics of truth was hostile to the plurality of opinions which authentic politics, based as it was on opinion, sought to preserve.

Finally, there was Marx, perhaps Arendt's main adversary in both her political books. Arendt fully granted the virtues of Marx's insistence on the worldly nature of politics, and insofar as praxis was interpreted as action not making, his influence had been salutary. But the Marxist tradition had gone wrong in two ways. First, in *The Human Condition*, Arendt contended that Marx had all but equated labour and work and elevated both over political action as the most important form of human activity. Thus Marxist thought, according to Arendt, lacked a notion of the political as anything but a reflection of economic needs and social interests, whether from the side of the bourgeoisie or of the proletariat. In other words, Marxism does not ascribe to politics an ontological status of its own.

She returned to Marx in *On Revolution* and analysed the way the Marxist tradition had placed the 'social question', that is, the problem of poverty, at the heart politics. But rather than being a master stroke on Marx's part, Arendt saw this as a deep and fateful mistake, one anticipated in her historical narrative by the difference between the American Revolution, which came close to being a political revolution in her sense, and the French Revolution, which succumbed to the temptation to try to answer the social question. It is a vast understatement to say that the meaning and status of the 'social' in Arendt's thought is problematic, for she used the term 'social' in at least three different senses. A first meaning refers to that realm where individuals associate freely on the basis of preferences and affinities; society in this sense operates by discrimination, of which literary salons in earlier days or clubs and associations in the twentieth century are examples. A second, more complex meaning of social refers to what we would call the economy, that is, the spheres of production, distribution and consumption, especially of the necessities of life. A final sense of the term is the more familiar modern sociological usage linked to the idea of mass society. What all three meanings share, at least according to Arendt, is that when they are made central to politics they become profoundly destructive of it. A state-run economy leads to the abandonment of freedom in the face of planning to abolish poverty, while a free-market economy, whose autonomy is guaranteed by the state, will eventually undermine political freedom and equality, as will a politics which entrenches political inequalities based on economic or racial differences among citizens.

Arendt and Contemporary Thought

The question of how to categorise Arendt politically is also quite problematic. Much of the originality of her political thought lies in her desire 'to think without banisters', a tendency which often seemed at odds with her idea of judgement, derived from Kant, based on 'common sense' and 'an enlarged perspective' at the core of her moral and political epistemology. While her emphasis upon plurality and her hostility to comprehensive ideologies sound liberal, she never had the liberal confidence in progress and strongly objected to the liberal vision of politics as essentially being about the satisfaction of interests and desires. She was too much a Kantian for that. Moreover, her concept of freedom was not a 'negative' one, primarily intended to refer to action in the absence of restraints or as instrumental in protecting individuals against tyranny. For her freedom as participation in the decisions that affect the common life of the political order was an end as well as a means.

In rejecting politics as a form of 'making', much less world-transformation or redemption, she seems close to the conservative distaste for political 'rationalism' and for the politics of identity or therapeutic self-expression. Her emphasis upon the need to construct 'lasting institutions' to preserve the public space of freedom was deeply conservative in the generic sense of the term. But Arendt was no blind devotee of politics past, including that of the Greek polis, and thus was at odds with her fellow German-Jewish émigré in America, Leo Strauss. Nor did the organic traditionalism often adopted by a certain kind of medieval-oriented conservatism have any appeal. Finally, from *Origins*' critique of Western capitalist expansion to her animadversions against economic and social contamination of the public realm by advanced capitalism in *The Human Condition*, Arendt was far from being an apologist for capitalism, free-market or otherwise, or for the politics which was devoted to the preservation of market freedoms.

Besides the critique of Marx already mentioned, Arendt also objected to the deterministic cast of the Marxist grand narrative of dialectical historical progress. But she was sympathetic with the political tradition of revolution and came to appreciate the importance of independent Marxist radicals such as Rosa Luxemburg and admired the work of two friends from her Paris days, Bertolt Brecht and Walter Benjamin. (She was later to write important, though not uncritical, essays about each figure.) In *On Revolution* she welcomed the emergence of the workers' movements as central to the revival of politics in the modern world. In other essays of the 1960s and 1970s, she welcomed the recent examples of popular insurgency, such as the civil rights and student movements, and anti-Vietnam War protests, which preserved and extended the public space of freedom.

Perhaps Arendt is best seen as a kind of civic humanist or republican in modern dress. Certainly, politics and citizenship take on a central role in her political vision. But she was also deeply suspicion of political indoctrination and the moral authoritarianism implied by most republican ideologies. Indeed, her notion of the public space and of political action has no essential connection with the state or constitutional political structures as such. Considering her enthusiasm for the council system of government, her politics seems more communitarian anarchist than anything else. Nor was she an advocate of the social and cultural homogeneity that most republican visions seem to imply. Rather, her emphasis upon plurality and diversity and her strong objection to basing any state on a single religious, ethnic or racial ideology place her closer to contemporary cultural pluralism or multi-culturalism of a certain sort.

Finally her politics, however it is labelled, has proved to be important in illuminating what is at issue in the transition stages in polities, as illustrated in the American civil rights movement, Solidarity in Poland and the Civic Forum in Czechoslovakia, and in post-apartheid South Africa. Neither reformist nor revolutionary, such movements sought to revitalise and extend the public space and to increase the access to political participation. Particularly in Eastern Europe and the crumbling Soviet Union, her work on totalitarianism was often invoked in the late 1980s and early 1990s. In the history of political thought, Arendt's belongs, as Margaret Canovan has noted, with Tocqueville, Burke, Montesquieu and Machiavelli as thinkers who mixed history and theory, and sought to identify the emergence of a new kind of politics or to think about politics in new ways.

More generally, Arendt's hostility to historical determinism and her emphasis upon history as a disjointed set of fragmentary provocations to re-assess what we are doing can sound positively postmodern. She was a 'splitter' not a 'lumper' and sought to make distinctions among phenomena rather than reducing one to another. She thus tended to essentialise the central terms of her political thought, even when she located their historical origins and development.[6] Indeed, her rejection of reductionism anticipated the postmodern questioning of depth-models of explanation and interpretation. Yet, Arendt was nothing if not a serious person; and irony about the world in general, as opposed to a lively melancholy in the face of painful historical realities, was foreign to her temperament. The idea that popular culture was culture rather than just entertainment was one she simply did not understand.

With this mandarin notion of culture, Arendt might be thought to have had some affinities with her fellow German-Jewish émigrés from the Frankfurt School. Though she shared some friends with them, namely Benjamin and theologian Paul Tillich, Arendt and Theodor Adorno were bitter enemies. But all personal and political issues aside, Arendt's peculiar kind of radicalism was far from the Marxist-inspired domination theory of the Frankfurt School. Where they typically looked to avant-garde culture or to the politics of happiness as negations of existing society, Arendt insisted that the source of freedom was neither psychological nor cultural but political. The possibility of collective action, not the creation of a non-repressive society, stood at the heart of her vision. It was left to the second-generation Frankfurt theorist Jürgen Habermas to effect a kind of theoretical rapprochement between the Frankfurt School and certain aspects of Arendt's thought, in particular her idea of the public space. Indeed, the complex genealogy of Habermas' concept of the 'ideal speech situation' would have to include Arendt's development of the idea of the public space in *The Human Condition*.

The most basic criticism of Arendt's concept of politics is that it is difficult to figure out what politics is 'about' in her thought. In excluding concerns with poverty, social welfare and social justice from 'the political', she seemed to empty politics of much content. This is a weakness if her ideas of the political and the social retain their spatial connotations. But several interpreters of her work have suggested that if the political is considered to be a cast of mind or mode of thinking, one which asks of any public policy how it contributes to increasing public participation in politics and strengthens the plurality among, and equality of, citizens, then the distinction between the political and the social makes a certain amount of sense.

But Foucaultians (not to mention Marxists) might well ask why Arendt fails to recognise the importance of power differentials and structural inequalities in blocking equal access to the public realm. No doubt, Arendt needs to be supplemented on this point. But it should be noted that in replacing domination or satisfaction of interests with action as the main point of politics, Arendt made the larger point that politics, empirically and normatively, was always about more than power or violence alone. Put another way, Arendt insists, against Foucault as it were, that there is a fundamental difference between persuasion and coercion, between speech and force. And any analysis of politics which fails to make room for such a distinction is simply inadequate.

Finally, Arendt's vision stands at odds with much contemporary theory on the issue of humanism, though she hardly ever used the term. In retrospect, there is considerable justification in seeing the underlying concern of her work as the attempt to rethink what it means to be human in the wake of the worst that the twentieth century witnessed. From this perspective, *Origins* was an extended intervention in the post-war debate about humanism between Martin Heidegger and Jean-Paul Sartre. She clearly saw that all the traditional underpinnings of human nature and common humanity, such as the transcendent force of religion, nature, tradition or history, had been discredited by what had happened in Germany and the Soviet Union. For her, the turn to race had been a disastrous but, perhaps, logical next step in trying to find an underpinning for humanity. But she was by no means in agreement with Sartre's location of the foundation for humanity in human subjectivity. From her apotheosising of 'the right to have rights' in *Origins*, to her attempt to define politics as an activity confirming being, to the conclusion of her Eichmann book, where she wrote of 'a crime against human status', against 'human diversity', and an act which 'violated the order of mankind',[7] the search for a foundation for talking of humanity or human nature was perhaps the central theme and pathos of her thought.

Notes

1. Hannah Arendt, 'Letter to Gershom Scholem', in Ron H. Feldman (ed.), *The Jew as Pariah* (New York: Grove Press, 1978 [1963]), p. 246.
2. Benhabib, *Reluctant Modernism.*
3. Arendt, *Origins*, p. 459.
4. Arendt, *Eichmann*, pp. 49, 149.
5. Arendt, 'Letter to Gershom Scholem', p. 251.
6. Benhabib, *Reluctant Modernism.*
7. Arendt, *Eichmann*, pp. 268, 269, 272.

Major Works by Arendt

Eichmann in Jerusalem: A Report on the Banality of Evil (New York: Viking Press, 1963).

The Human Condition (Chicago: University of Chicago Press, 1958).

On Revolution (New York: Viking Press, 1963).

The Origins of Totalitarianism, 2nd edn (Cleveland, OH: World Publishing, Co., 1958).

Suggestions for Further Reading

Beiner, Ronald (ed.), *Lectures on Kant's Political Philosophy by Hannah Arendt* (Chicago, IL: University of Chicago Press, 1989). A good account of Arendt's concept of judgement.

Benhabib, Seyla, *The Reluctant Modernism of Hannah Arendt* (Thousand Oaks, CA: Sage, 1996). One of the best theoretical analyses of Arendt's work.

Canovan, Margaret, *Hannah Arendt: A Reinterpretation of her Political Thought* (Cambridge: Cambridge University Press, 1992). A stimulating and independent reading based on archival as well as textual sources.

Honig, Bonnie (ed.), *Feminist Interpretations of Hannah Arendt* (State College, PA: Pennsylvania State University Press, 1995). A variety of treatments of Arendt's thought from feminist perspectives.

Villa, Dana R., *Politics, Philosophy, Terror: Essays on the Thought of Hannah Arendt* (Princeton, NJ: Princeton University Press, 1999). Essays on a variety of issues in Arendt's work.

Young-Bruehl, Elisabeth, *Hannah Arendt: For Love of the World* (New Haven, CN: Yale University Press, 1982). It remains the definitive biography of Arendt.

15

Claude Lévi-Strauss (1908–)

Christopher Johnson

Lévi-Strauss in the Critical Tradition

Lévi-Strauss was in some ways quite hostile to the philosophical tradition of Europe in which he was trained, as he came to regard philosophical questions as those which science could not yet solve. Anthropological structuralism was intended to be a human science, imbued with the full rigour and objectivity of the natural sciences, just as Freud had intended psychoanalysis to be a science of the human psyche. In that respect, Lévi-Strauss would not have shared Husserl's objections to scientifically oriented philosophy, nor Gadamer's hermeneutic conception of the human sciences. Indeed, he regarded structuralism as a super-rationalism. Having said that, Lévi-Strauss also wished to undo the subject/object dichotomy that had haunted Western philosophy, in that he did not regard the subject as the location or source of meaning, but language or signs. This position was central to Lévi-Strauss' opposition to Sartre's version of existential humanism, an opposition which he shared with Heidegger. In terms of the post-war intellectual attack on humanism in France, Lévi-Strauss was thus also allied with Nietzscheans, who saw existentialism as a defence of the 'last men', and Marxists, who saw it as a defence of bourgeois individualism.

As a social theorist, Lévi-Strauss had something in common with Marx, whom he acknowledged as one of his main intellectual influences. However, it is the mode of exchange rather than production which is central to Lévi-Strauss' understanding of society. Moreover, language or signs take on a materiality in his structural anthropology that would require a substantial revision of historical materialism. Such a revision was indeed undertaken by Althusser in his theory of ideology, which drew heavily on Lévi-Strauss' view that lived meaning is always mythical, and hence political ideologies are modern myths.

Just as the tribal shaman reintegrates a sick person into the community through symbolic means, so does the psychoanalyst use language. More generally though, Lévi-Strauss' understanding of the integration of the individual into society through the dominant language used by social and political institutions paved the way for a combination of structuralism and Marxism in a politically-motivated critique of the dominant discourse or ideology.

Introduction

It is difficult to underestimate the significance of Lévi-Strauss' thought for contemporary theory. On the one hand, he played an important role in raising the profile of anthropology as an academic discipline in post-war France, arguing for its special status in the family of disciplines loosely referred to as the 'human sciences'. On the other hand, his main theoretical contribution to anthropology, the method of structural analysis, was from the 1950s onwards also influential in a range of disciplines external to anthropology, from history and philosophy to psychoanalysis and literary studies. The name normally given to the intellectual movement that took its inspiration from structural anthropology is structuralism, and while Lévi-Strauss has been careful to dissociate himself from the various applications of his theory, it is the name he gives to his own theoretical practice.

Lévi-Strauss was born in Brussels in 1908. His original training was in philosophy, but like a number of his contemporaries he quickly became disillusioned with the subject and decided to concentrate on ethnology. In the mid-1930s he was offered a teaching post in sociology at the University of São Paulo, which enabled him to conduct a series of fieldwork expeditions into the Brazilian interior. The crucial experience, however, were the years spent teaching in New York during the war, when he met most of the leading American anthropologists of the day, and began what was to be a lifelong friendship and collaboration with the Russian phonologist Roman Jakobson. Decisively, Jakobson introduced him to the methods of structural linguistics, which he would go on to apply in his pioneering work on kinship structures and mythology.

Schematically, Lévi-Strauss' career can be divided into two parts. The first phase includes the fieldwork experience of the 1930s and the initiation of what would be Lévi-Strauss' first major research project, a cross-cultural analysis of kinship structures. It concludes with the publication of the *Elementary Structures of Kinship* in 1949. The second, and from the point of view of structuralism, the most important phase of Lévi-Strauss' trajectory, begins in 1950, when his move to the Ecole Pratique des Hautes Etudes also required a change of specialisation. His subsequent concentration on the anthropology of religions, more specifically, mythology and systems of classification, allowed him to devise new methods of analysis in what was a relatively undertheorised area of anthropological study. Inevitably, these two phases of Lévi-Strauss' career are not entirely distinct, and there are important lines of continuity between them.

Kinship and the Theory of Exchange

At the heart of *The Elementary Structures of Kinship* is a theory of exchange derived from Marcel Mauss' classic essay, *The Gift* (1925). The gift, as Mauss defined it, is a mechanism for the regulation of relations between different social groups or societies, binding them together in circuits of reciprocity. If you give something to another individual or another group, then the obligation of the other party is always to return the gift, to reciprocate. For Mauss the act of donation is therefore never disinterested and never arbitrary. The gift is never a pure gift: it is always motivated, consciously or unconsciously, by this primary function of articulation, the joining and relating of distinct social groups.

In the *Elementary Structures,* Lévi-Strauss applies Mauss' theory of the gift to the problem of kinship relations. For society to exist, humans must transcend the merely biological relation between individuals. Group members must not marry within the immediate group, but with members of other groups. This is the function of the prohibition of incest, the quasi-universal trait of human society which forbids the sexual union of biologically proximate individuals. The reason for this prohibition, argues Lévi-Strauss, is not a biological but a social one. What appears to be a wholly negative rule also has a positive dimension, the reverse side of the prohibition of incest being the prescription of exogamy, ensuring integration through intermarriage with other social groups. From this perspective, the prohibition of incest would be the most fundamental of rules, the first rule of social integration; in Lévi-Strauss' somewhat philosophical phrasing, it represents the passage from 'nature' to 'culture'. If, as follows from this, the kinship ties established through exogamy are the most elementary form of social bond, then they are not the only form. This is where Mauss' model of exchange is introduced. After Mauss, Lévi-Strauss sees exchange, or what he terms the 'principle of reciprocity', as the most important mechanism of social cohesion, and he combines this with his interpretation of the incest prohibition by considering exogamy as the exchange of women. In the traditional societies studied by ethnologists, the 'donation' of a sister or daughter to another social group creates the obligation in that group to return a sister or daughter, thus creating a lasting bond between the groups. A more complex configuration would involve a less direct transaction, whereby the donor would receive a wife not from the second group, but from a third party, and so on; the overall effect, that is, social integration, would be the same. Lévi-Strauss terms this 'general' as opposed to 'restricted' exchange. As in Mauss' model, the exchange of women would therefore be one of a number of reciprocal transactions binding together distinct social groups, but for Lévi-Strauss it is a special category of exchange in that its 'object' (women) is of the highest social value, and the relations it establishes are the most permanent and pervasive ones.

Saussure's Theory of Language

Lévi-Strauss' treatment of the question of kinship in the *Elementary Structures* is more extensive and also more technical than the above summary might suggest. Furthermore, in addition to Mauss' theory of the gift, there is another, perhaps less explicitly articulated theoretical influence discernible in the book, that of linguistics. It is the latter, rather than the more narrowly sociological model of exchange, which informs Lévi-Strauss' theoretical practice in the second part of his career, when he begins to specialise in the anthropology of religions. Historically, the kind of linguistics Lévi-Strauss takes as his model originates in the pioneering work of the Swiss linguist Ferdinand de Saussure, published under the title *Course in General Linguistics* in 1916. To make linguistics a rigorous science, Saussure argued, one had to focus on what was essential to languages in general as systems of signification, bracketing out such contingent factors as historical development, sociological context, or phonetic peculiarities. These variable functions of individual languages formed part of what Saussure termed *le langage.* Modern linguistics had, in his opinion, devoted too much attention to the historical or diachronic study of language, whereas a proper science of linguistics would be a synchronic study of *la langue,* that is, the abstract system of rules governing the act of linguistic enunciation at a given moment in time. *Langue* could be described as the legislative part of language, and *parole* (speech) as the executive part of language, the concrete instantiation of *langue* in the individual and particular acts of speaking or writing, for example. Saussure further defines *langue* as a system of signs, in which the sign itself is decomposable into two halves, the *signifier* and the *signified.* The signifier is the 'sensible' side of the sign, the carrier of sense (Saussure specifies that it is the 'acoustic image' of a sound, for instance, and not the sound itself), while the signified is the mental construct or concept corresponding to a given signifier. The relationship between signifier and signified is an arbitrary and accidental one, which means that their articulation is purely a matter of convention within a particular linguistic community (for example, 'horse' in English, *cheval* in French). This brings us to an essential feature of *langue,* which is that it is a system of signs based on the principle of *difference,* difference between different signifiers on the one hand, and difference between different signifieds on the other. The signifier 'horse' is identifiable only to the extent that it is phonetically distinct from other signifiers (for example, 'course' or 'Norse'); the signified 'horse' makes sense only in relation to a network of concepts from which it differs (in the same category, 'ass' or 'donkey'). Saussure puts it as follows:

> Everything we have said so far comes down to this. *In* langue, *there are only differences ... and no positive terms.* Whether we take the signified or the signifier, *langue* includes neither ideas nor sounds existing prior to the linguistic system, but only conceptual and phonetic differences arising out of that system.[1]

It can be seen from the above that Saussure bases his theory of language on a series of distinctions (synchronic/diachronic, *langage/langue, langue/parole,* signifier/signified), and two basic and related principles (the arbitrariness of the sign and the differential nature of *langue*). What is interesting from the point of view of Lévi-Strauss and structuralism is that Saussure's distinction between *langue* and *parole* and his comments on the arbitrary and conventional nature of the sign also imply a distinction between the individual and the collective. Saussure states:

> *Langue* is not a function of the speaking subject ... It is the social part of

> language, external to the individual, who by himself is powerless either to create it or to modify it. It exists only in virtue of a kind of contract agreed between the members of a community.[2]

Another point to note about Saussure's linguistics of importance to the subsequent development of structuralism is that he sees the science of language as forming only part of a more general science of signs, or *semiology*:

> It is therefore possible to conceive of a science *which studies the role of signs as part of social life* ... We shall call it *semiology* (from the Greek *semeîon*, 'sign'). It would investigate the nature of signs and the laws governing them ... Linguistics is only one branch of this general science.[3]

Saussure is generally recognised as the founder of structural linguistics. Two of his continuators in the field of phonology (the science of speech sounds), Trubetzkoy and Jakobson, are Lévi-Strauss' main references in linguistics, apart from Saussure himself. In 1945 he published 'Structural Analysis in Linguistics and in Anthropology', where, quoting Trubetzkoy, he summarised the four main principles of methodology in phonology: the reduction of conscious linguistic phenomena to their unconscious infrastructure; the analysis of relations between terms rather than the treatment of terms as independent entities; the use of the concept of system and the elucidation of the structure underlying the system; the discovery of general laws, either by induction or logical deduction. He goes on to suggest that in the case of kinship studies in anthropology one is confronted with the same kind of object as the linguist and that the same principles of analysis can therefore be applied. Like the system of language, systems of kinship are arbitrary systems of representation, systems of symbols, whose underlying structure does not necessarily correspond to individuals' conscious apprehensions of the relations pertaining in a given social group. Like the phonologist, the anthropologist should be looking at the relations between terms rather than the terms themselves. Just as the phonologist has reduced the diversity of sounds in natural languages to a limited set of basic sonic distinctions, so the anthropologist should be able to reduce the many different permutations of kinship relations observed in human society to a small group of oppositions.[4] Lévi-Strauss believes that, by imitating the methods of structural linguistics, the anthropologist can arrive at a truly scientific analysis of kinship systems, that is, an analysis which explains and simplifies its object without losing touch of its concrete reality.

Myth and Classification

After 1950, questions of social organisation play a relatively minor role in Lévi-Strauss' work, and the focus of attention shifts to systems of classification and representation, for which the pivotal text is the *Introduction to the Work of Marcel Mauss*. We have already encountered the notion of kinship systems as arbitrary systems of representation, as systems of symbols. In the *Introduction to Mauss* Lévi-Strauss extends this definition to the whole of social existence:

> Every culture can be considered as an ensemble of symbolic systems headed by language, matrimonial rules, economic relations, art, science and religion. All of these systems seek to express certain aspects of physical reality and social reality, and even more, to express the links that those two types of reality have with each other and those that occur among the symbolic systems themselves.[5]

The six systems mentioned here could be divided into two groups. The first three terms (language, kinship rules, economic relations) could be seen as the 'infrastructure' of social organisation, representing the most immediate forms of social interaction and exchange, while the final three terms (art, science, religion) would designate the relatively autonomous instances of creation, intellection and collective representation, the 'superstructure', as it were, of social existence. Together, all of these systems could be more generally conceptualised as different levels of communication in a given social space.[6] The problem is that the possibilities of translation between symbolic systems are limited and never integral; the different systems are essentially irreducible. Moreover, in the case of 'superstructural' systems such as art, science and religion, their expression of aspects of the physical and social world is never an exhaustive one: there is always an element of 'play' between the signifier and the signified. Though what passes as science in different societies attempts to regulate and reduce this element of play, the essentially finite nature of human thought means that there will always exist a 'surplus' or 'supplementary ration' of signification, what Lévi-Strauss terms the floating signifier.[7] The positive aspect of this limitation is that it permits the potentially infinite permutations of collective representations such as myth and artistic creation.

Another important idea put forward in the *Introduction to Mauss* is the notion of a mental unconscious common to all subjects, regardless of the contingencies of cultural variation. This unconscious is not the same as the unconscious in Freudian theory; rather, it is analogous to the deep-level structures of language as revealed by structural linguistics.[8] It is the transcendental ground which guarantees the ultimate intelligibility of systems of representation radically different from our own.

In the decade following the *Introduction to Mauss*, Lévi-Strauss proceeds to put the flesh on the bones of the theoretical programme initiated in this text. The most substantial part of his work on systems of classification (the taxonomies of the physical and animal world used in non-literate societies) is to be found in *The Savage Mind* and *Totemism*. Whereas traditional interpretations of these systems saw them as being entirely affective in motivation, expressing the mystical 'participation' of the individual with nature (for example, an individual who is a member of the bear clan would be regarded as being quite literally a descendant of the bear), Lévi-Strauss instead describes such representations as a 'logic of the concrete' or *bricolage*, a kind of DIY logic which takes items ready-to-hand in the natural world and processes them into units of opposition, constructing higher-order systems of signification in the same way that a language constructs meaning from different sound utterances. In the case of totemism, the distinctions established between different animal species, for example, are posited as being homologous with the divisions (distinctions) within and between different social groups. So the fact of belonging to the bear or eagle clan is not so important in itself as the fact that the bear is distinct from the eagle and vice versa. In totemism, then, one is faced with two parallel systems of differentiation: perceived distinctions between animal species are mapped onto social differences.

Lévi-Strauss' treatment of systems of classification is an intellectualist one, that is, he treats representations such as totemism not as the expression of an affective, pre-scientific way of thinking, but as a feature of cognition, a kind of intellectual tool with its own, rigorous logic. The same attitude informs his work on myth. 'The Structural Study of Myth' (1955) represents the first substantial application of the linguistic model to mythical discourse. Lévi-Strauss argues that not only is myth in principle subject to the same kind of analysis as language, it is also objectively a part of language, which is its primary means of expression. He therefore distinguishes between three levels in language: the two, distinct levels of *langue* and *parole*, as defined by Saussure, and a higher level of complexity, at which the myth operates, which is both dependent on the first two levels and detached from them. Myth is therefore a qualitatively different form of language, but it can be analysed in the same way as language. So Lévi-Strauss arrives at the following, basic propositions concerning the analysis of myth:

- Like any language, myth is made up of elements or constituent units, but of a higher order of complexity than the constituent units of language. One can therefore trace an ascending order of inclusion and complexity from phoneme (minimal unit of sound) to morpheme (minimal unit of meaning) to sememe (sequence of morphemes) to the 'gross constituent units' of myth, what Lévi-Strauss calls the *mytheme.*
- The meaning of myth is not to be found in its isolated constituent elements, but in the way in which these elements are combined.[9]

To isolate the 'gross constituent unit' or mytheme, Lévi-Straus breaks up the narrative sequence of each myth into the shortest possible sentences, each of which denotes the linking of a subject and a predicate. The basic characteristic of each individual mytheme must therefore be that of a relation. Along the horizontal axis of the myth, the diachronic unfolding of its narrative, the same type of relation can occur at differently spaced intervals, so that if one views the myth along its vertical axis, that of synchrony or structure, this relation will appear in its 'natural' grouping, alongside other, similar relations. The real constitutive elements of myth are therefore not isolated relations, but 'bundles' of relations of the same type. The 'meaning' of the myth derives not from its manifest content, the diachronic sequence of its narrative (which can often be absurd and senseless), but from the combinations, or more precisely, the binary oppositions, between these bundles of relations.[10]

Lévi-Strauss goes on to give a demonstration of the structural method, using the example of the Oedipus myth. He isolates four mythemes, or groups of relations in this myth, and sets them out as indicated in Table 1.

If one reads this table like a text, from left to right and top to bottom, then this reproduces the diachronic sequence of the myth or its surface narrative. However, if one reads the table from left to right only, one column at a time, half of the diachronic sequencing is lost and one is left with the underlying meaning of the myth. Thus the first column groups together relations in which there is an exaggeration of kinship ties, while the second column reverses this relation into one of undervaluation. The third column denotes relations in which there is a negation of the autochthonous origins of

Table 1

Cadmos seeks his sister Europa, ravished by Zeus			
		Cadmos kills the dragon	
	The Spartoi kill one another		
			Labdacos (Laios' father) = *lame* (?)
	Oedipus kills his father, Laios		Laios (Oedipus' father) = *left-sided* (?)
		Oedipus kills the Sphinx	
			Oedipus = *swollen-foot* (?)
Oedipus marries his mother, Jocasta			
	Eteocles kills his brother, Polynices		
Antigone buries her brother, Polynices, despite prohibition			

humanity (the destruction of monsters), while the fourth, referring to various impediments to walking properly, affirms these origins. Lévi-Strauss concludes that the Oedipus myth can be viewed as a kind of logical tool designed to resolve an irreducible contradiction between cosmology (the ancient Greek belief in the autochthonous origins of humankind) and reality (the fact that we are born of man and woman). The myth transcends this contradiction (born from one or from two?) by relating it to a derived question: born from the different or from the same? Hence the relation between the overvaluation and undervaluation of kinship ties (columns 1 and 2) is the same as that between the attempt to deny autochthony and the impossibility of this denial (columns 3 and 4). The fact that the relations expressed in columns 1 and 2, 4 and 3 respectively are mutually exclusive is at least compensated by the fact that it is possible to think of their mutual exclusion as being structurally homologous. The overall function of myth is therefore to overcome or *mediate* the essential contradictions of social life, without necessarily providing a direct resolution of them.[11]

Lévi-Strauss' analysis of the Oedipus myth is the starting point and the template of all his subsequent work on mythology. In the four-volume study *Mythologiques*, for example, he takes over 800 North and South American myths and submits them to the same kind of analysis: the isolation of individual mythemes and the determination of the underlying complex of relations between them. In each case, the object of analysis is not an individual myth, but rather the set of its variants. One considers all versions of the myth on an equal basis. In this way, the 'message' of the myth is distributed across the range of its different utterances in time and space. The effect of this perspective is to relativise the position of the individual subject in the production of mythical discourse. Myth is less the product of a finite, individual consciousness (its teller or author) than the collective expression of aspects of social existence over time – a metalanguage whose message is other than its manifest content. As Lévi-Strauss asserts, 'I therefore claim to show, not how men think [*pensent*] in myths, but how myths operate [*se pensent*] in men's minds without them being aware of the fact.'[12]

Structuralism, Philosophy and the Human Sciences

Structuralist theory was not only influential in anthropology. Very quickly, other French thinkers were to apply elements of this theory in their own, respective domains. The structuralist influence is apparent in Roland Barthes' work on the semiology of mass culture, fashion writing and literature. Michel Foucault presented his 'archaeology' of the human sciences as an attempt to view our own cultural history with the same sense of defamiliarisation and distanciation achieved in Lévi-Strauss' structural anthropology. In psychoanalysis, Jacques Lacan's proposed return to Freud was combined with a theory of the unconscious based on Saussurian linguistics: the unconscious, he claimed, is structured like a language. In literary studies, there was a revival of interest in theories of rhetoric and narrative discourse, which also drew on the earlier work of the Russian Formalists; this trend was evident in the work of Genette, Greimas and Todorov.

However, the influence and effect of structuralism, as it came to be called, was as much ideological as theoretical. The surge of interest in things linguistic was frequently accompanied by a rejection of the philosophical movement which had dominated French intellectual life since World War Two, existentialism, as exemplified in the philosophy of Jean-Paul Sartre. For many, structuralism constituted a point by point refutation of the main ideas of existentialism. Where existentialism privileged the immediate, first-person experience of the individual, structuralism focused on the anonymous systems and structures which precondition individual experience. While existentialism claimed itself to be a humanism, concerned with moral issues such as individual choice, responsibility and commitment, structuralism was a human science, operating at levels of abstraction which made questions of choice and agency seem insignificant. Where existentialism placed great emphasis on historical processes, structuralism was content to map the invariant (synchronic) structures resistant to the transformations of history.

Lévi-Strauss himself contributed to this general discrediting of philosophies of the subject. Already in the autobiographical book *Tristes tropiques* (1955), when describing his three principal intellectual influences (Freud, Marx and geology), he is dismissive of phenomenology and existentialism:

> Phenomenology I found objectionable in that it postulated a kind of continuity between experience and reality ... existentialism ... seemed to me to be anything but a legitimate form of reflection, because of its over-indulgent attitude towards the illusions of subjectivity ... Instead of doing away with metaphysics, phenomenology and existentialism introduced two methods of providing it with alibis.[13]

A few years later, in the final chapter of *The Savage Mind*, 'History and Dialectics', Lévi-Strauss launched a more direct attack on Sartre, rejecting what he saw as Sartre's narrowly ethnocentric view of humanity, which refused to take account of the diversity of human experience. Sartre had failed to recognise that the 'savage' is equally capable of complex and abstract reasoning, relegating his or her thought processes to the status of a 'primitive' (non-dialectical) mentality. The societies studied by ethnologists, like all societies, were subject to historical change, but in collective representations such as myth had chosen to present their pasts in a different way, constructing their social identity around the repetition of archetypal situations rather than in relation to a linear and chronological sequence of events.[14]

Lévi-Strauss' distinction between different modes of historical consciousness reflects the more general distinction he makes between 'hot' and 'cold', or 'cumulative' and 'stationary' societies.

The first are societies which progress through an accumulation of technical inventions and discoveries, continually building on previous knowledge to form great civilisations such as our own. Historically, the defining technology for such civilisations is writing, which permits both a stable historical consciousness and the retention of technical and scientific knowledge. The second category of societies are no less ancient or gifted than the first, but never manage to synthesise their discoveries in the same way as cumulative societies, oscillating around a more or less fixed level of development. Lacking the defining technology of writing, these small-scale societies nevertheless benefit from demographic stability, the conservation of their natural environment, a greater degree of political consensus, and more authentic forms of interpersonal contact than those observed in advanced industrial societies.[15]

Evidently, Lévi-Strauss' distinction between 'hot' and 'cold' societies is not a neutral one. He considers the effects of 'mechanical civilisation', as he calls it, to be ultimately harmful for the whole of humanity, establishing a global 'monoculture' in which all cultural differences are progressively dissolved. The ideological expression of this paradigm is the kind of philosophical humanism which takes its own, culture-specific representation of the subject as a universal and which enthrones that subject as master and possessor of the natural world. In societies without writing, on the other hand, the rejection of historical change (myth, he argues, is a kind of *anti*-history) and the subordination of the cultural to the (super)natural ensure that their relationship with the world is not simply an instrumental one, that their interventions in the natural world are checked and limited by the sense of its sacredness, its essential priority to the human, the individual and the social. As a discipline, anthropology would represent a 'new' humanism in the sense that it argues for the preservation of cultural diversity and takes the example of non-Western cultures as a possible alternative model of being in the world. What Lévi-Strauss had in effect done was to provide an alternative model of humanism which also claimed to offer a more scientific picture of humankind. At the vanguard of the new human sciences, anthropology therefore combined the scientific credentials of structuralism with a moral consciousness equal to the diversity of human experience.

The most effective response to the challenge of the human sciences in France came from a new generation of thinkers who had assimilated the lessons of structuralism but who were also prepared to think beyond it. Of this new generation, perhaps the most important figure is that of Jacques Derrida. In two seminal pieces, 'Structure, Sign and Play in the Discourse of the Human Sciences' and 'The Violence of the Letter: from Lévi-Strauss to Rousseau',[16] Derrida questioned the pretensions of structuralism to have left behind the problems of traditional philosophical enquiry. Like all arguments proclaiming the end of metaphysics, the structuralist critique of metaphysics was not sufficiently reflexive with respect to the history of its own discourse and the genealogy of its concepts. This was especially evident in Lévi-Strauss' different comments on the role of writing, which he had singled out as a defining criterion of differentiation between 'hot' and 'cold' societies. Derrida saw this gesture as characteristic of a long tradition of Western philosophy, which he termed 'logocentrism', which held writing to be a secondary and subordinate aspect of spoken language, an auxiliary and unnatural form of communication which tended to distort and pervert the immediate 'truth' of the spoken word. Derrida's reading of the history of Western philosophy is a symptomatic one, taking different 'moments' of that history (Plato, Leibniz, Rousseau, Saussure, Lévi-Strauss) as individual examples of a way of thinking that is as persistent as it is pervasive. The theory of writing that he derives from his critique of logocentrism is universal to the extent that it transcends the specification of any particular historical context. At the same time, his choice of Rousseau, Saussure and Lévi-Strauss, in particular, is not an arbitrary one. Lévi-Strauss had designated Rousseau as the spiritual father of anthropology and the founder of the human sciences, while Saussure was the father of structuralism. In the context of mid-1960s France, therefore, Derrida's deconstructive reading of Lévi-Strauss could be read as a strategic response on the part of philosophy to the intellectual hegemony of structuralism and the human sciences.

Standard critical accounts of structuralism have often interpreted Derrida's critique of Lévi-Strauss as marking the inauguration of a new phase of critical enquiry, that of poststructuralism. However, despite the importance and the pertinence of Derrida's reading of Lévi-Strauss, it should be remembered that in France the influence of structuralism was to persist for at least another decade, and that the term 'poststructuralism' was itself not a French but an American invention. Perhaps even more important is the fact that Derrida's theory of writing and difference, as Derrida himself recognised, would have been impossible without the theoretical inspiration provided by structuralism. In short, if terms such as difference and code, sign and signification, synchrony and diachrony have become part of the stock-in-trade of contemporary critical theoretical discourse, it is largely thanks to the original and essential mediation of Lévi-Strauss.

Notes

Page references for original French texts are in brackets

1. Ferdinand de Saussure, *Course in General Linguistics,* trans. R. Harris (London: Duckworth, 1983 [1916]), p. 118 (166). Translation slightly modified.
2. Ibid., p. 14 (30–1). Translation slightly modified.
3. Ibid., pp. 15–16 (33).
4. *Structural Anthropology 1,* pp. 33–51 (40–62).
5. *Introduction to Mauss,* p. 16 (xix). Translation slightly modified.
6. Ibid., p. 36 (xxxii).
7. Ibid., p. 63 (xlix).
8. Ibid., pp. 33–6 (xxx–i).
9. *Structural Anthropology 1,* pp. 208–11 (229–33).
10. Ibid., pp. 211–12 (233–4).
11. Ibid., pp. 214–16 (237–9).
12. *Mythologiques 1: The Raw and the Cooked,* p. 12 (20).
13. *Tristes tropiques,* p. 58 (61).
14. *The Savage Mind,* pp. 249–51 (329–32).
15. *Structural Anthropology 2,* pp. 28–9; 335 (40; 391).
16. Jacques Derrida, *Writing and Difference,* trans. A. Bass (London: Routledge, 1978 [1967]), pp. 278–93 (409–28); *Of Grammatology,* trans. G. C. Spivak (Baltimore: Johns Hopkins University Press, 1976 [1967]), pp. 101–40 (149–202).

Major Works by Lévi-Strauss

The Elementary Structures of Kinship, trans. J. H. Bell, J. R. von Sturmer and R. Needham (Boston: Beacon Press, 1969 [1949, 1967]).

Introduction to the Work of Marcel Mauss, trans. Felicity Baker (London: Routledge, 1978 [1950]).

Tristes tropiques, trans. J. and D. Weightman (New York: Penguin, 1992 [1955]).

Structural Anthropology 1, trans. C. Jacobson and B. Grundfest Schoepf (Harmondsworth: Penguin, 1977 [1958]).

Totemism, trans. R. Needham (London: Merlin Press, 1964 [1962]).

The Savage Mind, trans. R. Needham (Chicago: Chicago University Press, 1966 [1962]).

Mythologiques: Introduction to a Science of Mythology, 4 vols, trans. J. and D. Weightman (London: Cape, 1970–81 [1964–71]).
Structural Anthropology 2, trans. M. Layton (Harmondsworth: Penguin, 1978 [1973]).

Suggestions for Further Reading

Descombes, Vincent, *Modern French Philosophy*, trans. L. Scott-Fox and J. M. Harding (Cambridge: Cambridge University Press, 1980 [1979]). Essential for an understanding of intellectual context and the philosophical debates around structuralism.
Hénaff, Marcel, *Claude Lévi-Strauss and the Making of Structural Anthropology*, (Minneapolis and London: University of Minnesota Press, 1998) [1991]). A clear and accurate overview of Lévi-Strauss' anthropology, with useful synopses of the principal texts.
Johnson, Christopher, *Jacques Derrida: The Scene of Writing* (London: Phoenix, 1997). Takes Derrida's classic reading of Lévi-Strauss as an exemplary articulation of deconstruction and the theory of writing.
Pace, David, *Claude Lévi-Strauss: The Bearer of Ashes* (London: Routledge, 1983). A useful introduction to Lévi-Strauss' work. Examines some of the connections between the scientific and ideological components of structuralism.
Sturrock, John (ed.), *Structuralism and Since: From Lévi-Strauss to Derrida* (Oxford: Oxford University Press, 1979). An authoritative collection of essays on the main luminaries of structuralist and poststructuralist thought.
Sturrock, John, *Structuralism* (London: Fontana, 1993 [1986]). A lucid analysis of structuralist theory and its different areas of influence.

Names index

Subject index

Subject index